The Director Had a Heart Attack and the President Resigned

The Director Had a Heart Attack and the President Resigned

◆

Board-Staff Relations for the 21st Century

Revised Edition

Gerald. B. Bubis

iUniverse, Inc.

New York Lincoln Shanghai

The Director Had a Heart Attack and the President Resigned
Board-Staff Relations for the 21st Century

iUniverse books may be ordered through booksellers or by contacting:

iUniverse
2021 Pine Lake Road, Suite 100
Lincoln, NE 68512
www.iuniverse.com
1-800-Authors (1-800-288-4677)

ISBN-13: 978-0-595-41878-7 (pbk)
ISBN-13: 978-0-595-86226-9 (ebk)
ISBN-10: 0-595-41878-3 (pbk)
ISBN-10: 0-595-86226-8 (ebk)

Printed in the United States of America

Contents

Foreword

Early one morning last summer, I met Jerry Bubis for breakfast at a small restaurant in Minneapolis. Jerry is a 1950 graduate of our social work program and has been honored by our college for his distinguished career. He was in town for a few days and had several visits to make. Some time ago, he'd given me a copy of *The Director had a Heart Attack and the President Resigned: Board-Staff Relations for the 21st Century* to read. Excitedly, he explained his ideas to expand the text into a new edition. If you have not had the experience of sitting with Jerry to hear him talk about his passions, I can tell you that it is a joy. His eyes sparkle while he lays out his ideas. I thought that his book was not only great reading but also a useful manual for anyone wanting to know more about how boards function.

I told Jerry that it was an honor to be asked to write a foreword for his text. After breakfast, he was on his way to visit a former teacher, Dr. Gisela Konopka, who was also an emeritus professor from our school of social work. Jerry and I have talked many times about what an inspiration she was to her students and to her colleagues. During the writing of this edition of Jerry's book, Gisela died. Her death was not unanticipated; she was, after all, ninety-three years old. But it was unexpected in that she had continued to be a mentor for both of us. Somehow, I had anticipated her always being available to me. This book would certainly have been a source of discussion for the three of us.

As I was considering what to write in this piece, I found myself drifting back to Gisela's writings and thinking about her teachings on the power of people coming together to create change. One of the truths of which she would have reminded us was that boards (as well as agencies and organizations) are essentially different groups. Groups of different sizes and purposes but still essentially groups. Further, she would have reminded us as social workers to remember what we had learned as group workers and apply that knowledge to our work on boards. Gisela believed in the dynamics of group process and that through purposeful group interaction, change could occur. In her classic work on social group work, Konopka stated, "Groups are the basic expressions of human relationships; in them lies the greatest power of man. To try to work with them in a disciplined way is like trying to harness the power of the elements … like atomic power, groups can be harmful and helpful." Jerry has learned well from his teacher of many years ago. In this new edition, he provides numerous ways to harness the power of people.

While many of the examples draw from the author's experiences with Jewish organizations, the ideas are universal. Jerry's eighteen years of practice and twenty-one years in academia teaching board/staff relations has given him a rich background on which to build. One of the best examples of this is a tool that appears in a grid, which can be used to evaluate candidates for board membership. Jerry suggests a few "w's"—wealth, work, wisdom, wit, and wallop as criteria for board membership, as well as people skills, commitment to Jewish values (or the values of the particular organization), and that amazing word—*menschlichkeitism*. I have been on boards where the selection criteria were limited to who might be interesting and who would come to meetings.

A friend of mine told me that she was once on a board for almost six months and meeting monthly before it was clear exactly what her role should be. She had agreed to serve without seeing a job description for board members or having a discussion on her role. She joined the board despite her busy schedule because she felt passionately about the organization's mission and wanted to help in some way. It was only after joining that she discovered the board members did very little other than listen to staff reports, support the executive director's ideas, and review the budget. While questions were eagerly responded to, suggestions for change and new ideas were ignored.

Jerry reviews the essential responsibilities of board members and the delicate balance between board and staff roles. Boards are legally responsible for the actions of the organization they serve. They have the power to hire and fire staff, select leadership, and provide oversight. It is possible—maybe even predictable—that boards and executive directors of agencies will come into conflict. How that conflict is handled is critical to the future functioning of the agency.

A few years ago I attended a retreat for an organization on which I had been on the board of directors for many years. A newly hired Executive Director had quickly gained the full support and trust of the staff but was viewed with suspicion by the board of directors. In an exercise by an outside facilitator, the staff was asked to surround the director (who was lying on the floor) and carefully lift her a few inches off the floor, which they did with no trouble at all. In the next exercise the board was asked to do the same thing. The Executive Director froze and was clearly frightened although willing to give it a try. Board members expressed great reluctance at participating in the exercise and backed away. One staff member offered to take the Director's place. Without completing the exercise it was clear in the discussion that there were significant problems of trust and understanding between board and staff.

At a break in a recent committee meeting, I turned to my colleagues and asked about their experiences with board membership. One woman laughed and said that when she had re-located to a small town in Indiana, she volunteered to be a member on the local United Way board. With dreams of allocating funds to worthy causes, she instead found herself frustrated as her major tasks were to march in the Fourth of July parade, sell raffle tickets, and to help calm dogs at a picture taking for a "Santa and Your Pet" holiday fund-raiser. The real decision-making was done outside of the board.

The motivations for joining boards were quite varied. One man who had a passion for animals had served on the zoo board for almost twenty years because he also had the requirement to volunteer for a minimum of ten hours a month presenting animals to zoo goers on Sunday afternoons. Another man gave an example of an organization that had created an AIDS hospice primarily out of the work of two mothers who were frustrated with the lack of services available for their sons. While the organization had expanded due to the compassion, caring, and commitment of these women, they eventually became exhausted, and the need for a more formal board with members who could be more objective about the growth of the organization was identified.

One woman who has great expertise in personnel benefits and policies finds herself frequently asked to be on organizational boards to exploit her skills. In a recent effort, she found herself immersed in studying various benefit packages for employees and was rewarded for her efforts with extra compensation from the organization. Another colleague told of eagerly joining the board of a well-established social service agency and being told at the second meeting that they had decided to merge with another social service agency in the community. She spent months in sub-committee meetings conducting delicate negotiations around everything from a new name to merging leadership within the two groups. She has now become an expert in this area, has written a publication about the process, and is eager to find a new opportunity to share her experience.

One of the most controversial activities of a board is responsibility for finances. The ability to find and sustain funding is crucial. There is a cartoon I remember that depicts Moses coming down from the mountaintop holding two shiny and new stone tablets in his arms. In modern day terms, the stone tablets could be viewed as his "mission statement". Smiling, Moses is looking toward the heavens and saying "… and now, what about funding"? One of my most frustrating experiences was serving on a board for an organization that needed to move from being a for-profit agency to a nonprofit agency. It was hard for current board members to see the value in giving up their annual profits in exchange for having to assist with fundraising.

This book presents over ninety different scenarios that could provide for provocative discussion in the classroom as well as the boardroom. The scenario titles reflect the diversity of situations faced by boards and staff: "Development Director and Division Chair Compete," "Who's in Charge?," "Positive Changes without Negative Feelings," "Canceling Under-funded Events," and "Defining an Intern's Role." The Scenarios also raise more difficult issues such as Overcoming a Reputation for Sexism; Female Staff at a "Men Only" Fundraiser; Hurt Feelings Lead to Nasty Gossip; and Prominent Staff Executive has AIDS, Does Not Want Public to Know.

For new leaders who struggle with how to get started as well as experienced leaders who take the time to thoughtfully reflect on their own performance, the section on Tools and Exercises is equally helpful and provocative. Presentations such as Ten Basic Rules for Productive Meetings, Structuring a Meeting; Dealing with Difficult Members, and various mechanisms for analysis and evaluation of groups are very useful. Some chapters in this new edition are classics that have appeared previously including Peter F. Drucker's Lesson for Successful Nonprofit Governance and Toward a Contingency Model of Board-Executive Relations by Ralph M. Kramer.

Two new chapters to this edition are authored by Unitarian ministers. Reverend Lee Barker posits that respect is challenged and tested constantly between a professional and a board. He gives an example of an errant email message that led to stressful relationships and concludes that the power of a minister's work with a board is the world of hope and the world of trust. Reverend Stephan Johanssen makes the conclusion in his chapter on Beyond the Organizational Chart: Board-Staff Relations in Healthy Congregation that, "… just as good fences make good neighbors, good boundaries between organizational parts of a congregation do make for good relationships".

One chapter I particularly found useful was "Positioning Women for National Leadership" by Shifra Bronznick in which she reminds us that organizations have not fully utilized the talents and experiences of women. I am frequently reminded of this when I am asked to provide suggestions of faculty and alumni who might serve on community boards. Despite the fact that I give names of both men and women, the women are frequently overlooked and assumed to have less relevant experience. I am also reminded of the fact that women are less likely to see many of their life experiences as relevant to board membership and leadership. One woman's work in organizing Girl Scout cookie sales involved coordinating the efforts of hundreds of volunteers, balancing a budget and monitoring inventory. In my current role as parent of a hockey player who is twelve, I find myself coordinating schedules for car pools, collecting funds to support tournaments, event planning, and contributing to the long range goals of the organization. Former Secretary of State Madeleine Albright was asked in a radio interview what experience had best prepared her for negotiating with foreign leaders and heads of state. She replied, "arranging car pools and schedules for my children".

A former student told me the story of planning a family trip to England to visit relatives. The anticipation went on for several months. Every time a plane flew overhead, my student would say to her young daughter, "Before you know it, we will be sitting on that plane, flying to see Grandma". About the third or fourth time this occurred, the young child looked up into the sky and queried, "How do we get up there to get on the plane?"

Planning for successful relationships between board and staff does not just happen because of good intentions, eager anticipation or by accident. A successful relationship evolves because of careful planning, clarity of roles, shared mission and good communication. No one should be confused about how to get there. Jerry Bubis has given us a publication that offers a road map of how to achieve our goals in working with staff and boards.

1. Konopka, Gisela. (1963) *Social Group Work: a Helping Process*. Englewood Cliffs, New Jersey: Prentice—Hall, Inc. p.vi.

Jean K. Quam, Ph.D., L.I.C.S.W.
Professor and Director
School of Social Work
University of Minnesota
1404 Gortner Ave, 105 Peters Hall
St. Paul, Minnesota 55108

Preface

The first edition of this book was in formation for many years. My career has been a unique one. Eighteen years of practice were followed by twenty-one years in academia. The practice was primarily in Jewish community centers but included stints in Hillel, camp settings, and Jewish federations. In that time I was able to observe many boards of directors and work with more than a few in four different cities.

At the same time I became active as a citizen in a number of organizations, some essentially professional and others in the not-for-profit sector where I was a board member, officer, or president.

Moving into academia, I had the privilege of leading in the development of a graduate school devoted to educating professionals for Jewish community service. Over the twenty one years I taught courses on board-staff relations (among others) and became even more active on the board level in both general and professional organizations.

I have had the privilege of attaining posts at the national and later international level as a volunteer. After retirement, some sixteen years ago, my time took an even sharper focus both as trainer, consultant, and lecturer and as a volunteer on many boards of directors. By my estimate I have conducted classes, seminars, and workshops for close to 2,500 professionals and board members in cities all throughout North America, Europe, parts of South America, and in Israel.

I began collecting vignettes and scenarios from real life while keeping up with the literature in the field as best I could. I did some writing on the subject but increasingly felt that something was needed that could combine theoretical and practical material. This book is the outcome.

Over the past twenty-eight years I have had the pleasure of being a Fellow, and later a Vice President, of the Jerusalem Center for Public Affairs, where I learned much. I was deeply inspired from and through Daniel Elazar, of blessed memory (1934 to 1999), its founding president. Dan was a scholar and teacher to me but most of all, a dear friend whom I sorely miss even though he has been gone over six years. His output was prodigious over eighty books, countless articles, while editing three journals, teaching at two universities and heading up three think tanks. He encouraged me greatly in the creating of this book.

For articles not reprinted here I plead space requirements. For the focus of scenarios chosen and games simulations developed or utilized, I assume responsibility. Errors are mine even as I acknowledge the importance of the articles and, of course, their authors to me.

There are many people to thank in the preparation of the first edition of this book, beginning with the authors of the essays whose wisdom and insight inform much of what is called the best practice in the field. Joslyn Arnon and Barbara Zelonky were very helpful in screening scenarios and putting them into usable form. Most patient and especially helpful has been Sarah Felman, who caught many style and spelling errors, and helped put this document into its final form for the first edition. Mark Ami-El at the Jerusalem Center helped with his thoughtful and useful editing. My colleague, Steven M. Cohen, was of inestimable help to me.

There were many who helped underwrite the initial project at the Center, which was devoted to the issue of governance in contemporary American board-staff relations. A special thanks to Marcia Burnam, and thanks to Lionel and Terry Bell, Jack Cherbo and Elaine Hoffman, David Fox, Betsy Gidwitz, Richard and Lois Gunther, Arnold and Vicki Kupetz, Luis and Lee Lainer, Irwin Levin, Mark and Peachy Levy, the Polinger Family Foundation, Linda Rosenberg, Irwin Rosenbloom, Ed Sanders, and Sanford Weiner. The Jewish Agency for Israel's contribution assured the completion of that project.

My wife Ruby's patience and loving criticism has, as always, been hopeful and encouraging.

Ben Cutter helped in the initial reshaping of the book for more general use. Marla Eglash Abraham, a former student, faculty colleague, friend and now interim director of the School of Jewish Communal Service was of inestimable aid in critiquing my essay. Lisa Helfman, a recent graduate of the school, was of much help in initial editing the scenarios and exercises. Beth Kraemer Bubis has my thanks beyond measure for her extraordinary help. To all, I share my appreciation.

The feelings expressed by many colleagues that the core material of this book would be a great utility in the general nonprofit sector led to this significantly revised edition. It is my hope that this publication will prove a useful tool for all who work as staff or board members on behalf of bettering lives and advancing causes throughout the world.

Gerald B. Bubis
Los Angeles
2006

Introduction

Downsizing. Outsourcing. Entrepreneurial fundraising. Power-sharing. Re-engineering. Reinventing. Twenty-first century. Market share. Niche marketing. Mergers. Redundancy. Measurable outcomes. These and many other phrases and words swirl over e-mail, in articles, memos, and conversations relating to the pressures and events impinging upon the corporate sector in America. All these issues, concerns, and challenges also faced the not-for-profit sector at the end of the twentieth century, directly confronting those who would claim to lead communities into the future.

In the United States the voluntary system is unique insofar as its use of paid staff is concerned. The result, as noted in one of the essays in this book, is a dual driven system which, when developed and implemented well, gains much of its dynamism and creativity from the interaction between staff and board members.

Complications abound. There is not always clear sanction or clarification of what board members expect of staff and vice versa. In research I conducted with Steven Cohen of Hebrew Union College (formerly of Hebrew University), we confirmed the problem of low trust levels existing between staff and board members.

The challenge, then, is to recognize that leadership is needed; leadership grounded in values yet infused with competencies; leadership sanctioned by the constituents to lead because they trust the leadership.

The ultimate measure must be in behaviors, not in motivations. It is the staff's responsibility, together with successful senior volunteers, to help volunteers go from "doing good" to performing well. Many are ready to do so. Many are not.

It remains the staff's responsibility not to engage in stereotypical thinking when dealing with volunteers. The golden rule still does not hurt. It can never be trite to try to treat others as one would hope to be treated. It is incumbent upon staff to remember they are being paid to do a job well and that includes dealing with volunteers openly and honestly. The competencies of many of the volunteers today exceed staff competencies. They will only stay if they feel their talents and wits are being challenged to the utmost.

Research has confirmed that the competencies of board members, regarding both what they know and what they do, were seen by both staff and board members as being at relatively low levels. (Bubis, Cohen 1998).

This book contains a number of foundational articles devoted to governance. The articles which are reprinted cover a range of models of governance in the not-for-profit sector, as well as cautions and guidelines growing out of practice, wisdom, and/or research. Some of them are a decade or so old but retain timeless wisdom in the world of governance and board-staff relations.

The balance of the book is devoted to scenarios collected in the course of research or teaching. The scenarios are followed by a number of exercises to be used in both board and staff training.

The book's title? As part of the aforementioned, respondents were asked to describe a situation involving a problem in board-staff relations together with reporting the resolution of the problem. An anonymous respondent reported, "a new president began to run the organization as if it were his factory. He treated everyone on staff, especially the director, as if they were employees in his factory." What happened? How was it resolved? The answer—"the director had a heart attack and the president resigned."

The brief description of the problem coupled with the laconic answer fires the imagination. We wish that a more detailed description existed of the issues that arose between this particular president and director. Did the lay president assume that the director as an employee was to be the active listener and constant implementer of whatever he was ordered to do? What might some of the issues have been? Did any other board officers or board members come to the director's defense? What kinds of responses did the director engage in? Was he confrontational in turn? Did he ever suggest alternative scenarios to be utilized? How were the suggestions received? Was the chemistry between the two of them doomed to produce conflict from the start because the director was also confrontational and as insensitive as the short scenario suggests was the case with the president?

We will never know the answers because the anonymous respondent chose not to share details. What we do know, based upon the scenarios shared in this book, is that there is much volatility in many of the relationships between board and staff members.

There is a skew to these scenarios. The great majority of them have been shared by staff, meaning those working as administrators, human service workers, educators, social workers, fundraisers, and rabbis and ministers, who while working as spiritual leaders may still be hired and fired by boards of directors. They are drawn primarily from the world of agencies, including family services, campus organizations, city-wide funding bodies, and community centers. A number are also drawn from synagogue and church settings with issues arising between board members, clergy and/or educators.

Board members contributed some scenarios as well, but in smaller numbers. In some instances, scenarios are included that focus on relations between staff. These are included because of their potential negative ramifications for the board and its constituency if the problems are not resolved. In all instances, these are real scenarios which were chosen from a much larger sample set which I have accumulated over the years.

If you, the reader, would like to add to the compilation of scenarios, please share them with me by fax, 310-788-0713, or e-mail, grbubis@msn.com.

Dedicated to Daniel Elazar
1934–1999

Present Realities and Future Possibilities

Gerald B. Bubis

"I believe in the beloved community and in the spirit which makes it beloved, and in the communion of all who are, in will and in deed, its members. I see no such community as yet, but nonetheless my rule of life is: Act so as to hasten its coming."

—Josiah Royce (1855-1916), American philosopher

While it might be argued that community organizing began in the Bible, when Moses organized the people and delegated tasks in the name of building and preserving the community, Royce's sentiments written in the nineteenth century echo the same longing for community ties and involvement. Modern times featured the development of organizational specialization, opportunities for entrepreneurship, and the growing complexities confronting cultural or religious communities while still aspiring to become a beloved community.

Perhaps, on the face of it, the running of faith or interest-based not-for-profit enterprises might be seen as simple. Volunteers who are interested come together under one banner or another and, where necessary, hire people to do their bidding, implement their policies, and otherwise engage in the day-to-day running of the organization to the satisfaction of their bosses, the volunteers.

This past century in America saw the proliferation of literally hundreds of voluntary organizations. They took on a multiplicity of tasks: assisting in immigrants' socialization; providing relief; teaching English; finding jobs; maintaining cemeteries, churches and synagogues, religious schools, libraries, and hospitals; responding to social ills; aiding in the settlement of displaced populations; reuniting families; publishing newspapers; printing books; sending kids (and families) to camp; building orphanages, homes for the aged, YMHAs and YMCAs; organizing unions; dealing with local, state, and national governments; rescuing the captives; developing debating societies; setting up special facilities for those with asthma and tuberculosis; setting up free medical and dental clinics and kindergartens. The list could be expanded.

Thousands of caring people have given of their time and resources to build diverse communities with wide ranges of services and institutions. The cacophony created by this wide-ranging and varied multiplicity of opportunities demanded increasing attention. Sometimes slowly, sometimes quickly, sometimes unevenly and with little forethought, people were hired to provide such services. Volunteers still worked side-by-side, hand-in-hand with those they hired. There were conflicts. Clarification and re-clarification was needed as to when volunteers performed functions unique to them by virtue of their status, purse, or role. Reciprocally, paid staff began to professionalize and evolve more coherent methods of services.

Today, a wide spectrum of beliefs and practices must be manifest on organizational boards. Issues arise in all agencies and organizations that call for reflection of core agency values as a major guide to decision-making. At the least, the past should have a vote, if not a veto, to quote a famous rabbi. Knowledge of the organization's constituency, their history, cultural norms and values should take part in weaving the organizational fabric.

The business of the nonprofit world is people-oriented. Additionally, while all organizations using any kind of public funds must do so efficiently, they must also understand the difference between efficiency and effectiveness.

Agencies and organizations which use sectarian references in their names do well when they continue to manifest that which is unique to them as a group, even as they remain part of the community around them.

Inexorably, agency roles and functions have been reviewed and revisited. Over the decades, appropriate skill desiderata were identified, leading to professional training programs and schools, certification programs and allied graduate education programs devoted to educating paid staff with a view to enhancing practice and clarifying those values, methods, and skill sets for those who serve in the nonprofit arena.

A literature has evolved, sometimes born of practice, sometimes reflective of research. Literally hundreds of articles and books have been printed devoted to the concerns, issues, and challenges involved in building up the voluntary sector.

The articles in this book represent some of the most challenging points of view, findings, and practice excellence that are in print today. They provide a context for this article which in part draws from the teachings of many over the decades, combined with my practice wisdom which now spans five decades.

The challenge is to learn from but not be stalled in the past, while trying to synthesize the utilizable for tomorrow.

Models of Governance

In a democracy there are many ways to structure decision-making. Here we will review and analyze: 1) the various models of governance in nonprofit settings which exist in America today, 2) the roles filled by volunteers as governors, 3) the roles of staff in the governance process, 4) the sources of friction, 5) the skills needed by all concerned in the governance process, 6) some of the paradoxes which confront all of us who function as board or staff members, 7) the place and use of boards and committees in the governance process, 8) effective use of agendas, 9) practical suggestions and cautions for dealing with the increasingly complex challenges to the governance process.

The Legislative Model

The foundational premise of the legislative process is based upon an adversarial approach to problem-solving. That process is grounded in hearings, deliberations, and debate with heavy staff input.

This process ultimately produces outcomes which accommodate to the exigencies and contingencies of the power and tensions behind the advocates for and against a given piece of legislation. In this world, the notion of passing a measure by a fifty-one percent vote is acceptable even as the antagonists hope to persuade their respective adversaries to vote with them. Amendments abound. It is the rare piece of legislation which comes out of a committee process in its originally proposed form. Representativeness, both covert and overt, is thus an important part of the process. When concerns overlap, adversaries can become allies, if only temporarily. The public insists on being heard.

Ultimately, much of the ratification process is open to public scrutiny, intentionally and otherwise. The press, television, and other media become the watchdogs of society. They, of course, have toppled incumbents. Ultimately, a recurring re-ratification process is at work. Even though voter turnout is poor, even though election fraud is not an unknown phenomenon, even though cynicism often abounds, the "elected" officials ultimately respond to a sense of representativeness, the cost of elections notwithstanding.

Checks and balances, however imperfect, exist between the three branches of government, and in places such as California, with a referendum system, some would suggest there is a fourth branch of government.

At its worst the system can lead to corruption, excessive attention to lobbyists and those they represent, excessive cost in the pursuit of office, and what some would perceive to be the excessive power of incumbents.

Within the not-for-profit community there are other identifiable models.

The Federation System

The closest possible analogies to the federation system are the Catholic Church, with its complex and comprehensive network of religious, educational, social services and social action structures, and local chapters of United Way. The comparison for the Catholic Church breaks down in that the Church does not have a board and committee governance system.

Within the Jewish federation system—the federations themselves, community centers, family services, vocational services, Hillels, homes for the Jewish aging, community relations committees, and the like—the tendency is to operate with a consensus system evolved between board and staff members. Permutations exist born of organizational cultural differences, the power of certain personalities who come and go, the strength of a board, and its membership and constituency.

It is the exception to have major policy changes which are ratified by only fifty-one percent of the board members. The committee process undergirds the whole system, which is where much if not most of the organization's governance business is evolved. This may or may not be a tidy process. The seriousness of the participants, their access to helpful information, the roles of the chair and the staff, often explain the levels of trust that the system as a whole invests in the committee process.

This can be a ponderous process at times. Concerns that all spheres of influence are engaged prior to any important decision results in the accusation of issues being processed past the point of relevance, and indeed this is sometimes the case. These systems are often seen by some as "ponderous pachyderms," to quote one observer, when it comes to making decisions in a reasonable time frame.

In the opinion of many, the search for consensus has served the system well. The nature of the enterprise, counting as it does on voluntarily given money, most of which comes from a relatively few, cannot ignore donors' wishes. The power of the purse is not a new phenomenon in the life of not-for-profit organizations. With that said, it is true that most large givers remain remarkably trusting of boards and their committees. They tend to be underrepresented in the governance process, if one measures that involvement by board and committee membership and actual attendance at meetings.

The governance systems are, for the most part, self-perpetuating. Sitting boards create nominating committees which are most often appointed by the president. While thought is given to some sense of "Representativeness" on boards, there is no check and balance system and elections for board membership and contested elections are a rarity.

Professional and Trade Associations

Contested elections for office are the norm. Candidates lobby for votes, solicit support from members, and invest time and energy in the election process. Platforms are developed through an elaborate membership process which seeks to welcome maximum involvement through hearings, opportunities to serve on committees, structures of involvement through sophisticated publications, and other means of communication. Staff people are not advocates for or against candidates, but rather play a maximum role in serving the organization itself. There is a balance of input between board and staff into the governance process.

Groups which mirror this model include the National Association of Social Workers, Alliance for Nonprofit Management, American Medical Association and the American Society of Association Executives, to name a few.

Umbrella Organizations and Cause-driven Organizations

Organizations in these categories are branded together by their respective missions. Their boards tend to be structured for geographic, economic, racial, demographic and/or professional diversity depending on their respective missions. On the local level, board members are generally appointed by constituent organizations with more and more frequent instances of constituent representation as required by law. The balance between board and staff powers is delineated in a careful way, and the consensual model of governance is the norm. Those that are national in nature are, by definition, more likely to be staff driven. As always, there are some notable exceptions where personalities have taken on a cause and have attempted to model the organization around their own charismatic personalities. Transparency and accountability of budgets, oversight functions by boards as outlined later in this essay, as well as all the other legitimate functions of a board of directors are often lacking. The chief executive officer and/or charismatic public figure, separately or jointly, wield great power and are unlikely to be held accountable to any public scrutiny unless overtaken by some particularly egregious public behavior, larcenous activity, or truly excessive misuse of funds, however legal it might have been.

Groups with reflect this model include The Salvation Army of America, the Council of Churches, YMCA of the USA and Greenpeace.

Community Based Organizations, Churches and Synagogues

Most nonprofit organizations function in essentially autonomous ways. Churches vary, with some being highly autonomous while others are restricted by virtue of respective denominations national structures and power-sharing arrangements. Local boards still tend to have a comparatively great amount of freedom in the governance processes. The relative power and roles of clergy and local agency executives defy easy classification. There is a wide range of models of power sharing, use of power in decision making, developing and implementing policies, programs, evaluative tools and the like. The models listed above offer many of the wide range of possibilities and are also present in local settings. More specific models practiced by many community based organizations (e.g. the Carver model) will be elaborated upon later in this article.

The principles, guidelines, best practice measures and evaluative possibilities do not vary, with rare exceptions.

Models of Governance

Organization	Board And Officer Selection Process	Balance Between Staff And Board Input In Governance	Primary Legislative Style	Representative Nature Of Governors
Federation System	self-perpetuating	dual driven	consensual	elitist
Public Legislative Model	contested	elected officials utilize staff	adversarial	representative of constituencies
Professional and Trade Associations	contested	dual driven	adversarial	representative of constituencies
Umbrella Organizations	appointed	dual driven	consensual	representative of constituencies
Cause Related Organizations	self-perpetuating	unpredictable	unpredictable	non-representative
Charismatic Organizations	self-appointed	none	none	none
Community based organizations	proportional by consensus	based upon personalities	consensual	representative

Essential Board Responsibilities

Boards of directors classically have had the following responsibilities:

Vision
Mission
Paths of Implementation
Legal Oversight
Hiring and Firing of Staff
Agency Oversight
Selection and Election of Leadership
Policy Formulation
Resource Development
Evaluation Procedures
Board Recruitment
Development
Planning
Program Development
Interpreters to the Community

The extent to which staff is engaged or primarily responsible for these responsibilities is discussed in the body of this essay.

Vision, Mission and Paths of Implementation

Essential to the function of a board are these three responsibilities. While I place them on the top of the board's list, I want to emphasize that staff must play an important and vital role in helping to shape these essential elements to an organization's on-going well being, vitality, and growth.

This is the day and age of streamlining, "compassionate conservatism," budgetary cutbacks, entrepreneurial fundraising, mergers and acquisitions in the NGO sector, and perhaps of greatest peril, public distrust of long-serving conventional organizations and agencies. It becomes imperative that a board focus as never before on its purpose, and what it seeks to accomplish in the grandest and greatest sense. This envisioning process must envelop all who are key elements to the cause for which the organization has been structured. It is best that board members, staff, clients and community members be involved in some phase of this process for it both sanctions and sanctifies the very reason for the organizations' existence.

Out of this grand vision a more specific and focused mission statement must emerge. This must be the task of the board to ultimately ratify, embrace, underwrite and assure that it permeates the very fiber of the organization's essence and reason for being. Staff helps shape the vision, but board members must "own" it. This ownership manifests itself in the next component of this tri-fold responsibility—namely specifying paths of implementing the mission. It is imperative that a board spends its primary energies on these responsibilities, for they are long-term in nature, layered and laddered in their complexity.

It is one thing to set out a grandiose vision regarding the plight of children in impoverished countries, as an example, then follow it up with a brilliantly succinct mission statement which summarizes in haiku form what your organization will do to ameliorate the condition of those children you choose to serve. It is yet another, however, to plan carefully for the human, physical, fiscal, social, psychological, economic and political resources your organization will have to bring to bear to fulfill your mission. It becomes even more difficult as you attempt to remain accountable through measurable outcomes, and modify environments, people, attitudes or resources.

Legal Oversight

Many of us sometimes forget that by law the board is the legally assigned entity responsible for general oversight of the organization. Under the law, the board has fiduciary responsibilities. It must assure society that the purposes for which the organization was incorporated are being fulfilled in a responsible manner. By law, it must be able to assure the organization's donors that the money given in trust is being utilized in a manner which meets accounting and auditing expectations, and government rules and regulations.

The sources of those funds today may be both private and public, but a reporting system must be in place which includes public posting of audited reports. Thus, the public, private, and government funders, members, and clients, if they wish, may review the fiscal status of the organization in which they are interested. (The law exempts religiously incorporated organizations from reporting to the state under the same disclosure requirements which must be met by other not-for-profit organizations.)

While the board has the legal right to oversee *and* implement *all* the other functions a not-for-profit organization engages in, through the decades many functions have been delegated to staff. While this is the case, the general oversight functions of a board cannot be delegated. What does take place is a process wherein the degree to which staff is involved in each instance is of varying visibility and importance, depending upon a number of criteria which will be discussed below.

Hiring and Firing of Staff

Perhaps the second most important power of a board over and above its generally legally expected oversight function is the hiring, evaluating (and when necessary firing) of the executive director.

This process can spell the success of an organization beyond measure. Careful review of expectations, requirements for the job, the chemistry between a candidate and a selection committee, thoughtful and full delineation of needs, revelations of past successes and failures in the organization, sensitivity to the needs of candidates and their families, are the *sine qua non* of a good selection process.

A thoughtful and appropriate candidate is evaluating and measuring the community and the organization as much as he or she is being evaluated and measured in turn.

The list enumerated above is applied with varying degrees of sensitivity and sophistication by different organizations/agencies. Parties to this process should be hoping for disclosure of relevant information and realities.

The very style of the meetings with candidates sets a tone. Where is the candidate interviewed? How formal or informal is the setting? Is the committee representative of those with whom he or she will work? Are the real opinion-makers and power-brokers part of the process? How realistic is the employment package? Does housing represent an issue in hiring the most appropriate candidate?

If this is a two-career family, is community leadership sensitive to helping the spouse or partner relocate? Will education costs for the family need partial or full funding? Some leaders have been known to stint in the interviewing process and conditions of employment, little appreciating that fine staff are in a sellers' market.

Over the years, the hiring of staff below the executive level has been delegated to the chief executive officer. Two points need to be made: 1) In almost every organization, volunteer counterparts are present as mirrors of staff. The volunteer chairing the young adult division should then be involved in the hiring of the new staff person and such should be the case in almost every instance where there are chair counterparts to staff roles; 2) All of the cautions and suggestions listed above are appropriate guidelines for the hiring process to the degree it is possible. The wise executive remains sensitive to this process, confident that the outcome will be less turnover, greater staff loyalty, and a greater sense of commitment by volunteers to the professional staff and to the organization itself.

Agency Oversight

Most organizations have instituted committees which initiate or are asked to shape suggested policies to assure the smooth and ongoing functioning of an agency. Insofar as possible, it is increasingly the practice in the more progressive organizations to include appropriate staff as voting members of the committees, but the preponderance of committee members remain volunteers. While the general oversight of the agency must remain primarily within the volunteers' domain, the process will not work well if the staff functions (which will be detailed later) are not performed well, consistently, and in a timely fashion. All that follows flows from the oversight functions of the board, which in complex structures will count heavily on the staff's input. As is constantly rediscovered by all involved in the governance process, the whole governance system is based upon trust—trust that the committees perform their jobs well, presenting options or recommendations to the board which are grounded in knowledge, creativity, probity, and appropriateness. The committee, in turn, counts on the staff to help them examine options and assess positives, negatives, and consequences of their actions. Knowledge that is gained in this process encompasses the multifaceted aspects of this sometimes laborious process.

Consider this reality in the following true scenario:

> The personnel committee (which has staff representation on all matters except salaries and benefits) has been asked by staff to review the agency's policy on continuing education. Over the years the amount allocated for staff training was reduced because of agency budget cutbacks. From the board's point of view, it was legitimate to make the cuts across the board. From the committee's point of view, it had always felt uncomfortable about the cuts, but had not opposed them.
>
> Staff has prepared data showing the importance of staff training as a function of staff retention. Throughout the country, agencies with a well developed staff training program geared to the needs of the agency and the staff have a far lower turnover rate than is the case in agencies spending very little on staff training. The proposal put forth by staff for committee consideration was that 1 percent of the gross personnel budget should be added the first year and from that time forward be built into the budget as an ongoing cost, as was the case with pensions, medical benefits, etc.

Did the staff have a "right" to initiate this process? Is the turnover rate of staff and continuing staff education a legitimate part of the oversight function? What are some actions the committee could take prior to, and during, a board executive meeting and subsequent board of directors' meeting? What might be some unstated considerations against the proposal? Are there questions not raised here which should be considered? How much of this "review" process should take place between the chairperson and the staff person who is working with the committee? Does staff have the "right" to raise the proposal with the executive committee and the board even if the proposal is rejected by the committee?

Selection and Election of Leadership

The demographics of organizational life confirm that a gerontocracy exists within many agencies' and organizations' boards of directors today. The organizations which make no provision for replacing this cadre of caring leadership will be doomed at worst and despairing at least because of insufficient planning for finding, selecting, and training new leadership.

Whose responsibility should this be today? What are the criteria for leadership which should be utilized?

Historically, community leadership has always included people of means. Simultaneously, there were knowledgeable participants involved in the governance process. As Daniel Elazar (1980) has pointed out, the leadership was seen as having earned the right to these roles. They were trusted by members of the community to represent the values and aspirations of the community. Seen as they were as members of that community, there was a feeling of a sense of what Elazar has labeled "kinship," which emphasized the commonality of destiny and concerns. This led to what Elazar has called a "consent" process. The community trusted the leaders to serve them well. While Elazar drew his model by tracing the Jewish community from Biblical to modern times, it is highly applicable to the voluntary sector as a whole.

Constitutional Principles of the Polity

1. *Voluntary Citizenship*: that "citizenship" in the polity, i.e. voluntary government is a matter of choice, and that the decision to become a "citizen" must be expressed by some positive act of affiliation.

2. *Associationalism*: that the basic unit of the polity is the "voluntary association"—a group who agrees to join together to pursue one or more self-selected goals.

3. *Federalism*: that relations between and among these associations are (largely) based on federal and confederal (rather than centralizing or hierarchical) principles.

4. *Aristocratic Republicanism*: that the polity is ultimately responsible to (and sovereignty ultimately resides in) the public as a whole, but that leadership is vested in an "aristocracy" of trustees normally defined by their readiness to contribute substantial money and energy to the polity.

5. *Consensual Decision-Making*: that decisions are reached by seeking a consensus among active leaders and that open conflict is avoided wherever possible.

6. *Shared and Divided Authority*: That authority in the polity is exercised by a variety of leadership groups, representing different bases and primary spheres of authority, with no group monopolizing authority in any sphere of activity.

7. *The Covenant of Mutual Responsibility*: that a primary purpose of the polity is to insure the well-being of every person as an expression of mutual responsibility. (Geffen, 1997)

We can infer by extension that leadership in the community, no matter what interests it serves, must be understood as stewardship on behalf of the community which should at its best represent a consciousness upon the part of the leaders of the ultimate purposes of their organizations. Simply put, the leadership of an institution should not lose sight of the reasons for the creation of the institution, nor that their "custody" is temporary.

Serious questions must be asked by those involved in nominating committees. There are those who would not have staff involved in the process. Again, the function of choosing leaders is primarily a board function, but staff can play and, I would argue, should play an important role in the process.

All those who staff committees should be conscious of their responsibility to identify those who should ultimately serve on a board. They are the antennae for senior staff and volunteer leadership, especially in large agencies. Awareness of criteria should have some internal consistency within the agency. Everyone must be thinking about tomorrow's leadership and the agency's needs.

A shorthand way of remembering what an organization should want at the board level has been subsumed by the five W's. They are listed below in no particular order and with a caution. The five W's are rarely found in one person. What is essential, however, for the best functioning boards is a balance on the board level and the hope that at least three of the five W's would be present in one board member.

The W's stand for Work, Wisdom, Wealth, Wit and Wallop—and, as you will see, I have added three dimensions.

Work

There must be some board members to perform the functions so essential to the success of the enterprise. A willingness to read and react to reports, attend meetings, and take on a fair share of the tasks, whatever they may be, must be evinced by a significant number of board (and committee) members. These tasks are all related to the governance functions and must flow from an expectation that everyone understands the difference between functioning as a volunteer in a service role and one who is engaged in the governance process.

Wisdom

Every community has a group of experienced people, wise to the ways and wiles of community life. They have knowledge of how best to effectuate change and who the decision-makers and power-brokers are. Their acumen is born of having served and observed having succeeded and failed, having perspective without haste, yet aware of timing and its requisite role in decision-making. They are creative and innovative, not resistant to change but able to counsel caution when others might not see the pitfalls of precipitous action or radical change before readiness is apparent.

The board cannot be over-peopled with idea-givers who are always suggesting that everyone except themselves should ever act. Yet there are those with whom counsel should be taken at the expense of serious consequences if counsel is ignored.

Wealth

Certainly in this day of resource development, few boards can succeed without a significant group of people for whom the organization's cause is paramount and is manifest through the significant sharing of resources as well as time. Heroic giving sets challenges, offers models for others, and translates visions into reality. It is always a difficult challenge to find donors who are not already committed to a cause, yet sometimes those who give to others in exemplary fashion join boards when asked without having committed to a gift. Agencies and organizations do this in the hope of convincing the new board member and potential donor of the uniqueness of their needs, and, indeed, there is often success with this approach. There is a danger of keeping such a person on a board who after a cycle of a year or so has not responded, for as others come to be aware of the non-support there is a negative signal which can come to stultify fundraising efforts with other board members.

If the potential donor is making significant non-monetary contributions, fulfilling at least three of the five W's, there must be serious weight given to keeping the person involved.

The children of significant givers and the widows and widowers of past givers are also potential sources of support. Those who give funds but do little else are important to the organization. However, a board made up solely of givers would also be a potential disaster (a problem never present to that degree in real life).

Wit

Board membership can be onerous at times and difficulties can abound. Tensions can become endemic to the governance enterprise. It is often forgotten that when all is said and done, emotional pay for board and committee members must exceed emotional pain. It is very helpful in the selection and election process to make sure that a significant percentage of the board is composed of people who, in addition to the other W's being sought, also have a sense of humor, see sunshine when others see clouds, and are optimistic, yet grounded in reality.

Wallop

No organization can function outside of a network. As "no person is an island," so it is with agencies and organizations. However they are viewed, their perceived importance and status often turns on relationships. There must always be those among the board who not only possess the wisdom to analyze but the ability to connect. Making the phone call to open a door, set up a solicitation, introduce the president and executive to that highly important contact, are important assets for any organization. For an organization which is new, or has a new mission or services, this often is an indispensable component in the process of building and expanding services.

Again, the important thing to remember is that a board member should ideally manifest at least three of the five W's. The selection and election of leadership must be viewed as one of the most serious functions of a board. The input of staff is essential, given the need to have a multiplicity of sources for potential leadership.

There are yet other attributes than the five W's which are essential for maximum performance of boards and committees. These would include what I would call interpersonal skills, *menschlichkeitism*, and a commitment to the core values and mission of the agency grounded in integrity and ethical behavior.

People Skills

One might think it elementary to expect board members to be able to get along well with people, be sensitive to and about others, and have the capacity to communicate wishes, expectations, and positions in a polite manner. Unfortunately, as is evident in many of the scenarios which appear later in this book, this is too often not the case.

At the heart of all decision-making processes is the ability to form, nourish, and maintain relationships. When a person is on the board because of "wealth" and "wallop," the reality of a decision-making process can be overcome by the feared ramifications of wrestling with an eight hundred pound gorilla.

To say the least, strong yet positive board and staff leadership sometimes is needed to deal with board members whose presence is important and whose behavior is problematic.

Menschlichkeitism

This attribute, often elusive yet, like love, easy to recognize when it exists, assumes good people skills but goes beyond them. The word is *Yiddish*, evolving from the word *Mensch*. A *mensch* is a person who is morally grounded and who functions with great integrity. *Menschlichkeitism* is that innate and outstanding quality of goodness and niceness, both of which qualities are essential to facilitating effective, positive and successful board-staff relations.

Board members who say thank you to staff are sensitive about agency goals and their achievement in both moral and common sense ways. Those who possess this attribute recognize the organization as a tool for human betterment and not an end in itself. They are often the people turned to for help in resolving difficult conflict situations. They manifest the W of wisdom in the ways they respond to stressful situations, difficult pressures upon the agency as a whole, and board and staff members.

Lucky is the agency or organization which has such jewels in abundance. For those not so blessed, the "mining" of these special souls is often a job first initiated by staff at many levels beyond the executive positions.

Commitment to Values

Wise is the organization which is conscious of the need for some board members who not only have institutional memory but are grounded in knowledge and living born of ethical (or at least grounded) values and beliefs. I do not wish to be misunderstood. I am not advocating that only those whose call to serve is based upon a traditional Judeo-Christian ethical framework are desirable for board positions, yet boards manifesting excellence in practice and service now appreciate this dimension as a refraction for measuring the fidelity of the agency's mission. Every agency or organization thus is responding to some kind of calling, whether secular or religious in its origin, when crafting its vision.

Policy Formulation and Planning

In the governance process, viable agencies and organizations spend considerable time and energy in the matter of policy formulation. The functions of yesteryear do not necessarily respond to the needs of tomorrow. Nothing is permanent in its present form, neither problems nor solutions, and, as a result, smugness can destroy a successful enterprise. Insensitivity to the changing nature of issues and the velocity of change itself converge to emphasize the ever-increasing importance of the processes and outcomes which must guide an agency into the next millennium.

Vision and Mission must precede all other processes. While no organization ever achieves its visions in full, the nature and direction of an agency's priorities must be based upon their stated mission. Serious agencies encourage think pieces from staff with alternate scenarios. A growing number ask key volunteers and staff to work on scenarios together. Strategic planning, in varying stages of commitment, is the chosen path of most—but typically only after the die is cast, budgets are set, facilities are procured, modified, or dispensed with and reality sets in.

Jim Collins begins his insightful book *From Good to Great* with the sentence "Good is the enemy of great" (2001). His book, as so many know, focuses on ways of moving organizations from being good to being great. He emphasizes the need for leadership to assure the appropriate mix of talents and values which combine in an alchemy which assure organizations being able to move to the highest level of functioning and product—whatever that product is. It is no less true in the not-for-profit sector. The differences between superior and average organizations are often traceable to the degree to which creative synergy and trust exists between staff and board members. This phase of agency activity often finds a high degree of involvement and input from staff because of the specificity of knowledge needed to inform the board as they form their judgments in turn.

To suggest that boards formulate policy and staff implement policy is to simplify what is in reality a complex set of relationships. It *is* true that the ultimate judgments as manifest by the vote of the board in the minutes is in the "hands" of the board members, yet no thoughtful board should pass policies without consulting with staff. Normally, much of this happens when there is a sound committee process, yet issues arise where it is clear that differences exist between people with honestly held positions. It is imperative that board members receive pertinent data and hear the reasoning of the staff, especially when it is clear that everyone concerned, including board and staff members, have strongly held positions.

This is not a setting for wars. As indicated earlier, for better or worse, consensus is the dominant way of resolving issues. There are no "winners and losers" if consensus is not possible and close votes end up deciding the destiny of an issue or program. Additionally, it does not follow that in such instances the staff's position is always the best one to follow. The greater issue can often be how staff is handled in such situations. Are they told to remain silent unless spoken to? Are they forbidden from circulating memos with what is considered by some to be controversy-laden content? Some of the scenarios noted later in this book note such instances.

In the policy formulation phase, is it moral for a staff person to only call those he knows agree with him or her to attend the meeting? Is it more permissible if a chair or a president does the same? When is silence on the part of staff or board members appropriate? As on the battlefield, are there times when one is realistic enough to lose a battle in order to win a war?

I am one who does not believe that threats to resign by either board or staff members is an appropriate approach to be used to "sway" people to one's position. There are those rare times when resignation is the last but the appropriate action to take when the directions, practices, and decisions of the organization are completely antithetical to one's own value system.

Short of that, whether board or staff member, one's own passion should always be grounded in facts, concerns, and outcomes which lead one to his or her position in the first place. Acting with political acumen, trying to influence the influential, and circulating material are legitimate tools and tactics in the process as long as they are guided by a moral compass which is not exploitative of people or the organization itself. To me, manipulation is anathema which has no place as a tool in organizational life.

A couple of true vignettes might bring these comments to bear in context.

> A community relations executive had set a process in motion which followed long and well established practice in the agency. A public issue was put on the ballot which fell within the purview of the urban affairs committee (UAC). Hearings were held on the issue, material with pro and con arguments were distributed, and after serious and full deliberation a vote was taken on the issue with a large majority approving the proposed ballot issue. The recommendation was sent to the executive committee for review and acceptance well in advance of the UAC meeting and election day itself. Normally when this process is followed, the executive committee would accept the committee's recommendation and then it would recommend that the UAC take a public position in support of or opposition to the issue.
>
> The UAC chairperson was opposed to the ballot issue and had made his own position known early in the process. The urban affairs committee members were particularly sensitive in their process in light of the chairperson's stated opposition. Nevertheless, after careful and due deliberations they had made their recommendation which was in opposition to that of the chairperson's. The chairperson realized that the recommendation would be sent to the executive committee for acceptance or rejection and called a meeting of the executive committee without a clear agenda, ordering the staff not to call those on the executive committee known to be in opposition to his position. The chairperson called his friends urging them to attend the meeting. The executive committee, at the UAC chair's recommendation, voted to table the recommendation and not bring it up to the board for a vote.
>
> By the time those who had supported the ballot measure were aware of what happened, it was too late to bring the matter to a vote before the actual

election. A number of the UAC members resigned in the aftermath. They did so with a protest letter shared with the leadership.

If you were the UAC executive, what would you have done? Under what circumstances should the issue have been discussed, even though it was after the fact? Does the fact that the UAC chair is very wealthy make a difference to your decision? What would be some arguments for and against doing nothing?

> In another community, a prominent Palestinian notified the UAC leadership that she would be available for a private meeting with community leadership. The UAC chair responded to the staff by refusing to allow staff to arrange such a meeting. The staff person involved felt this unilateral action was uncalled for and proceeded to phone some of the chairperson's peers, reporting what had happened. She was encouraged to arrange the meeting, making sure that those invited represented a cross-section of community leadership. The meeting was well attended and helpful in exposing leadership to a PLO leader and for perceptions on the peace process.

Did the staff person exceed her role in the policy formulation process? What are some of the consequences which could be predicted in future relationships between the staff person and her supervisor or with the volunteer leader?

It is rare that black and white answers exist. I would suggest that strength of relationships, the ability to assess consequences, the readiness to respond with appropriate action, and the inner compass which we all possess are the guides to what each of us would do.

Fiscal Resource Development

Traditionally, in most organizations where fundraising is a major component of practice, the rule of thumb was for a volunteer to solicit a volunteer—peer to peer. Traditionally, staff provided important information as needed, ranging from confirming a potential giver's assets to his or her philanthropic interests and history.

Fundraising events tended to be coordinated by staff with varying degrees of input from volunteers, which differed depending upon community culture, and volunteer interest and time availability. The volunteers engaged with women's organizations, auxiliaries and events, for example, traditionally have extensive and creative input into their planning and implementation processes. By strict definition of differences in the roles of staff people and volunteers, they are engaging in a kind of micro-management which is a "no-no" in most instances. In truth, people must remember that none of the models, suggestions and assessments of "practice' is written in stone. Rigidity on anyone's part in working in these settings is a totally undesirable trait. At times it difficult it is to draw lines between board and staff functioning.

As the sources of funds have become increasingly complex, so have the realities of what is needed to sustain the services the agencies offer. Foundations, philanthropic funds, government in the national, state, and local arenas, and corporations are an increasingly significant source of funds. They supplement and in some cases supplant personal donations as well as institutional fundraising campaigns as the traditional and primary source of funds. Marketing has helped many agencies become more and more entrepreneurial in selling goods and services, in many cases with agencies setting up revenue generating entities, often at the urging of planning and marketing staff. (For insight as to the increasing importance and need to develop entrepreneurial emphasis for resource development see the website for Social Enterprise Alliance at www.se-alliance.org).

The individual donor remains important, especially those who contribute five and six figure gifts annually, but the technical knowledge needed for grant writing and the time requirements for nonprofit generating centers have often tilted the role of staff toward much more engagement and importance. It is no longer uncommon for many agencies to count on individual donors for less than twenty percent of their budgets. Human service agencies under sectarian auspices often expend far more tax dollars than donor-based funds. Many agencies, as a consequence, have re-defined themselves as "non-sectarian", opening the possibility of qualifying for public funds. The role of staff thus becomes ever more important in these instances.

These developments do not diminish the need for board input and involvement. The nature of that involvement, however, might now result in more time devoted to strategic thinking than the day-to-day tactical matter of dollar by dollar and donor by donor fundraising.

Human Resource Development

As agencies have become more complex, the demands for increasingly diversified educational backgrounds have also come to the fore. Billions of dollars a year are raised and expended in nonprofit agencies (from all the sources, including fees for services).

Tens of thousands of professional-level employees work within communal infrastructures. Ironically, as issues and concerns facing the American community have become more complex, the educational level of its professionals has fallen.

There is a smaller percentage of people with a master's degree than was the case a decade or so ago. The downsizing of agencies and subsequent localizing of seeking personnel has increased the need for staff training exponentially. This need has not been met adequately and only the most sophisticated of agencies insist upon structured and serious training and education services for staff.

To the extent that the concern is being responded to, human resource departments have come into being. Nationally, the umbrella organizations have tried to respond, but their efforts tend to be under-funded and not as extensive as needed.

Long-term vocational plans developed with and for staff take place rarely compared to times past. One result of these trends is a huge turnover in the field (best estimates—half of those beginning in the field are gone within three years), so much remains to be done. Board members' roles in these areas are uneven. Many of the most powerful board members should be serving on human resource committees but rarely do. Much more interpretation is needed at the board level before sufficient funds will be available to upgrade significantly the content and opportunity for staff training, evaluation, and general staff development, to say nothing of compensation packages attractive enough for the best and the brightest to make their careers in the nonprofit sector.

Simultaneously, my earlier discussion of attributes for board membership tried to make the case for much more conscious screening and thought to the board selection process. I did not, however, point out that in best-practice agencies the human resource departments encompass volunteers as an arena of concern. More and more time must be given to the board membership evaluative process than is presently the case. In those few superior agencies, this includes peer review. As part of a committee process, there are logical steps to take: 1) board members should first be encouraged to develop criteria, 2) board members ought to evaluate their own performance on an annual basis at least, and 3) board members should also evaluate and rate the performance of the other board members.

What follows is a tool for use by nominating committees for initial screening of candidates for board membership. The grid below can be used for rating and ranking potential board members: The lowest a candidate would be weighted on each of the criteria would be "1," while "5" would be the highest weighting given.

There are eight criteria, so the lowest score (assuming no zeroes are used) would be eight and the highest would be forty. Each board nominating committee could discuss the floor they desired as the minimum for each new board member, and in deciding whether or not to continue incumbent board members for further terms.

The grid is also usable in selecting potential committee members. In each instance, there will be a correlation between the level of criteria and the strength and attractiveness of the organization. A highly respected agency delivering palpably excellent services or otherwise fulfilling its functions at a highly efficient and effective level will tend to attract more people who would score at the higher levels and vice versa. Thus, it is imperative for each nominating committee to ground its weighting decisions in reality.

The collective weighting by averaging a board as a whole (adding all scores divided by the number of board members will equal the board's average) gives a nominating committee another tool in considering how the agency governance system is doing vis-à-vis the criteria being sought for board members. A sample evaluation grid follows on the next page.

A Tool for Evaluating Candidates for Board Membership

Criteria	Measurement of Criteria for Board Membership					
	1	2	3	4	5	Total
Wealth						
Work						
Wisdom						
Wit						
Wallop						
Interpersonal Skills						
Menschlichkeitism						
Commitment to the core values and mission of the organization						
						Grand Total

Key:
- 9-15   Likely to provide little to the organization.
- 16-25   Sufficient to provide a base upon which to build.
- 26-32   Likely to be good board members
- 33-40   Great possibilities

In using this scale, other criteria can be added. Some boards or committees will want to add gender, ethnicity, geography, or organizational background as additional criteria.

Board training is an additional area of concern for more human resource departments and staff than in times past. Recent research in Jewish Communal organizations (Bubis and Cohen, 1998) found that a significant percentage of board members are very dissatisfied with their own competencies and performance as board members. This self-revelation must be dealt with so as to help assure that the best and the brightest among volunteers can be counted upon to be tomorrow's governance team.

Program Development

Settlement Houses and precursors to family services began over 150 years ago in Americanized form, following the ancient practices of community obligation to serve those in need. The Ethical Culture Movement (1876-1988) is an example of those early American versions, founded by Felix Adler in New York City. In its first few years of existence, the movement would establish the Society for Ethical Culture and spawn the first free kindergartens to exist in New York and San Francisco and create the District Nursing Service (later called the Visiting Nurse Service) in its first few years of existence.

Over the decades, board members' inputs changed from being direct deliverers of service to functioning as governors. (Voluntarism in delivering services directly, working with people, is still a vital part of nonprofit organizations, but our focus here is on governance, not direct service.)

Program development obviously refers to the services delivered by an agency or organization. There are increasing complexities involved in deciding the extent and degree to which the services offered by an institution are within their mission and competencies.

As insinuated before, successful marketing has become a focus of measure of today's nonprofit world. Grave issues arise when the values and language of the market place overtake the nonprofit settings. A board which takes its governance roles seriously constantly asks itself questions having to do with the value base that shaped and influenced the agency or organization in the first place. The "mission", which should draw so heavily upon the core values and obligations referred to earlier, can easily be lost if one begins to think of customers, niche marketing, packaging of services, and the like as the *sine qua non* of that which should drive an agency. It is, of course, desirable to use the latest useful tools and techniques in shaping responses to change, yet, in my opinion, there remains the need to simultaneously retain some balance between the impulses of the present and the imperatives of the past.

Business methods and entrepreneurial tools are important, but the board in its zeal to balance or expand budgets must be careful to examine issues. What are the values which underpin and impel an organization's mission? Are there service delivery proportions which must be maintained regarding sources of funding, in order to maintain those core values? When agencies redefine themselves as non-sectarian in order to receive funds, have they confused the difference between being non-sectarian and sectarian with an open door policy?

Agonizing issues await board members in matters of program development and much work, preparation, and guidance is often needed from staff. In turn, they cannot play an adequate role in these charged times if they are not grounded in knowledge which will best equip them to function as resource-teacher-guide-goad in the process.

Thus, a very dynamic interactive process is at the heart of the success of appropriate service delivery in today and tomorrow's world.

Interpreters to the Community

No longer does the agency count alone on board members explaining to peers and community representatives for its public relations efforts. To suggest that it ever was the case is to simplify the past. It remains important for board members to be knowledgeable and passionate interpreters of an agency's mission and services, but that is insufficient. The roles of marketing, public information, and public relations are sophisticated, demanding, and expensive.

It would be impossible for board members or volunteers to perform these functions today except in very small organizations. That does not diminish the role of the volunteer but rather refocuses it. As noted previously, the subtleties having to do with remembering the verities of one's mission and its grounding in values and the interaction of board and staff is vital in this process.

I have put forth in primer form the functions of a board and tried to emphasize the governance dimensions. Board members must serve primarily on the bridge of the ship, looking at great and informing questions which set into motion the direction of the ship of service on which they serve.

As one of the articles in this book points out, a board heavily engaged in micro-management (to keep the metaphor: spending an inordinate amount of time in the boiler room) is doomed if that situation becomes permanent.

Staff Functions

Over the past century, staff roles have evolved from a narrow definition of a secretary and/or implementer of policy to a seriously educated and sophisticated person who is engaged in helping to shape agency directions and priorities.

A person defining him or herself as a professional has a combination of values, skills, and methods grounded in a body of knowledge which help define the roles and functions he or she then performs.

Among the many successful executives in the nonprofit arena today, there are those holding doctorates in English literature, public administration, and law. Alongside them are those with MBA's, MSW's, and bachelor's degrees. Horror stories can be told of those brought in from other fields to begin their careers as executives of some of the most important and prestigious agencies in the world, who quickly disappeared from their jobs and indeed from nonprofit life. Only those agencies or organizations demanding licensing escape these realities.

It would appear that an important variable is the socialization or acculturation process which normally takes place for those who succeed. The successful staff person quickly recognizes the paradoxes that exist and is able to adjust to them while working to modify them when necessary or harness them when possible to serve the organization.

Among the most obvious paradoxes are: 1) the tension between consensus and creativity; 2) the models volunteers often use in their own management styles and the tension between those styles and governance styles in the not-for-profit sector; and 3) the tension often born of the search for and lip service given to the partnership model in governance and the fact that staff *are* employees.

Consensus and Creativity

The previous section discussed the utilization of consensus as the major mode for resolving differences and evolving policy. Unless those affected by the decisions agree to them, serious consequences await. Major donors who are disaffected can and do withhold gifts. Members and clients who are ignored can show their displeasure by seeking services in other venues. The community as a whole can turn against an organization and withhold its psychological support or even become vocal opponents to the agency, setting up competing services or totally ignoring the positive activities and roles of the agency.

Stories from across the country abound of disaffected big givers, soured constituents, and angry community activists turning against or away from long accepted agencies and services. All these developments, together with the listing of the attributes of a professional, underline the fact that much of the practice of a professional is grounded in art.

In turn, this approach to consensus has to face the reality that when one looks at the most innovative and imaginative responses to changing needs, they are grounded in creativity. This creativity is typically unfettered by committee meetings and process, or by buy-ins and permissions from a multi-layered bureaucratic system.

There is challenge to consensus driven agencies. Can an organization with a consensus driven style pursue and include daring innovators, board and staff, who are unfettered by conventional thinking as they seek solutions for today's new problems? Do synagogues and churches not face many of the same challenges? I would suggest that they do.

Dr. Ian Mitroff, head of the Institute of Crisis Management at the Marshall School of Business at the University of Southern California, has been a consultant for General Motors, Tylenol, and the U.S. Defense Department. He has conducted much research about creative problem solving and crisis management and has pointed out a number of cautions when confronting dilemmas of this sort.

1. Some complex problems have no solution and all complex problems *may* have multiple solutions. Each solution may be "good" but not necessarily appropriate.

2. No magic exists in finding answers, but certain processes will lead to more frequent solutions than others. These processes must allow for risk-taking, experimentation, and adaptation.

3. Overkill with *irrelevant* information can paralyze problem-solving. The minimum essential information has the best chance of illuminating issues. The fewer the specifics and the more the focus on overall issues will more frequently lead to the best *chance* for problem solving.

4. *True* problems are *never* simple.

5. Contrary to conventional thinking, complex problems can rarely be broken into a series of simple problems. This is because all complex problems interact and affect the whole.

6. Technical, scientific, and economic aspects of problems are inseparable from human aspects. While studies are important, the readiness to accept findings, the dynamics explaining resistance to "science" or change in general, are variables which can never be ignored.

7. Total objectivity does not exist on anyone's part in the problem-solving process, for reason and emotion are never totally separable.

The professional then must find the ways to utilize the mastery of processes while moving to the greatest degree possible to encourage risk-takers and innovators to enter and remain in the system (Consultation with Mitroff, 1985).

The Entrepreneurial Model and the Cooperative Model

More than ever before, the place and power of the successful entrepreneur is essential to the success of agencies today. The entrepreneur is a risk-taker who is still often in charge of the entity through which s/he made his wealth. No stereotyping is intended, but consulting and countless committee meetings geared to careful processing of decision-making is often not the norm in the world of the entrepreneur.

The entrepreneurial model is not confined to the successful business person. Artists and many scholars are used to acting boldly in their respective fields, testing the given, questioning norms, stretching boundaries.

These worlds often collide with the world of established nonprofit organizations. There is no easy answer as to how to make the best use of the talents from these worlds which so value creativity and innovation.

At the least, careful orientations should be conducted to assure clear understanding of expectations that people have of the organization. The organization's representatives must in turn be honest as to their sense of how the potential volunteer leader will fit into the governance process. The organization itself will do well to examine its approach to governance, and the degree to which staff persons play a pivotal role in this process. The creative staff person must constantly question him or herself as to how well the needs and interests of volunteers are served even as they are asked to serve in turn.

It is incumbent upon staff to be especially sensitive in this regard. This does not suggest that the consensual model is not appropriate as the major way of decision-making. It does suggest that more conscious care be given before meetings are called and when they are called that they have clearly defined purposes. (See further discussion of this issue in the later discussion of the staff role in meeting preparation.)

Other Evolving Models of Governance

All who have served as staff working with boards or have served on boards have their horror stories, times of triumph, satisfaction, frustration and despair. The scenario section of this book concentrates on the issues and instances of concern. Consciously and perhaps wrongly, the success stories are not recounted. My intention was to concentrate on how to handle problems through anticipation and the ways of delineating goals and roles of those who serve either as staff or board members.

Inconsistencies and problems abound. Very often disappointments come to know no bounds because expectations were too high and clarification of the possible was not addressed sufficiently. How often have board and staff people lamented about the size of the board as being too great; or, the number of board members who rarely if ever attend meetings? What are people to make of the following tendencies among some (and a growing number of) organizations: those that drastically cut the size of the board, limit its frequency of meetings, consolidate power within the hands of a few board members as the CEO, now so frequently called the President, follows a "business" model of governance, accountability and transparency?

At a time when most of the Western world is moving towards decentralized approaches in governance, many NGO's are doing just the opposite. Often this move is further motivated by the almost voracious and insatiable need for dollars as our national government "privatizes" by removing long used sources of public funds which underpin much of the private sector of the panoply of services they offer.

I earlier referred to the balance needed on a board of people representing work, wealth, wisdom, wit, wallop and what I called "menschlichkeitism." It is rare that one person embodies all those attributes. When, as is increasingly the case today, those with the most wealth dominate the not-for-profit boards, a destabilizing of the agency governance structure is possible. Those most supportive in monetary terms are often too busy, or, for any number of other reasons, little interested in taking part in governing the agency. In turn, there are others, who because of prior experiences or fears, spend the bulk of their time on a board trying to micromanage the agency and spend little time on the real governance issues and concerns discussed elsewhere.

My colleague at Hebrew Union College, Dr. Steven Windmueller and I published our study of the largest not-for-profit merger in the twentieth century (Bubis, Windmueller, 2005). We noted a number of patterns which evolved out of a legitimate concern to develop a sound governance structure. The goal was to bring mega givers into the governance of the newly merged organization (United Jewish Communities) while attempting to maintain some balance with those board members who were representatives of the various constituencies served by the newly merged organization. One of our recommendations originated from a small number of very astute people involved in the merger process. To strike a balance in organizational life's golden rule—"those with the gold rule"–we suggested a new form of bi-cameral governance. The "upper house" (think senate or House of Lords) would be composed of the wealthiest of the people involved locally or nationally in one way or another with the newly merged organization. They would have no major role in governance as such, but would be kept involved and engaged at their levels of interest. How effective was the organization? Was it clear in its vision, mission and goals? How proactive was the organization? How could it best remain relevant in a changing world?

Klausner and Small correctly clarified an important issue in board governance (2005). This research had confirmed that *boards of directors often rightly emphasized their governance role but wrongly assume that all board members must participate in the governance process itself.* The failure of organizations is in not differentiating more clearly the varying tasks and roles of a board. These can be divided and separated to the end that *some* board members take on the governance functions-oversight, evaluation of the CEO, plus the myriad of other roles I identified earlier (Essential Board Responsibilities). Within large boards, it may be necessary to give honor and status to those desirous of supporting the organization financially and using their own status to do the same. Klausner and Small make a strong case for what they call a "bifurcated board", where some members are "governors" and others are non-governors. This new structure responds to the organizations needs and the levels of interest and commitment of board members. As they say, "there is no reason to pretend that all directors actually govern, nor is there reason to ask or expect them to" (Klausner & Small, p 46).

These approaches answer the dilemmas often faced in wanting to maintain as many stakeholders as possible close to the organization while evolving a truly effective governance (not micro-management) system for the organization. Frequent communication opportunities for members will better assure their becoming truly involved. This is more likely to lead to active participation on committees and in other activities for those ready and desirous of doing so. Some who are board members because of the prestige and power can do so. A balance of roles by various individuals still leads to a desired outcome, that a board fulfill its obligations with board members' talents and interest present which in total results in the maximum use of people on boards.

Staff in turn must strike a balance and decelerate the frequent drive to centralized power in the hands of a few. In my opinion, however "effective" a highly centralized model of governance and management may be in the short run, it will endanger the healthy growth of the organization in the long run.

Sources of Friction

There are a number of areas where staff and board members report conflicts, sometimes catastrophic, sometimes minor. A later section of this book describes over ninety scenarios involving various examples of these conflicts.

Most of these can be categorized and classified. They seem to fall into the following categories: 1) misunderstanding and/or misperception of roles; 2) the expectations which grow out of these perceptions; 3) the lack of clarity of the respective powers of staff and board members in governance; 4) unshared trust levels; and, 5) insufficient communications and uncertain and/or incomplete information.

Misunderstanding of Roles

There are many dimensions to this concern. Staff must remember they have a job at the least and a calling at best. Webster's dictionary reminds us that the meaning of vocation is rooted in the notion of a religious calling—a summons to serve. To be a professional is to have a vocation (a calling) grounded in knowledge and competency and standing for (professing) a set of values and beliefs grounded in that role.

Staff persons who have a job will not be imbued with the same expectations for themselves that their truly professional colleagues have. There is a caution to be shared. It does not follow that even though one views his or her work as a calling in the best sense of the word, that board members will always recognize this nor appreciate it. Staff, in turn, must be sensitive to the wide variety of motivations and realities which guide or explain the involvements of board members. At the least, volunteers have an interest in the agency in which they serve and the mission which guides its services. At their best, board members are driven by passion for the agency and its good works. Their time, energy, and resources are devoted to the particular agency in disproportionate degrees which confirm the authenticity of this passion.

Neither the seriousness of the "calling" or "professing" of staff nor the passion of the volunteer are by themselves sources for potential conflict. Difficulties can and do arise between a passionate (and not necessarily disciplined) board member and a staff person who views his or her work as a job. The opposite is true when an ardent and intensely committed staff person is working with a board member with a low level of interest in the organization.

Attitudes can be detected, body language interpreted, and voice tones used which spell potential points of conflict. Staff or board members who call at unreasonable hours, or who expect immediate and total attention or response, are certainly a recipe for potential disaster. The resulting insensitivity, both public and private, in the expressions of expectation each has of the other has consequences which are easy to set in motion and often difficult to undo. Little touches ranging from notes of thanks, public expressions of jobs well done, appropriate mementoes from board to staff member and vice versa can go a long way to keep relationships stable even when there are disagreements as to role and task fulfillment.

The roles and functions which are within at least the purview of board oversight were reviewed previously. The blurring of roles and the resultant difficulty of clearly and permanently setting up fences between staff and board functions was underlined and must be repeated for emphasis.

Expectations Growing Out of Unshared Perceptions

The potential for difficulty is ever present. The single biggest variable in the hands of staff is their constant need to be conscious of what they say and do.

This brief sentence, which in social work jargon is called the "conscious use of self", is one of the great differences between staff and board members. It is staff who must do initial thinking about an agenda, an announcement, a meeting, a strategy and its consequences. The order of an agenda, the timing of an announcement, and all the nuances which will be discussed later often can make the difference between a successful event or meeting and a failure. Staff must check rooms early for good seating arrangements, lighting, temperature, water, pencils, pads, and the myriad details appropriate to the event. An auditorium-style seating arrangement when intimacy and face-to-face contact is desired spells problems.

More complicated is the need to think of appropriate tactics, strategies, scenarios, and consequences when complicated and divisive issues confront an organization. Memos, informal discussions, and notifying key people of upcoming issues are but some of the roles staff persons take upon themselves as a result of being conscious of the need for proactive thinking and thoughtful analysis.

The conflicts, when they arise, are often born of the lack of clarity or sanction as to who is charged with these responsibilities. A letter or a speech written in the name of the president is appropriate if the president expects it. An agenda developed by staff with "instructions" for the eyes of the chair is an excellent tool if the chair desires it or understands why they need it. Woe is the staff person who has not ascertained what is expected. All cheers for the staff person who appreciates the complexity and diversity of the varying expectations different volunteers have of staff.

Any given staff person may be working with numerous committee chairpersons simultaneously and, just as is the case with a therapist with many clients, differentiated approaches are needed. These approaches must be geared to meeting the needs and desires of the volunteers, for they are the reason staff is there in the context of the needs of those engaged in governing the agency. Thus, the art of functioning as a staff person is not only grounded in a series of skills, but bound together by practice wisdom. Having a particular set of skills is imperative, but knowing when and where to apply them is where art and wisdom conjoin.

The new director who has quickly been able to appropriately assess the shortcomings of the organization is to be congratulated. If he or she is constantly referring to how they rectified those shortcomings at their last post, the knowledge is manifest but the wisdom is lacking. There is no greater turnoff to all who hear who are told how "we" did it this way when I was in (fill in your favorite successful organization or city).

Wisdom demands being able to assess the timing of the application of knowledge as well as the ways that would be most appropriate to effectuate desired change. The honorary life board member, now eighty years old, full of his or her own wisdom but perhaps fixed in their ways more than one might wish, has to be made an ally to effectuating that change. Regular meetings by a thoughtful and sensible executive geared to picking the brains of this walking history book, asking for advice, building trust, and testing new ideas, can avoid pitfalls and enlist an important ally for change in the process.

Woe to the executive who underestimates the help or the blocks which such a board member would be able to effectuate. The wise executive is going to think through the potential power for progress or blockage that each board member has and selectively apply the skills discussed above in order to help effectuate change where necessary, while retaining the best of the past.

The new executive, and other staff, for that matter, learn the blood lines, marriages and partnerships which interconnect decision-makers. Business and other investment connections are important to know about. So are feuds, divorces which have alienated, and children who are friends.

The wisdom and roles of board members, in turn, must be ascertained. Who are the peace-makers? Who has a confrontational style? Are there gruff grizzlies that turn out to be teddy bears once the facade is penetrated?

I remember having my first breakfast as a new executive director with the president. After a pleasant breakfast with chit-chat to match, before I could raise my agenda with him, he announced in a gruff, tough way, "Jerry, did anyone tell you that I eat executive directors for breakfast?" I quickly responded with a smile on my face, "With this one, you'll get severe indigestion." After he controlled his waves of laughter, he suggested that we get on with our agenda. We ended up with a harmonious and fruitful relationship.

What if I had responded with other than humor? I came to find out that he tested new colleagues and employees in the same way. Being conscious of one's role at all times, must be accompanied by the challenge to use one's self, as it were, wisely and appropriately.

Certainly an area which needs serious attention is planning for meetings in order to maintain consensus while getting the organization's business done.

When I was a young sub-executive, one day my mother-in-law, who was very active in a women's group which had many meetings, turned to my wife and inquired, "What does Jerry do for a living? All he seems to do is go to meetings." Indeed, it would seem at times that the nonprofit world is suffering from meeting-itis. One wag has suggested that, given the fact that all sound continues to exist after it is first initiated, science will one day find a way to retrieve past meetings and confirm that indeed the camel *was* a horse designed by a committee.

One of the difficulties with meetings is the fact that so few people, at the mention of a meeting, begin by questioning the need for a meeting. There are many good reasons to have meetings and they will be discussed. There are often many more meetings than necessary. Staff and the executive will be feted if they find ways to reduce them in frequency, streamline the meeting itself, and find new ways to make decisions other than the conventional structure of a group of volunteers formed into a committee and staffed by professional staff. Phone, video conferences and use of email are but some of then techniques in expanding frequency today.

Lack of Clarity of the Respective Powers of Staff and Board Members in Governance

I previously made the assertion that *all* power in a voluntary organization resides by law in the board of directors. In theory, whatever staff persons do is because their actions and roles are sanctioned by the board. In small organizations this is often a simple matter, for if there is any paid staff, they are usually performing technical functions. Board members make and implement policy, define their mission, and deliver whatever services they perceive to be relevant in implementing their mission.

As indicated previously, the development of the concept of professionalism in the early part of the twentieth century modified this model greatly. The result over the decades has been the development of what some choose to call the partnership between staff and board members in the shaping of organizations, how they are governed, and deciding what services they will offer (or stop offering). The increasing complexity of organizations, changing time demands on board members, and the skills and knowledge that many, if not most, board members have, change the dynamics of the organization *and* the relationships between board and staff, and, indeed, between board members themselves.

The greatest problem, as an outgrowth of these complexities, is clarifying the often blurred line between board and staff members which was discussed previously. Staff people who are not on the executive level are often caught between the expectations that board and committee members might have as to how they set their work priorities and their supervisors' expectations of them.

Staff can then be caught in a contradictory set of expectations from which they must quickly extricate themselves. (A number of the scenarios cited later in this book bring to life the difficulties which may arise as a consequence of this development.)

It is incumbent upon the staff person to remember that not all supervisors are sensitive to the needs of the agency or the staff person. The staff person's responsibility is to protect him or herself while still trying to perform the job at the highest possible professional level. Through supervision, clarifying the nature and extent to which board members' requests or expectations are legitimate can help the staff person to do the same with the board member.

A dedicated board member may be anxious to perform his or her job as competently as possible while being unaware of the limits of time that may constrain the staff person. Lack of clarification to the board member of the limitations of staff and the organization in fulfilling board members' expectations thus can be a source of great frustration which can grow into anger and separation from the organization under the worst scenarios.

Frank, full conversations with volunteer leaders are always needed so that whatever realities exist shape the expectations of volunteer leaders. In turn, however, there is a caution for staff. Creative staff persons learn how to use time and energy in often wildly and widely diverse ways in order to fulfill the expectations and needs of the system. In this work, as in other settings, there are one-ball jugglers and multi-ball jugglers.

Working at the governance level of a complex organization is demanding, exciting, and at times dangerous to the life of the professional. The pressures can result in mistakes, enemies, and other complications on many levels.

Shortcutting the process in order to save time can have its own disastrous outcomes. While there are ways to streamline governance in communal organizations (which will be discussed later), woe be to those who regularly ignore the need to supply information in a timely fashion to all who need to know. As research demonstrates (and is reproduced in this book—Bubis and Cohen, 1998), trust levels drop precipitously between staff and board members when some of these things happen. The strongest executive with the most indifferent board is foolish not to remember that he or she is an employee or steward of the enterprise. No one can predict the circumstances under which the most laissez faire board will get aroused when repeated actions by staff are so obviously within the purview of board responsibility.

The clarifying process once again is the best tool in avoiding the worst of misunderstandings and inappropriate expectations. Six words can often do it. "What do you want of me?" is a good place to start the clarifying process, leading at best to a mutually crafted set of expectations that board has a right to expect of staff and, once again, vice versa. The reciprocal nature of healthy relationships between board and staff cannot be underscored enough.

A number of other questions should be in staff's minds in clarifying roles. "What do you want and expect of staff?" should lead to what board members can expect from each other and what staff can expect from each other. There is often a fine line between governance and management. The problem is often not that the line (ever-moving) is crossed, but what kind of goodwill, understanding, and trust exist in the overall relationships between board and staff. Note that I have never defined board members as clients in this relationship for I do not perceive them as such. They are, at bottom, bosses, however rich and mutually evolved the relationships.

Senior staff has to struggle with the extent to which they establish intensive friendships with board members. Indeed, there are many executives who make it a practice not to allow serious personal relations to develop, while others count among their closest friends a selected number of board members.

In large organizations it can be heady stuff to be invited to the homes of the rich (and sometimes the famous). As a rule, the invitation has been extended because of the position one holds, and it is good to remember this. It has been said that where you stand is defined by where you sit (Miles). Indeed, there is always the concern a professional should have as to kinds of scenarios which might unfold and call for brave and at times unpopular stands by the executive. This is not easy at times, but then who promised eternally thorn-less rose gardens?

Unshared Trust Levels

A number of factors enter into the building up or lowering of trust levels between staff and board people. All are grounded in experience, anecdotes, expectations, and/or misunderstandings. Unfortunately, none may relate to the specific experience of two specific people. Thus, the behavior of a former staff person might color the expectation—positive or negative—that a given board member has of a new staff person.

Humans frequently develop prejudices or conclusions about others based upon an experience about which they generalize. "Our past executive never shared easily and openly with us. Therefore, I conclude that all professionals are the same and I will deal with the new staff as I feel I should have (or did) with the old staff." "I found out the executive was charging personal phone calls. I'll never let another executive get away with that again, so as president I am going to demand to see all phone records." "I found out that the former executive did not get bids on new stationery as she should have and gave the job to the son of a college friend. I am going to make sure bids are handled by a board committee."

"In the last agency in which I worked I shared many confidences with the chair of our personnel committee with whom I developed an especially close relationship. I came to find out that everything I said was shared by the chair with her spouse who constantly breeched confidences and shared them with his circle of friends. I will never be open and honest with a volunteer leader again." "I went through a period of a rocky relationship with my spouse and discussed it at some length with our president. Later on, I found out she shared these stories at her bridge club and word got back to my husband. I have vowed to have a totally professional relationship with everyone in my new job."

"Our last executive was the crème de la crème; thoughtful, articulate, highly competent, visionary—all of the great attributes one could ever hope for. Our new executive is okay, but it is not the same. There is no way I am going to confide any dreams that I have for the future with our new guy. I am going to work around him because I just don't believe he knows what Jack knew and I'll be damned if I will give him a chance because he will probably fail soon anyway."

"I heard the new exec does not watch a budget carefully and ran a big deficit. Any time he tries to suggest anything that costs money, I am going to veto it even if it is a good idea and we can afford it."

All is not bleak and dark. Good experiences lead to high trust and this trust is often transferable from an experience with one person to an expected or beginning experience with another.

This discussion has a mirror image to it. Experiences of staff color their reactions in turn. The scenarios in this book are replete with experiences shared by staff which inevitably lead to concern about board members, at the least, and low trust of them, at worst. The outcome of low trust by one or more people in any set of relationships is potentially disastrous. When it involves community work, there are ramifications far beyond the two people involved. The extent of low trust in the field between board and staff is quite widespread (Bubis and Cohen, 1998) and should be a matter of serious concern. There are no easy answers to dealing with trust issues, for they are born out of experiences. It is for staff to be conscious of all they must do to maintain or attain high trust levels. Keeping appointments, following up on promises made, engaging in full disclosure, remembering who "owns" the enterprise, are but some areas around which staff need to be eternally conscious.

Insufficient Communication and Uncertain or Incomplete Information

When one tries to isolate those tools which lie mostly in the hands of staff, certainly the communication and information which is controlled by staff must be high on the list.

It should be clear by now that in this day and age of highly sophisticated and well educated volunteers, staff have few unique attributes or tools which are theirs and theirs alone.

Staff should know more about the details of their agency's functioning. They are expected to have an in-depth perspective or understanding which would give them access to information and control of that information and its dissemination.

Volunteers in the world of governance need information related to the issues confronting the agency and its future. Serious oversight requires regular and utilizable fiscal information. Are income projections on target? Have unexpected expenditures arisen or, while rare, unexpected savings occurred? Does everyone understand the difference between an accrual and cash flow budget? Does the executive keep information which might be "painful" from the board?

There was one executive who at year's end would defer paying one month's bills so as to "balance" his budget. These past few years have seen enormous deficits revealed in what had been thought to be well-run agencies. While a board is charged with the primary oversight responsibility, if the chief executive officer, chief operating officer, and/or chief financial officer are not sharing information in a timely fashion and a helpful form, disaster awaits. Board members are frequently cowed about asking questions, fearing ridicule if their questions prove to be inappropriate or are seen to be so at the time of the questioning.

It should be staff which takes the lead in recommending safeguards, consulting frequently with the management team to assure that all is well. Deficits cannot always be avoided. Examples of this from Jewish communal life can be found in times of emergency when the Jewish community's response has been to assume deficits in the face of dire consequences. Operation Exodus and Operation Moses rescue operations for Soviet and Ethiopian Jews and the response to Hezbollah's actions are three such examples. In communities at large, the responses to famine and genocide in Africa, natural disaster aid relief in South America, or the refugee situation in the former Yugoslavia are analogues.

At these moments, staff must play key roles in developing scenarios which demonstrate options and outcomes, positive and negative, so intelligent policy decisions can be formulated.

How often, in turn, are board members in some organizations confronted with the opposite of a paucity of information? Can you remember a meeting you attended as a staff or board member where a weighty tome was placed in front of the board members accompanied by the announcement that the board would be expected to pass the recommendations contained therein at the board meeting?

If you are a staff member, can you recall instances where you have been expected to change an approach or program because of arbitrary decisions suddenly shared with you for implementation because of capricious board action?

Desirable Staff Skills

There is much to ponder when reviewing the potential for conflict and discord, yet it is comforting and important to remind ourselves that agencies and organizations function remarkably well, given all that can go poorly. Let us now examine those talents and skills which contribute to exemplary professional practice. They are:

1. The capacity to understand systems, their problems, possibilities, and limits.

2. The capacity to communicate well through the written and spoken word.

3. The capacity to facilitate interaction between people and, through them, units within and between organizations.

4. The capacity to master fiscal matters.

5. The capacity to have consideration and respect for others (not just volunteer leaders).

6. The capacity to envision change without defensiveness.

7. The capacity to promote others' capacities and productivity.

8. The capacity to analyze and produce homeostasis when needed and enable others to prepare for change when needed.

9. The capacity to share information, power, and responsibility.

The Capacity to Understand Systems, Their Problems, Possibilities and Limits

Just as an artist can approach a picture and analyze form, color, structure, and content, so does the artful practitioner approach work in an organization. There is an almost unconscious assessment process in the computer of the mind which leaps into action. What accounts for its success or failure? Is it human resources? Fiscal resources? A combination of both or a lack thereof? What do people think of the organization, those within and outside of its structure? How importantly or unimportantly is it viewed by those who use it and/or support it? How is the community affected by its presence? What sure loss would there be if it ceased to exist tomorrow? How loyal are its staff and its volunteer supporters? What is unique about it? Does it duplicate the work and services of others? How cooperative is it in dealing with issues and handling problems? Are the services affordable? Could they be better offered by someone else?

The Fifth Discipline: the Art and Practice of the Learning Organization, (P. Senge, 1994), is a key tool in understanding organizations as systems and in applying those concepts to the questions listed in this section. As Senge writes in elegant simplicity, "for managers facing an array of problems which resist current ways of thinking, managers who want to know: "How do I fix things?" You can't just "fix things", at least not permanently. You can apply theories, methods and tools, increasing your own skills in the process. You can find and instill new guiding ideas".

The Capacity to Communicate Well through the Written and Spoken Word

How many "ahs" and "ums" does it take in a spoken sentence to prevent the listener from concentrating on the words being uttered between the fits, starts and stumbling of the speaker? How long does a person speaking in a monotone have until the listener turns off, as indicated by glazed eyes and/or rolling eyeballs? What does a poorly parsed sentence, delivered orally or in writing, indicate to the listener or reader? Ask yourself how clear you are in communicating to people, how you sound and how your words read when you write something.

I am not the world's greatest teller of tales, orally or in writing, but I have learned over the years to get all the help I can use, and use all the help I can get, in both departments. Outlines of what I want to say or write about are a great help. Generally, I have come to realize that reading from a paper may make things easier for me but are a burden on a group of listeners, however large or small. I have found that eye contact is essential, and if there is time, humor preceding the points I want to make help establish a bond. In my writing, I accept the need for an objective editor who, at the least, will untangle a much too complicated sentence, or, at best prod me into making my points more clearly. These skills are essential for good practice, but are often underestimated in their importance.

The Capacity to Facilitate Interaction between People and, through Them, Units within and between Organizations

It seems almost a truism that the best practice is one that meets a litmus test. Do the ways in which I do my work bring about the valuable and desirable goals on behalf of the people and organizations which society sanctions as truly important?

There are today artful practitioners who are cynical about what they do, proud of their ability to manipulate people into paths which suit the professional, without regard to greater social purpose.

The world we live in is in need of a great deal of repair, yet human and fiscal resources are limited. I am not so naive as to believe that professionals will help organizations "die," any more than I expect professionals to leave practice voluntarily because they are inadequate to the expectations that society has of them.

Yet those I admire the most are selective about where they choose to work. They do not abuse relationships by being insensitive to the needs and priorities of those they serve. Rather, they see themselves as change agents or advocates who work on behalf of and with the communities they serve. They create collaborative partnerships in order to leverage resources and serve the best interests of their constituents. Their highest level of concern is for the integrity of the services and programs offered and the ethical behavior of lay and professional leadership of the organization. These professional tend to have a macro or larger understanding of their community and work, towards inclusion over exclusion. In short, they see partnership as value added and not as territorial infringement.

The professional at the end of a career who is fulfilled is one who can truly say "I did well at trying to 'do good', and I did so collaboratively."

I have seen a lot, done more than a bit, and met thousands of professionals. I can truly say that in distilling the profile of those I admire most and who have accomplished the most, no matter the size of the setting, they meet the criterion I write about here.

The Capacity to Master Fiscal Management Skills

As the complexity of the nonprofit world continue to increase, so too have the funding sources needed for organizational fiscal health. Each source may require different sets of reporting and verifying expectations, particularly with respect to foundations and government funding.

Historically, most agency executives and senior management staff made their way up the administrative ladder with little or no special fiscal management skills. In the current climate of the nonprofit arena, an executive director who does not understand the difference between accrual and cash flow financial statements will not survive. Ironically, the same can be said about board members, a significant number of whom also lack these skills, at least on that consumer level.

Projecting income and expenses are essential tools in management. Smaller agencies often cannot afford financial officers and must count on a bookkeeper to share information in a timely fashion. The staff person who has risen to management level without these skills must be secure enough to recognize what is a serious professional deficit. They must take the steps to learn these skills informally or otherwise. The rise in the use of MBA's in the not-for-profit sector is often a response to the dissatisfaction board members come to have with senior staff.

Increasingly, the sudden dispatch of directors can often be traced to the consequences of poor fiscal control within their agencies. Timely reports in accessible formats are essential, together with time to discuss ramifications and consequences related to fiscal matters. Superficial discussions with skeletal information to a board or appropriate committee are an insult to the board members, at best, and an approach which can backfire, at worst. Full disclosure is a good principle to follow. Ownership of problems as well as ownership of successes must be shared, and it is the wise practitioner who remembers that it is ultimately the board which is in legal command and which has legal ownership of the not-for-profit organization.

This section could perhaps be best summed up in one aspiration—that *all staff persons at whatever level share the goal of providing board-centered leadership.*

The Capacity to have Consideration and Respect for Others (Not Just Volunteer Leaders)

I am thankful to a wonderful and insightful secretary with whom I worked when I was a young executive. I was new to the city and had been hired to direct a community center whose leadership had raised the money for a new building. Prior to my arrival great thought had been given to the building design and furnishing in general terms, but little planning had been done to involve people in shaping the actual programs which needed to be developed.

I resolved to set up a series of focus groups and worked at a furious pace. I was in different homes four and five nights a week, probing, questioning, and listening to people as they shared their dreams, hopes, and expectations for the new center. Every morning I would march into the now completed building, walk hurriedly to my office, establishing eye contact with no one, uttering nary a word of greeting to anyone, then calling "my" secretary into the office to tell her of all the material, reports, and communications that would have to be generated as a result of the evening before.

One day she asked me if she could close the door. After doing so, she turned on me and in a strong and firm voice proceeded to tell me that I was a son of a b—h. Yes, I had worked hard since coming to town, but I had never had a smile for staff, never thanked them, and never realized that a two-hour meeting the night before could generate ten hours of work for the staff.

The conversation was one of the great learning moments of my life. I have much to thank her for, and while I still do not have it down pat all the time, I know that I make every effort to thank people, be sensitive to human amenities, and not just turn on the charm when I am with people of power. How often I have observed colleagues who could get Academy Awards for their acting as they "turned it on" for volunteer leaders while busily treating staff disdainfully or insensitively. Yes, we all were taught this in kindergarten, but the integration of learning has proven to be spotty at best in too many of us.

The Capacity to Envision Change without Defensiveness

Many years ago there was a character called Rufus in the cartoon strip *Gasoline Alley*. He was a handyman who worked for Uncle Walt, the family patriarch. Uncle Walt would often suggest new ideas for Rufus, ranging from putting up a new fence to re-roofing the garage. No matter the suggestion, simple or complex, Rufus would reply, "I know I ain't going to like it."

This resistance to change is often evident in too many colleagues who, for whatever reasons, resist and resent the new. They find it possible to find (invent?) all manner of reasons to defend the present and resist change in whatever form or to whatever extent it is needed.

The voguish terms of "reinventing organizations" and "transformational leadership" are often heard, with big gaps between the stated and the done regarding the actual changes instituted in many organizations.

In partnership with their staff counterparts, board members must engage in envisioning the needed changes and indeed are often involved in creating and/or managing in their own work setting.

Consider, for a moment, the pace of technological change over the past ten years—faxes, laptop computers, e-mail, websites, micro-surgery, teleconferencing, portable phones—to name but a few, have become globally accessible. What a revolution! Yet how many of us can transfer the implications these new tools (and many others) have to practice and governance? The board or committee member who works in a state-of-the-art world expects the visionary kind of thinking which stimulates him or her all day long.

The not-for-profit sector may have other goals than business, but the tools inherent in much of what is needed by way of creative and proactive thinking are no less real and required than in the for-profit workplace.

While creativity applied in proactive ways is not a talent possessed by all, research does tell us that brainstorming *can* help in the process. Wise executives can nourish creativity, openness to new ideas, solution finding and continual organizational learning. They must do this by establishing and maintaining a work culture that embraces brainstorming, innovating, taking risks and being allowed to experiment and fail.

Alternatives to forming another committee are discussed. When I have suggested some alternatives, I have seen colleagues blanch and quickly proceed to explain all of the reasons why the proposals would not work.

The hoary story still resonates with truth. Remember the young man carrying a violin case who got lost on his way to Carnegie Hall. He approached a policeman and asked how to get there. The policeman's one word answer is not for the boy alone, "Practice." Yes, part of what we must do is to take the time to develop scenarios, act them out, discuss them, apply them and modify them, and eliminate our defensiveness in the process.

Professor Ian Mitroff, referred to earlier, feels the test to this capacity is to ask "what if" questions. About 25 years ago in his career, he was a consultant to the management team of General Motors. He asked them what would happen if a foreign car company were to come along that developed a car utilizing less fuel that was more easily built, and was less expensive than comparable General Motors models. What contingency plans did they have? He was also a consultant to Tylenol's management team shortly after Tylenol perfected its "tamper proof" bottle and he asked them the same question. Unknown to him, at the same time, Professor Avraham Sela, who was a consultant to the Israel Army's general staff on Palestinian Arabs, asked them what contingency plans they had in case Palestinian children started to throw stones at Israeli soldiers. The answers were identical—"It can't happen so we have no plans."

Today, proactive, anticipatory planning, and alternative scenarios to deal with the fast moving agenda facing the multitude of communal, religious, or interest-based institutions must be the hallmark of professional practice. Almost anything *can* happen, for good or otherwise. Much of this thinking *must* come through the board with the active involvement of staff. That is the *real* stuff of policy formulation and policy-making. The process itself is an adventure, sometimes dangerous, but most always stimulating and exciting.

The Capacity to Promote Others' Capacities and Productivity

As I have observed hundreds of senior staff in action over the years, I have been able to confirm the patterns of those I have come to admire the most. These observations were confirmed in research (Bubis and Cohen, 1998) when we teased out the attributes most admired in volunteer *and* staff leadership.

All of this goes back to kindergarten. The successful kindergarten teacher gives praise for a job well done. He or she follows parenting rules which celebrate positive traits among children. When limits have to be set, the successful parent and teacher utilizes the sandwich method of criticism—first saying something positive, followed by the suggestion or criticism related to the need for changed behavior, and once again followed by another positive comment.

Effective professionals know how to say thank you to staff. They send notes—sometimes small gifts. They encourage good practice and acknowledge thanks in many ways. More importantly, they constantly make clear to their key volunteer leadership that there is a staff team which is producing results when things go well, while as senior staff they accept responsibility for shortcomings when they occur. Staff persons, in turn, are given opportunities to demonstrate their growth by being given increasingly complex assignments.

Senior staff must always be aware of the "Peter Principle" and make every effort not to get staff into roles and functions beyond their capacities. In turn, a superior who is a mentor in the best sense of that word strikes a balance between allowing a staff person to grow by being allowed to make judgments and plans, and being told or advised on paths to take or avoid because of the supervisor's experience and knowledge. As people grow on the job, the latitude to do their job must be expanded. Trust *of* staff and *between* staff is key to quality productivity.

Staff persons quickly recognize the kind of system in which they work. If creativity is truly encouraged, productivity will increase. The bureaucratic response of caution and negativity which some staff fall into reflects an agency culture which discourages innovation and experimentation. The permeation of a system begins at the top. This culture must be seen as encouraged by board members too, but the assumption here is that the executive and his or her management team encourage a horizontal and vertical process which is evident to both staff and board members.

The Capacity to Analyze and Produce Homeostasis When Needed and Enable Others to Prepare for Change When Needed

Good senior staff people understand that change can be painful and is often resisted. They also know that sometimes change is glacier-like in its speed and at other times has a velocity akin to the calving parts of the glacier when it meets the sea. No organization can long cope with change which is so pervasive and unremitting that it destroys all that is familiar and comfortable. Radical change, when and if it does happen, must be followed by time periods which allow for integration and stabilization of the new.

Staff people look to senior staff for reassurance, smiles, and any sign which refutes the rumors and affirms the success or failure of a project. Internal e-mail, minutes shared, plans circulated, and figures shared are but some of the tools needed to keep staff focused and aware. Thus, there is the collective sigh of relief or further resolve appropriate to the reality.

Secret planning at the highest level breeds discontent and destabilizing of trust. It is rare that confidentiality is truly an effective tool in an organization. The sunshine law which calls for open meetings in the public sector has much to commend its use in the private, not-for-profit sector.

The training which may be needed for change or, at its worst, the development of humane ways to help people find new jobs when changes are involuntary as the result of diminution of resources or refocusing of resources, gives messages to those who stay. Loyalty in organizations is earned, not granted, and can only result when confidence abounds that senior staff and board are cognizant of the best of methods to prepare for and manage change.

The Capacity to Share Information, Power, and Responsibility

These points are corollaries of the capacities noted previously, but are highlighted separately because of their importance.

It is the rare instance when information cannot be shared with all concerned. Wise management utilizes newsletters, periodic summaries, and staff meetings to note progress, share difficulties, or outline possible scenarios facing the organization.

Does the organizational leadership realize that a financial shortfall is a distinct possibility if radical action is not taken? How many pabulum reports are shared with staff and board members that are so vague as to reveal nothing? Can a board member take his or her charge seriously if there is no serious engagement by staff of various scenarios, including unanticipated consequences?

Where does power lie in an organization? Is it truly shared between board and staff? Can the collaborative model truly function if power is narrowly confined and decisions of real importance are centralized in the hands of a few?

The senior staff people play a key role in maintaining or changing the culture of an organization. The steps which need to be taken are not difficult and often would meet with little resistance. Board members who are not in the "inner circle" which exists in most organizations count on staff to help assure an open process of governance, which is a shared hope of staff persons who work at the "lower" levels of the organization.

The strength and security of staff is thus put to a test because the control of information is such a powerful tool in any organization. Staff people at all levels often come to mirror the best or the worst of what they find in an organization. Thus, practices set by senior staff have great ramifications. Junior staff people have their mettle tested because at this point they can often become cautious and bureaucratic, fearful of testing the parameters of the organization's resiliency and flexibility.

Leadership is supposedly an attribute sought in all staff as it is in board members. Staff people at any level who are truly leaders will question poor practice. They will attempt to modify their professional environment by doing what they can to counter the practices they see as controlling or in others ways not sharing information, power, and responsibility.

Getting minutes out on time, sharing executive committee minutes with board members, keeping minutes at committees, writing minutes which actually reflect what happened, are small steps in this process.

Information is power, but over and above the information level, staff's responsibility must always move toward sharing other manifestations of power with colleagues and board members. Who gives reports? Who is thanked publicly and in print and under what circumstances? How are people *really* involved in decision-making? Are actions pre-decided so that actions taken on the board level are pro-forma? Does an agenda allow for discussion, new motions, and serious time for examination of issues? These are the signals one looks for in ascertaining the level to which this combination of practices is manifest.

New Trends in Board-Staff Relations

Experience and research confirm that there are new trends in board-staff relations, some good, some problematic. The problematic trends include: 1) increasing blurring of roles without clarification; 2) increasing internal power struggles; 3) increasing dehumanizing and brutalizing of staff; and, 4) increasing stereotyping of volunteer leadership.

Blurring of Roles

Many nonprofit, community-based organizations have become complex systems and, as a result, it is not always easy or possible to keep roles clarified as perhaps purists would wish. Staff people who are truly invested in the organization in which they serve want very much to affect and influence policy directions. They often feel they know more about the organization's potential and problems. Research confirms that many staff wishes to play a powerful role in shaping policy. The same research confirms a resistance and sometimes hostility by volunteers who feel policy formulation is their domain. The reality is often such that staff are increasingly consulted and involved in policy formation if trust levels are high. At board meetings, many organizations follow the hospital and university model and grant the chief executive officer voting privileges. In most others, senior staff people attend executive committee and board meetings. Depending upon the organizational culture, there is a wide variety of participation levels in the discussion which precedes policy formulation. Indeed, a new observer might find it difficult to identify who is a board member and who is a staff member.

The obverse is also true. In some organizations, board presidents insist on being able to attend staff meetings and take part in discussions. In yet other instances where technical knowledge is required (legal, bylaws, information systems, fiscal management, and communications committees, to name a few), the staff are often less active and, in many instances, board members play dominant roles as resource, education, and information specialists to other committee members.

The issue here is not that any lines were "crossed" and that staff and board members were fulfilling roles they had no "right" to fulfill. Rather, it is the understanding everyone has as to the most effective ways to use the talents of those assembled. The agreement must begin with the president and the executive.

The executive is still most likely to be a generalist whose own skills and abilities are not grounded in a specialty within governance. The executive must recognize that the infrastructure he or she controls is there to serve the purposes of the organization and not vice versa. Clarification helps minimize the conflicts and consequent lowered trust levels which are the outcome of blurred roles.

Internal Power Struggles

The opportunities for internal power struggles abound in complex organizations. By definition, most large organizations are an amalgam of hierarchical and matrix management. There are, on the one hand, increasingly powerful staffs and committees that are related to levels of influence, decision-making, and access to the budget. The nursery school or after school care program planning committee are essential in a church, synagogue, or community center. Their power and the power of the staff who work with them are not seen as having the authority and responsibility of the agency-wide budget committee or strategic planning committee.

At the same time, larger organizations are frequently structured into regions. The intent is to share power and responsibility while allowing for easier access to the most powerful volunteer and staff—the president and the executive. That should be the intent, but it often does not work that way in practice. The result is that responsibility for activities, programs, or fundraising may be delegated with no concomitant power or authority accompanying the delegation of responsibility.

The expectation on the part of those that delegate, then, can be for better outcomes, whatever they may be, but with no thought as to what the results are when authority and responsibility are separated. The regional office that is expected to produce more money this year than last but is given little to no say in the dispersal of the money raised will try to find ways on both the volunteer and staff levels to change the status quo. Contrary to "good practice," staff will thus be asked to function in collusion against the heads of the organization to which they are responsible. In yet other instances, staff will try to use board members to help in expanding their power base in the organization.

Exemplary agencies appreciate that authority (power) and responsibility are inseparable. Accountability on all levels must remain the expectation in healthy organizations.

If an organization desires to maintain the best and the brightest of board and staff members, it must have in place opportunities for growth with increasingly complex assignments and responsibilities, accompanied by the necessary authority.

A budget which originates from a committee or region and is then monitored by that same committee and region is grounded in an entirely different set of expectations and attitudes than is the case when committees are either notified of the budget they have or, in too many instances, are not even aware there is a budget or how much it entails.

In some cases, the process and product is totally staff driven. The result in both instances is volunteers who have no appreciation that they can change the agency climate and its practice by asking questions, stating expectations, or making suggestions for change.

Everyone wants power and authority in one role or another. An agency which faces a series of challenges or challengers which are both hierarchical and vertical and involve volunteers and staff in sometimes colluding and sometimes colliding roles cannot possibly function at its best.

Wise leadership seeks to open the system to shared opportunities and options which best serve the pursuit of the agency's mission and goals. Non-action can result in weakening the organization, at the least, and destroying its leadership's capacity to function, at worst.

Dehumanizing and Brutalizing of Staff

Anecdotal information gathered through descriptions of first-hand experiences in how staff people are often dealt with by board members should be a matter of grave concern. Volunteers reading this might ask themselves some questions. What tone of voice do you use when speaking to staff? Is it different than when you speak to your peers? Do you see staff as paid by you and therefore answerable to you personally without regard to whether or not staff has an assignment to fulfill? Have you asked staff to perform errands or otherwise partake in personal service to you including getting you coffee at meetings? Is the staff you like the best the most obsequious? Do you bristle when staff contest with you or otherwise take a position which you disfavor?

Many of the scenarios in this book reflect actual instances when many of the stances referred to come to life.

Executives report being fired on a Friday and being asked not to return on Monday. Key staff people across the country have had experiences of being forced from a job because their personality proved grating or otherwise disappointing to a key giver in the organization.

While some scenarios point to the need of junior staff to be protected by senior staff, they themselves may feel (or be) vulnerable and thus severely restricted in the role of protecting and mentoring junior staff. Until this subject is discussed at the highest levels, staff at all levels are vulnerable.

Sessions at regional and national organizations, written materials, five-minute videos, continual clarification of role delineation, and open discussions at executive and board meetings on the "care and feeding" of staff are needed much more frequently and intensively than is presently the case. Retreats with board and staff members together, while difficult to do, are regular tools for those agencies which decide to deal with this problem.

While this essay is focused on board and staff relations, I would be remiss if I did not note that dehumanizing and brutalizing of staff *by other staff* can and does take place. It is not central to the theme of this essay, but it is to be decried and both staff and board must be aware that it exists.

Board members might consider an ombudsperson being appointed who would function in a totally confidential role, being made available for a kind of hot-line to hear staff complaints under carefully delineated circumstances. I realize the suggestion has some complex pitfalls to it should staff be vindictive or immature. There have been instances, however, where staff persons have not been in unions, have not had friendly supervisors or superiors and had no channels to pursue their issues. They have feared for their job security and have had no recourse to pursue. An ombudsperson (mediator) under carefully structured circumstances and guidelines evolved with both board and staff input and sanction might prove a helpful tool in such instances.

Stereotyping of Volunteer Leadership

The bulk of the scenarios in this book are drawn from responses of staff during training programs I have facilitated or in response to research where volunteers seem somewhat resistant to putting their experiences in writing. As a result, some staff unfortunately may over generalize and/or even slip into stereotypic thinking about volunteers.

There *are* board members who engage in dehumanizing and other insensitive behaviors when working with staff. When I have witnessed these behaviors, there have been times that I have realized that these particular board members were not discriminating. They unfortunately tended to treat family and employees in their own businesses in the same way.

In such instances their behavior must be confronted, preferably by a peer or high level staff member, one who is secure enough to be able to escape any negative consequences generated by the board member or volunteer in response.

Generally speaking, the motivations of volunteers are positive. They wish to serve for any number of reasons, which can range from a sense of noblesse oblige or following in a parent's footsteps to a desire to "give back" after climbing the socioeconomic ladder. Sometimes people wish to make business and/or social contacts and find nonprofit venues great places to do so.

Boards and Committees in the Governance Process

As noted earlier, under law the board of directors is the legal trustee for the operation of a not-for-profit organization. I also outlined a series of functions that are shared to a greater or lesser degree with staff when using the collaborative model in governance.

John Carver and Miriam Mayhew Carver, in *Basic Principles of Policy Governance* (1996), have developed a model they call "policy governance". They advocate a different approach to the governance roles and responsibilities in a not-for-profit organization. They posit a number of principles to guide the board of directors:

1. The trust in trusteeship.

2. The board speaks with one voice or not at all.

3. Board decisions should be predominantly policy decisions.

4. Boards should formulate policy by determining the broadest values before progressing to more narrow ones.

5. A board should define and delegate rather than react and ratify.

6. The pivotal role of governance in identifying and delineating goals.

7. The board's best control over staff means is to limit, not proscribe.

8. A board must design its own products and process.

9. A board must forge a linkage with management that is both empowering and safe.

10. Performance of the CEO must be monitored rigorously, but only against policy criteria.

The summary which follows is included to emphasize the indispensability of a board which uses its powers well and in a focused way, while granting staff appropriate latitude to do their jobs. At the same time, the Carvers' view of board and committee responsibility is at variance with the conventional practice in many nonprofit organizations. A careful reading is required to discern the outcomes of their judgments and recommendations, especially as they relate to use of committees.

Trust in Trusteeship

The board as the representatives of the "owners"—the public, the donors, the service recipients—must remember that it represents those owners. The board must always be sure it knows who it represents and has developed and utilizes the ways to know what the "owners" want or need.

Agencies such as a family service most often see themselves as representing givers, while some see themselves as a combination representing givers, agencies, and organizations which make up the community. They balance their board membership accordingly.

Community centers, on the other hand, tend to have two kinds of boards. In one instance, a board may represent the members either primarily or solely. Yet others are representative of a trustee model which makes little or no attempt to have heavy representation from members. Others are just the opposite, with a preponderance of board members from the center membership.

No one way is correct. What is essential is "establishing the nature of governance, particularly in training board authority and accountability to their source."

The Board Speaks with One Voice or Not At All

This caution is not meant to squelch dissent or debate. It is intended to insure a wide diversity of viewpoints with sufficient opportunities to debate options and discuss consequences before a vote. Differences are thus encouraged, but after decisions are made a disciplined board respects this and supports the decision as if with one voice.

In the Carvers' opinion, the volunteer head of the organization should not intervene between the CEO and the board. It is their opinion that primary emphasis and focus of the board chair (volunteer) should be on the board and its board committees.

Furthermore, in their opinion, committees are often wasteful of everyone's time because most are set up to "instruct" staff, which breaks down the administrative structure. They are not against committees per se, but strongly advocate a careful focus on ascertaining the purpose of the committee and how it contributes to the governance function of the board in the process. In short, they see little or no need for committees to advise staff who should be operating under clear guidelines developed by the board and judged accordingly in their job performance.

In their opinion, a finance committee which crafts "options and implications concerning long-term reserves from which the board will make a choice" is legitimate, whereas if the committee is advising the CFO on how to construct the budget, it is not. Board committees should thus focus on such issues as recruiting and/or nominating board members, envisioning long-term goals, or dealing with the public. The focus must be on governance and not management issues.

Board Decisions Should be Predominantly Policy Decisions

The Carvers define policy "as the value or perspective that underlines action but goes on to delineate strict rules as to its form (Carver/Carver 1997, 17)."

Therefore, they explain, policies should be the expression of a board's soul and embody the beliefs, commitments, values, and vision of the board and by extension, that of the agency. Thus, a board is truly involved with wrestling, arguing, discussing, debating, and distilling policies without the intervention of the board chair, the CEO, executive committee, or any other committee. Such a board is not reacting to documents or statements but is proactive in creating them as the frame for staff action. It is the board's responsibility to proscribe and prescribe the frame for the functioning of staff. This should be done in four categories (Carver/Carver 1997, 35):

1. *Ends.* The board defines which consumer results are to be achieved, for whom, and at what cost. Written with a long-term perspective, these mis-

sion-related policies embody most of the board's part of long-range planning.

2. *Executive limitations.* The board establishes the boundaries of acceptability within which staff methods and activities can be responsibly left to staff. These limiting policies, therefore, apply to staff means rather than to ends.

3. *Board-staff linkage.* The board clarifies the manner in which it delegates authority to staff as well as how it evaluates staff performance on provision of the ends and executive limitations policies.

4. *Governance process.* The board determines its philosophy, its accountability, and the specifics of its own job.

The Carvers go on to say that these four policy categories are designed to be exhaustive. Beyond the bylaws, there should be nothing the board needs to say for the purposes of governing that does not fit into one of these categories.

Board policies under "policy governance," generated by the board, not parroted or approved by it, get at the very soul of governance. If the board's wisdom is not reflected in these policies, a central feature of real board leadership has been missed. When policy-making is properly construed, the board *is* its policies.

Boards Should Formulate Policy by Determining the Broadest Values before Progressing to More Narrow Ones

In the Carvers' opinion, the four policy categories are to be seen as the equivalent of the largest bowl in a set of nesting bowls. That outer bowl or boundary confines and defines the parameters of all that follows and a board in its wisdom *then* decides how much more specific it desires or needs to be in policy setting. All policy decisions that are made should go in order of *descending* importance and never out of sequence. In that way, a board will come to understand and respect the difference between true governance and micro-management. After that process is followed and the appropriate policies have been evolved, the CEO should then be depended upon to interpret limitations and applications of the policies (Carver/Carver 1997, 20-21).

The Carvers give two examples to explain this approach. They are both useful, especially in a broader discussion of communal organizations in general:

> "For example, a board policy that states "the job result of the chairperson is that the board behaves consistently with its own rules and those imposed from

outside the organization" is broader than a more detailed statement (within the larger one) that "the chair will make sure meeting content will be only those issues that, according to board policy, clearly belong to the board to decide."

Similarly, they continue:

"The board will link governance and management functions through a single (paid) chief executive officer" might be augmented by a more detailed statement ... "The executive director is accountable to the board for achievement of provisions of the board's executive limitations policies and can only be evaluated against these criteria."

A Board Should Define and Delegate Rather than React and Ratify

The premise here is that a board which primarily engages in a ratification process is caught up in that process without regard to the criteria which should be taking most of their attention (Carver/Carver 1997, 36-37). The end result is that a board is most often tied up with minutiae which are management issues if policy is clear. In turn, as a result, their energies and talents are diverted or not allowed to be used in the greater purposes which probably attracted them to the organization in the first place—visioning, setting directions, and enhancing that which is needed to move toward the fulfillment of the organization's goals. In turn, the CEO is unable to function at his or her highest level of competency because of the constant need for permission to act.

The board *does* have the responsibility to monitor staff, but based upon policies evolved before the fact which allow staff to function within whatever latitude the board has decided to allow—remember the nesting bowls. The result is truly creative use of staff alongside creative use of board members. Nitpicking should be held to a minimum and so should micro-managing. The policy guidelines thus become not only the parameter for staff action but the criteria against which staff can be judged.

Budgeting is used as an example. Once policies are in place that become the guide for budget development, a line-by-line approval approach should not be countenanced by board members. They, in turn, must be confident as a result of their monitoring process that policy guidelines are being followed by staff. Both staff and board benefit in that staff are able to work within the policy frameworks, and not be second guessed about issues where the board has already developed guidelines.

Ends Determination is the Pivotal Duty of Governance

According to the Carvers:

> The justification for any organization lies in what difference it can make. A nonprofit organization exists so that the world in which it operates will be a better place. The ends of an organization are the reason for its existence. It is obvious that careful wise selection of ends is the highest calling of trustee leadership.
>
> Focusing on ends ensures that the board tackles the difficult questions by mobilizing board time, mechanics, and concern around what good is to be done for whom and at what cost. *The board cannot forget these questions, even for one meeting* (emphasis mine).

Traditionally, committees are asked to look at various dimensions of a difficult problem. Strategic planning committees are divided into subcommittees which report to the board through the filter of the strategic planning committee itself and then the executive committee. The Carvers call for the board to constitute itself more as a think tank. By clearing their agenda of items which are historically management issues, there will be time enough to do this. Focusing on ends—measurable outcomes—results in a vigorous use of time and talent precisely because of the consequences of such outcomes.

This approach calls for a board to turn away from whether or not to build buildings, raise salaries, or craft programs, but focuses on the reasons the organization exists at all. The Carvers caution that even those boards which do engage in serious discussion of ends often settle on matters that are measurable—how many are served? What is the cost per person, per square foot, and the like? These discussions must be preceded by the serious and difficult work of revisiting what an organization *really* wants to accomplish beyond maintaining itself tomorrow because it did good things yesterday.

There are cautions. When considering constituencies to be served, for example, that is an ends issue. Arranging how to do it is a means issue. Most organizations of a communal nature are undertaking serious strategic studies, redefining their missions. Most of them think vertically rather than horizontally. For example, if a faith-based institution decides that serving the elderly is a high priority because that is a desirable outcome (goal—ends), should they first decide whether or not they truly believe that one should "do unto others?"

The outcome of such processes is not guaranteed. What is guaranteed is that serious discussion, debate, education, and examination of options and consequences of actions would take place. There would be wider involvement and engagement than is the case in a traditional allocations process. The outcomes would be grounded in a serious examination of the ends desired.

The test in all of this lies in the consistent ability to differentiate ends issues from means issues. The Carvers emphasize the idea that an issue is only an ends issue if—and only if—it directly describes what good, for whom, and at what cost. The language of ends issues articulates what the organization will be doing and describes what will be different for others.

This is not to say mission, goals, objectives, and program do not remain essential. It is to say that the primary (some would say sole) business of the board is ends issues. All else is within the staff purview, according to the Carvers. This approach has the goal of releasing board members' thinking and energy to the most difficult part of governance—what is the business of this organization? Micro-management must be removed from the board room and clear guidelines of delegation must be established in order to do that. But how do you then get appropriate accountability from staff?

The Board's Best Control over Staff Means is to Limit, Not Prescribe

The Carvers acknowledge that accountability is essential. A board focusing on ends without financial controls in place is not doing its job. Over and above ends there are board responsibilities focused on how the organization conducts itself. What an agency does and how it does it are means, not ends. For the board there is the requirement that it structures itself and conducts its business so as to accomplish its oversight functions. Staff means become the way staff is organized (or organizes itself) and takes the appropriate actions to "accomplish the ends or to safeguard the operations that produce them." Here especially, the Carvers' model departs from the usual modes of practice, for they feel that programs, personnel practices, budgets, equipment, and the like are means issues and thus lie within the purview of staff, not board. They do not advocate that a board remove itself from its oversight function, but rather accomplish it in ways that anticipate the controls and guidelines which must be in control. These guidelines are then the boundaries establishing the parameters within which staff can function. Staff is not told how to do its job, but the CEO is told in writing what would be unacceptable means for staff to utilize. Thus, guidelines on fringe benefits would be decided by a board committee, but the decision on what group insurance to buy or how vacation accrual would work would be developed and implemented by staff.

For this model to work, staff must have *clear* guidelines so that policies covering *all* unacceptable actions or situations are clearly stated. This must be done in enough detail as to make the board's intentions clear, with opportunity for staff to ask for clarification as materials are developed.

Using the nesting bowl analogy, the guidelines must begin with the broader outlines and get increasingly specific *as appropriate*. It is obviously the board's prerogative to decide on the degree to which detailed proscriptions are needed, but they must be consistent. On the other hand, the board proscriptions can be a safety net for the board and the staff. To make this process work, the board's responsibility is to become knowledgeable in the areas where proscriptions are being developed.

I referred earlier to the issue of some sectarian agencies redefining themselves as non-sectarian in order to receive government funds. It would be the board's responsibility to explore this issue in order to ascertain if the government departments require that redefinition or would accept the agency's defining itself as being sectarian but with an open-door policy to potential clients regardless of race, origin, or religion. The same holds true for the inverse. These are complex matters demanding decisions grounded in serious knowledge. With this model, serious study and debate would engage the board before coming to a decision. This approach sets a large frame for action by the staff and eliminates the constant return to the use of committees for what are really means issues and the staff's job to perform—and perform well as measured by the expectations previously set forth.

The Carvers point out that the end result of this approach is to make it possible to govern with fewer pages of board pronouncement, less micro-management by board members, and greater CEO accountability. The board is then able to use the majority of its time focusing on its special ends responsibilities: providing leadership in exploring, deliberating and creating strategic vision.

A Board Must Design its Own Products and Process

The board must deal with its own means—how it will conduct itself as it conducts its business. A board with consciousness to its commitment focuses always on whom it serves, who it represents, and how it will maintain contact with its constituency. It will think of what it "produces"—what its "products" are. There will be careful thought given to the job and power of its chair, when it will use committees, and what their focus will be.

Committees must be helpful to get the board's jobs done and *not help staff with theirs*. For this process to work, even as the board thinks through the chair's essential jobs, there must be linkage to the staff with parallel concern and clarification as to what is expected from the CEO and staff. The chair and CEO work together but are not responsible to one another. Thus, the chair cannot fire the CEO, for that should not be his or her responsibility.

To make this approach work, the board carefully and fully discusses what it expects of its chair and its CEO, and proceeds to become increasingly detailed in its expectations to the point that members are satisfied that its words become policies.

Who decides what information is shared by chair and CEO with the board? What guidelines are set vis-à-vis the parameters for deciding when an organization co-sponsors activities—supports them financially? How are appointments made to committees and committee chairs? Each board must make its own list as short or as long as it wishes and develop iron-clad statements as a framework for action.

This process not only defines how governance will unfold but how board will relate to staff. Only a serious process followed by living seriously by the process' outcomes can make this approach work.

A Board Must Forge a Linkage with Management that is both Empowering and Safe

Obviously, the most important relationship in the organization is between the chair (chief volunteer officer) and the CEO (Chief Executive Officer). It is a relationship that can be misunderstood and misused. Indeed, the very title of this book attests to that fact and reality.

Choosing the CEO is one of the most important board functions, followed by a working relationship with the chair which is effective in helping everyone perform their tasks well and productively.

The relationship between staff and board members at its best is like the "Fred and Ginger show." The seemingly effortless ballroom dancing of Fred Astaire and Ginger Rogers was grounded in practice, trust, and clarity or what each expected from the other, a seemingly symbiotic relationship at times which also allowed "star turns"—individual identification and prominence when it was appropriate to the overall team effort.

The CEO must be empowered to act with a great deal of latitude which must be exercised in product and ethical ways. Too little empowerment results in an under-utilized executive. By extension, the rest of the staff is also under-utilized. Too much empowerment results in a rubber stamp board which has abdicated its governance responsibilities. The balance—the Fred and Ginger balance—is achieved by applying and living by the principles previously outlined.

Power and responsibility between board and staff is dynamic, but the fluidity must be born of a shared vision of governance and management. This model calls for delegation solely through the CEO, including what is expected and how he or she will be evaluated. The bottom-line evaluation has to do with revisiting the expectations which were developed with the CEOs aid as to the organization's fulfillment of what the Carvers call the organization's end policies.

The linkage between board and management would always be grounded in the absolutely unwavering expectation of honesty, integrity, openness of communications, and high performance. While mitigating situations can arise regarding performance, it is imperative that the board be absolutely consistent in its demands regarding its expectations.

Performance of the CEO Must be Monitored Rigorously, but Only against Policy Criteria

A board must show great responsibility in monitoring the CEO. This process must only be conducted using existing board-stated criteria. How often (after the fact) are the measurements/objectives changed and CEOs let go because some board member did not like their style? The immutable rule, according to the Carvers, must be that if a board has not specified how it ought to be, they should not ask how it is.

Financial monitoring must be grounded in the prior specific understandings of the expectations of the board. One does a great injustice to a CEO who, for example, is hired to head an educational institution, who admitted having no skills and competencies in financial management and is then judged incompetent in fiscal management.

None of this model is meant to preclude setting up a system where information is shared in a timely manner for governance purposes.

This model, on the face of it, may seem very familiar to the practice in most organizational systems. Its difference is in focusing the board on ends issues and moving it away from management concerns. Staff, through the CEO, is held accountable, but far fewer committees are involved in the management process. Thus, staff people have wider latitude to do their work. There is no laxity in the monitoring process, but board members' energies are focused on grappling with the important longitudinal concerns, directions, and priorities that is the work of a thoughtful board. Their energies, talents, and priorities are instead turned to reviewing management and program reports, requiring no action other than ratification.

This model envisions much more time for proactive thinking on the part of the board, with energetic direction and help from staff.

This approach often requires new ways of thinking. What follows is a detailed excerpt on implementing what the Carvers call "policy governance" from their book *Basic Principles of Policy Governance* (1996).

Policy Governance brings an entirely new way to operate and to think about the expression of board leadership. Beware the comment that "we're already doing things this way." This comment will almost always be masking a superficial understanding of Policy Governance.

With an incomplete grasp, one can mistakenly see the model as merely reiterating familiar bromides like "boards should deal with policy," "boards should stick with long-term planning," or "boards should set goals and then leave managers alone." While there is some limited truth in these representations, Policy Governance involves a far more thorough reordering of how governance is conceived. The following sequence helps boards put Policy Governance into action. It is intended for boards bravely implementing on their own.

1. *Be sure that board members and the CEO understand the model.* Without good theory, actions aren't as meaningful and don't cohere. Until a board fully grasps the ideas and philosophy of this new technology of governance, implementation will be like putting new wine into old bottles. Board members' words may change, but governance will not be transformed. The board can test itself to see if members fully understand the model. For example, consider discussing whether each of the various issues an organization faces is an ends or means issue. Or take a board member's fear about finances, personnel, or other staff means; discuss how that fear could be used to amend an executive limitations policy.

2. *Make a full board commitment to this major change.* There is no reason that the decision must be unanimous, but it should represent the board's voice as a body. If moving to Policy Governance is only what the chairperson, CEO, or influential committee wants to do, it will fail.

3. *Put the board's commitment to move ahead on paper.* This step creates, in effect, the board's first governance process policy. For example, the board might adopt a simple, general statement such as, "We will govern with an emphasis on vision rather than internal preoccupation, encouragement of diversity, strategic leadership more than administrative detail, clear distinction of board and chief executive roles, collective rather than individual decisions, future rather than past or present, and pro-activity rather than reactivity.

4. *Develop all policies except ends.* Ends will be saved until last. First the system as a whole must be put into place. Develop all the executive limitations policies. Some board members will be put off by the negative wording, but remember that it is designed to produce a positive effect. Next, develop all the governance process policies. The first step in creating these policies has already been taken (in step 3). Now add other policies dealing with the chairperson's role, board member commitment, committee principles, committee products and authority, and board job description. Finally, develop all the board-staff linkage policies. Having completed policies that define its own job and the limits that apply to staff actions, the board can now safely contemplate a philosophy of strong executive delegation.

5. *Adopt a single temporary ends policy.* It may seem odd that the most important of board policies is saved until last. The policies already mentioned clear the clutter, trivia, and ritual actions from the agenda. Moreover, ends take longer to work through than the foregoing policies, and in fact, their development never stops. In other words, it works best to get everything else out of the way and then work on ends forever.
Since developing ends policies is slow work, and since a long delay before operating with the new principles is asking for trouble, adopt a tentative policy to plug the gap. My clients often adopt a statement that says, "Until ends policies are developed, the ends of the organization will remain as previously stated explicitly by the board or as found implicitly in previously adopted board documents." It is best to get started on real ends policies to replace this temporary one as soon as possible after implementation. At this point, all the policies necessary to begin operating with Policy Governance have been drafted.

6. *Do an administrative and perhaps legal check.* When a board has policies in the Policy Governance format and uses principles of the model, virtually all other board documents and pronouncements except bylaws become unnecessary. In fact, the motion putting all the policy drafts into effect will, at the same time, repeal personnel policies, budgets, old policies, and other approvals. Most previous board documents (personnel policies, budgets, salary schedules, and so on) with which the new policies will conflict can simply be given over to the CEO.
Before taking such a severe—albeit essential—action, you must be certain that the new policies do not conflict with law or with the bylaws. If the new policies conflict with the bylaws, change the bylaws. If the new policies conflict with law, then alter them so that the law is not broken.

7. *Have the first few agendas ready to go.* The immediate problem that the board will encounter after setting the model in motion will be the concrete matter of what to do that next board meeting. Even if you plan to

do nothing at the first post-transition meeting but have a discussion of ends and the difficulty of defining them, that is much better than falling back on previous agenda formats to avoid the anxiety. Absolutely do not have the staff create board agendas, although the board should invite staff members along with others to argue various points of view with regard to large, long-term ends issues. Remember that the board agenda is a matter of governance process, so the board chair has the authority to use any reasonable interpretation of whatever the board has said about agendas.

8. *Design the first steps in connecting with the ownership.* The ownership is the legitimacy base to whom the board is accountable, for whom it is the actual or "civic" trustee. Lay plans to form and meet with focus groups, confer with other boards, or have relevant statistical data gathered. Connecting with the ownership, like setting agendas, is a matter of governance process, so the complementary board and chair roles in the matter are similar: the board establishes its broad-brush intention and the chair fills in the details.

9. *Set a specific date to inaugurate the system.* To the extent possible, avoid phasing in the new paradigm; after prudent assurance that all is in order, switch completely to it in one move. Treat the transition like jumping from one trapeze to another. When you do decide to jump, don't jump halfway or jump in phases.

The time required for going through this implementation sequence varies greatly depending on the circumstances and the people. For a national or international board that meets three times per year, the sequence ordinarily runs a different pace from one that meets monthly in a community. A board of nine moves more quickly than a board of thirty. Most of my clients have taken from six to twelve months to implement the process.

But make no mistake, completing the nine steps above means only that the real governance work can begin. Three efforts will demand the majority of board time and energy forever. First, the ends will need continual attention in perpetuity. Second, finding ways to gather owners' input is not easy. Third, sufficient self-evaluation and redevelopment are needed so that board leadership can continue to improve. These three activities are unique leadership tasks, embodying the challenge and the channel for board members to be strategic leaders.

The approaches to governance reviewed here are not definitive. Many models exist and three have been reviewed here—the one most widely used in the traditional nonprofit system (the "collaborative" model), the "bifurcated board" (Klausner and Small), and the Carvers' "policy governance" model.

A Tool for Board-Staff Use

Regardless of the thrust of the philosophical directions of governance, there is practice excellence that can be discerned in the field. I have developed a Self-Rating Scale on Board-Staff Relations (see end of chapter) which allows an agency or organization to take measure of how it is doing in this area. This instrument is meant to help an agency or organization assess itself.

The essays and other material in this book are intended to help strengthen organizations while challenging them to use new ways of governing when appropriate. At the same time, there are pitfalls to be avoided by both staff and board members in the governance process, and parts of this book are particularly focused on those questions and issues.

The self-rating scale at the end of this essay is one such tool. It stands by itself and is self-explanatory. This scale can be reutilized periodically as one way of evaluating governance as a whole and the board-staff process as the essential part of how community "business" is conducted.

In too many instances, tensions do exist between board and staff members, born in part because of lack of clarity of roles, in part because of uneven competencies (more frequently found among board members than among staff), in part because of changing expectations, and in part because of the stakes involved.

The changes in nonprofit organizational life are enormous as a result of changing demographics, sources of funds, and varying generational goals and expectations. This book must be seen in the context of these all too real, changing, and often unpredictable realities. Most importantly, however, organizational missions and goals must be remembered. Organizations whose primary focus is fundraising often are faced with great dilemmas. By their nature, they must spend the bulk of their efforts in working with the elite who account for the greatest source of funding. At the same time, fundraising organizations may also be in the business of building community. Such organizations must grapple with implementation of hybrid approaches to serve their mission.

Board-staff relations must be seen as a tool in meeting the challenge of governance in a totally voluntary world. In our post-modern world with a multiplicity of options, people choose how to live their lives—as individuals or as part of one or another community, emotional, spiritual, sociological, religious, or various combinations of those dimensions.

In almost all of them, staff devotes their lives in service of the particular organizations or communities which offer them dignified opportunities to serve and grow professionally and personally. In turn, there are volunteers who give of their time and resources because they have chosen to do so. Both staff and board members may well be in search, in personal terms, of highly overlapping personal and spiritual fulfillment opportunities for meaning and legacy.

Keeping all this in mind should help board and staff people maintain perspective on what they do and why they do it. There are many issues which do not involve money as much as they involve constant focus and redefining of mission in the context of the needs of constituents, not the needs of organization. If the bulk of a board's time is given to organizational maintenance without reference to the larger purpose, the best and the brightest will move on to organizations which offer them those opportunities and the same is true of the best staff.

When all is said and written, a sense of purpose must permeate what we do. Yes, there *are* problems in governance and board-staff relations; this book would not have been published if such were not the case. Certainly much has changed for the better. The commitments of both staff and board to the nonprofit enterprise is more positive; the engagement by both groups, while different, is more intensive today than in yesteryear. We still strive for the beloved community Josiah Royce craved so passionately albeit with the technology, purpose and adaptability of the nonprofit sector of the twenty-first century.

Self-Rating Scale on Board-Staff Relations

	Low 1	2	3	4	High 5
Job descriptions exist for staff *and* board.					
Board members and their staff counterparts mutually develop annual goals in descending order of importance.					
Board members and their staff counterparts mutually develop contracts of expectations of one another.					
Notices for meetings are received by board members 10 to 14 days before the meeting.					
Information in the agency is shared in a timely way and in usable form.					
Minutes are kept regularly and shared in a wide and functional circle. Thus, executive committee members receive all committee minutes and reports.					
Board members receive executive committee minutes and at least quarterly financial reports.					
Committees have staff representation with voice and vote except those committees requiring only board membership (contract and salary negotiations).					
Agendas are developed mutually by board and staff.					
Objective criteria exist for board membership.					
Board and staff are evaluated regularly against mutually developed criteria.					
Board membership is rotated regularly.					
Committees nominate committee chairs for ratification by the volunteer agency head (sometimes called chief volunteer officer, president, or board chair).					
Boards and committees are diverse and representative of the community in which the agency or organization serves.					
Constituents have easy access to officers and senior staff.					
Board meetings are open to the public.					
In organizations serving large geographic areas, key meetings are rotated to expedite access.					
Communications to constituents encourage opportunities for communication from constituents.					

In organizations whose functions include fundraising, planning, and programming, recognition of volunteers is not confined to major fiscal supporters.					
The organization is gender neutral in board and officer membership.					
The organization is gender neutral in its hiring and promotion functions.					
Debate and discussion is encouraged at board and committees as a tool for achieving consensus.					
Staff people are not fired as a result of the actions or desires of any one volunteer.					
Trust between board and staff members exists in ways that are easily observable.					
There is respect between board and staff for each others' contribution to the fulfillment of the agency's or organization's mission.					
Both board and staff members are proud to be serving the agency or organization.					

Scoring

The highest single rating is 130 — the lowest is 26. Ask all board and staff to fill out the rating scale. Add the ratings of each form and divide by the number of people filling out the scale.

26 to 40	There is much work to be done across the board.
41 to 60	Examine the areas of agreement and disagreement to see if special attention is needed to any particular dimensions of board-staff relations.
61 to 80	The agency is moving in the right direction and should continue to emphasize and create additional positives.
81 to 100	The agency has much to be proud of and should build on its achievements.
101 to 126	Eureka! The place to continue to put one's resources, abilities, and future.

References

Gerald Bubis, 1981. "Professional Trends in Jewish Communal Service," *Journal of Jewish Communal Service*, vol. 1 vii, no. 4 (Summer).

Gerald Bubis, 1994. "Jewish Communal Service—Profession or Field of Work?," Jerusalem: Jerusalem Center for Public Affairs.

Gerald Bubis and Steven Cohen, 1998. *American Jewish Leaders View Board-Staff Relations.* Jerusalem: Jerusalem Center for Public Affairs.

John Carver, 1990. *Boards that Make a Difference: A New Design for Leadership in Nonprofit and Public Organizations.* San Francisco: Jossey Bass, pp. 9-12, 33-34.

Gerald Bubis and Steven Windmueller, 2005 *From Predictability to Chaos?? How Jewish Leaders Re-invented Their National Communal System.* Center for Jewish Community Studies.

John Carver and Miriam Mayhew Carver, 1996. *Basic Principles of Policy Governance.* San Francisco: Jossey Bass.

Jim Collins, 2001. *Good to Great.* New York: Harper Collins Publishers Inc.

Daniel J. Elazar, 1980. *Community and Polity: The Organizational Dynamics of American Jewry.* Philadelphia: Jewish Publication Society.

Rela Geffen, 1997. "Fundamentals of the Jewish Political Tradition: Constitutional Principles of the Edah." *Serving the Jewish Polity: The Application of Jewish Political Theory to Jewish Communal Practice.* Jerusalem: Jerusalem Center for Public Affairs, pp. 55-56.

David Kaufman, 1999. *Shul with a Pool.* Hanover: University Press of New England.

Michael Klausner and Jonathan Small, Spring 2005 "Failing to Govern? The Disconnect between Theory and Reality and How to Fix It" *Stanford Social Innovation Review*, vol. 3, Number 1, pp 43-49, 2005

Ian Mitroff, 1985. "Mission Impossible? Teaching Corporate America to Think Strategically," unpublished manuscript, p. 6.

Peter Senge, 1994. *The Fifth Discipline Fieldbook: Strategies and Tools for Building a Learning Organization*. New York: Currency and Doubleday.

Toward a Contingency Model of Board-Executive Relations

Ralph M. Kramer

Introduction

One of the distinguishing features of voluntary nonprofit organizations in the human services is the structured interaction between board members and the executive in their governance. Because of their interdependence, this professional-volunteer relationship between executive and board member is usually described as a "partnership" (Conrad & Glen, 1976; O Connell, 1976; Trecker, 1970; Weber, 1976). Most of the practice wisdom is based on this metaphor which assumes consensus and collaboration between equals, even though it is widely recognized that there are silent, limited, and junior partnerships. While partnership may be the "espoused theory" (Argyris & Schon, 1974), the "theory-in-use" of most executives, i.e., the concepts they use in perceiving their roles and relationships and that guide their behavior, is more complex and involves elements of power-dependency and even conflict. The concept of partnership is too limited in scope and does not adequately reflect the broader range of conditions under which there is not only collaboration, but also disagreement and dissensus between board and executive, and which require different roles, strategies, tactics, and resources (Brager & Holloway, 1978; Derr, 1978). Because the partnership model is closed, it obscures the political and shifting nature of the board-executive relationship which can be viewed not only as an exchange of resources, but also in terms of power-dependency, and which is influenced by the type of organization in which they function, the type of situation and issues to be faced, and the differences in their personal attributes and resources (see Table 1). Consequently, while useful for some purposes, the partnership model is insufficiently conducive for self-reflective and corrective analysis by which professionals can learn from their experience and become more effective.

72

Elements of an Analytic Framework for the Study of Board-Executive Relations

Organization
structure, size, age, type
fiscal system

Executive	*Board Member*
Professional status, expertise, interpersonal competence, ideology, self-image, reference groups, role repertoire, self-role congruence, duration of employment, personal attributes and leadership style	SES, prestige, duration of service, knowledge, skills, access to resources, financial support, service beneficiary, other loyalties, welfare ideology and commitment, self-image and reference groups

Interpersonal Role Relationships
History, status differentials, definitions
of role and situation, power/dependency
tradeoffs and resource exchange

Situation
Crisis/routine, time
constraints

Issue
Substantive character,
salience and controversy-
potential

In this article, we will identify and analyze some of the leading factors influencing board-executive relations, with particular attention to power and the potential for the domination of one or the other. After examining some of the conditions in which the relationship can lean in one direction or the other, an alternative, contingency model of board-executive relations is proposed.

In developing a new framework for the analysis of board-executive relations, we shall draw on concepts of social resource exchange, role theory and symbolic interactionism as well as interest group, power, and conflict theories. Overall, we assume that these behaviors occur within the context of a political-economy model of organizational behavior. Instead of the mystique of "partnership," the relations between board and executive can be analyzed using the concepts of (1) status, (2) norm, (3) role, (4) responsibility, (5) authority, and (6) power. A comparative overview of these concepts is summarized in Table 2.

Power and the Potential for Conflict

Although power is at the core of conflict and political economy models of organization (Zald, 1973; Gummer, 1980; Hasenfeld, 1983), few attempts have been made to conceptualize board-executive relationships as a key variable in policy making and the allocation of organizational resources. Studies of the governance of voluntary agencies tend to focus on issues of representation, elitism, and "minority rule" along with other departures from democratic norms (Fayence, 1977; Steckler & Herzog, 1970; Marmor & Marone, 1981). There has been relatively little follow-up on research findings published in the 1960s which point up the unequal distribution of power between board and executive, as well as sharp differences in their statuses, values, reference groups, agency identifications, and other relevant social-psychological attributes (Nettler, 1958; Kramer, 1965; Knight, 1968; Robins & Blackburn, 1974). Indeed, similar findings by independent investigators of opposing welfare ideologies raise the question of how voluntary agencies can operate in the face of sharp disparities in values between policy makers and managers who are structurally and functionally bound together (Nettler, 1958; Stein, 1961; Senor, 1965; Kramer, 1965). The failure to pursue some of these leads reflects also the underdevelopment of practice theory for professional interpersonal encounters that are socio-political rather than clinical in content (Bolan, 1980; Schon, 1982; Specht, 1983).

Discussions of power in the board-executive relationships are rare, despite the recent finding that "conflict between executive directors and trustees is all too common in not for profit organizations, especially in middle-size and small nonprofits where differences may become personal" (Unterman & Davis, 1982, p. 36). Perhaps the reluctance to recognize openly the existence of power in such social relations exists because "to unmask the actual distribution of power may serve to reduce the power of those operating behind the mask" (Gross, 1968, p. 77).

**Comparison of Board Members and Executives on
Six Attributes**

	Board of Directors	Executive
Social Status	Volunteer Trustee Employer Community notable	Professional/expert Full time employee Director of social agency
Behavioral Norms	Altruism and best interests of community Proscription of self-dealing and conflicts of interests Stewardship and collaborative partnership with executive Participation in and support of the agency	Ethical, professional performance Subordination of personal interests to those of the agency and the decisions of the Board Helping relationship to board members, including leadership development
Roles	Policy maker/trustee Employer Interpreter, supporter & advocate	Multiple & diverse: enabler, guide manager, educator, expert, etc.
Responsibility for to	Governance: policy making/adoption Resource acquisition, allocation and control Appointment of executive & adoption of personnel policies Community relations Community (membership, contributors & constituencies) & clientele	Implementation of policy via administration of program Appointment & supervision of staff Assisting the board & liaison between it and the staff Board of Directors, clientele, staff, community & professional interests
Types of Authority	Legal (formal/official) right as trustees to govern, receive and allocate funds Hierarchical — over executive	Professional expertise Hierarchical — delegated by Board to implement policy (administer program), employ, supervisor and evaluate staff
Power (resources for influence)	Status & authority as a corporate trustee Prestige as a community notable Legitimation of the organization Access to resources Personal knowledge, skill, time, energy Duration of service and intensity of commitment	Status as a professional with expertise Administrative authority & responsibilities Full time commitment; duration & continuity of service Access to and provider of organizational information Informal relationships with key persons

In this way, the partnership model of board-executive relations may deflect attention from issues of control in these "private governments."

There are a number of conceptual problems in estimating power because of its multiple sources and effects. To reduce some of these difficulties, power can be viewed as an interactive relationship whereby the power of one person derives from the dependency of another (Hasenfeld, 1983). To avoid some of the pejorative character of the word "power," we shall refer to "resources for influence" (Brager & Holloway, 1978) to distinguish it from the notion of control. As Zald (1968) points out, board member and executive each bring distinctive resources of varying importance to bear on their relationship, and "it is the balance of resources in specific situations and decisions that determines the attribution of relative power in the encounter between boards and executives" (p. 98).

What are some of these resources for influence accruing to boards and executives by virtue of their respective statuses? It is first necessary to distinguish between the resources of the board as a group with its corporate, legal authority which serves to legitimate the organization, and the board member as a person who has other resources for influence. Individual board members may have prestige as community notables; hence, their names are a resource. There is, for example, some evidence to show the positive relationship between the prestige of its board members and an agency's level of funding from the United Way (Provan, 1980). They may also have access to funds, their own and others', or to other volunteers or goodwill for the agency. By means of peer and other interpersonal relationships, board members can form coalitions representing different interests that can exert influence within the board or in the community. Apart from their community connections, board members may have knowledge, skill, time, and energy, all of which are reinforced by the duration and intensity of their commitment to the agency.

Sources and Determinants of Executive Influence

The power of executives stems largely from their status as professionals, their administrative authority and responsibilities, and their informal relationships. As professionals, they are presumed to be knowledgeable about agencies and their operations as well as the fields of service in which they function. Their professionalism also implies a full-time, if not a lifelong, career commitment. There is also the influence that is based on continuity; presumably, the longer the duration of their service, the greater their influence. Other aspects of the organization, such as its size, also determine the influence of executives. Levy (1982) has noted:

> The executive is in many ways invested with virtually unlimited power over many things and persons. The larger and more bureaucratic the organization, and the more autonomous the executive, the greater the opportunity to exploit or abuse such power with relative impunity. The smaller the organization, ... the more direct and unsettling the experience for victims of such exploitation and abuse and the more personal the effects may be or may feel (p. 61).

The size of the organization is also related to its potential for conflict; e.g., the larger the organization, the longer the lines of communication, the more tenuous is control between levels of authority, and a greater likelihood of factionalism and vested interests resisting change.

Because of their location in the communication structure of the agency, executives have access to and control over information which can then be shared selectively with board members and staff (Brager & Specht, 1973). The executive probably receives and gives more information than anyone else and acts as a communication link between board and staff. As noted earlier in the discussion of responsibility for policy making, the expertise of executives and their access to information make it possible for them to identify, select, and define the issues that eventually comprise the agenda for the board of directors. Executives help define the situation for the board through their responsibility for the preparation of virtually all the written material board members receive, such as minutes, reports, budgets, memoranda, analyses of policy alternatives and their likely consequences, etc.

Apart from carrying out their professional responsibility "to inform, educate, and guide the board," the extent of the executive influence on the issues selected for attention will also be affected by their substantive character, as well as the decision-making situation. For example, board members' influence may be greater if issues are particularly salient for them, such as the allocation of funds, facilities, and other tangible resources, or if an important policy precedent will be set, or if personnel practices or inter-organizational or community relations are involved. If, however, an issue can be defined as clinical-technical, professional, or administrative, then it is quite likely that board member opinions may not be sought or counted for very much. Also, certain types of decision-making situations will tend to optimize the power of one or the other. The board will probably be dominant in time of crisis, when an organization is facing major changes or threats, or when the time has come for executive succession (Zald, 1969). On the other hand, when the situation is more routine, or when there are severe time constraints, then the matter may well be left in the hands of the executive.

In addition to the resources for influence that are essentially structural, i.e., inherent in the professional status and administrative position of the executive, power can be mobilized through informal, interpersonal relationships with the chairman, individual board members, and key persons in the community. As a gatekeeper, the executive provides access to recognition and prestige for persons whose names can be proposed to nominating and other committees which continually seek volunteers for community service tasks. By suggesting names to various community and national bodies, one is in a position to influence who may rise to leadership and who will sit in judgment and make decisions in the future (Kahn, 1978; Feldstein, 1982). By selective sharing of information with certain persons, one can give them more status because of their possession of inside information. In addition, the executive has a form of input control whereby s/he can influence the selective recruitment and socialization of new board members who are required by the annual turnover of a portion of most boards of directors.

Other structural features of the board of directors reinforce the informal power of the executive including the relatively large size of many boards which are only nominally policy-making.

> The large board is preferred because it satisfies volunteers' desires for nominal involvement while leaving the director in control.... Some trustees also prefer a large board because they enjoy the public platform, the business context, and the opportunity to avoid individual responsibility (Unterman & Davis, 1982, p. 30).

In addition, boards tend to meet infrequently, and most board members give relatively little time to their tasks. Conversely, frequency of meetings has been associated with greater perceived influence of board members (Tulipana & Herman, 1983). Another consequence of a large board, apart from the marginal attachment and the limited, episodic participation of most board members, is "the maneuverability which comes from ambiguity" (Brager & Specht, 1973, p. 236). This refers to the diffuseness of the board of directors' collective control as employer of the executive, i.e., the total board rather than any single member is responsible for hiring and firing the executive. This allows the executive to maneuver among the different factions on the board which is rarely monolithic.

The ways in which executives utilize their professional authority and responsibility in interpersonal relationships (i.e., their power) will be determined by their ethical commitments and professional ideology. The extent to which they value open sharing and disclosure of information, truthfulness, loyalty, justice, fairness, etc., will shape much of the use of power (Levy, 1982; Forester, 1982). Guiding the executive's behavior may be a view of the board as a nuisance or unnecessary burden, a group to be overcome rather than an indispensable resource whose development is an essential part of professional responsibility and which requires appropriate values, knowledge, and skill. These two extremes reflect the strain between a technocratic and a democratic ideology found among voluntary agency executives. The former refers to the belief that experts or professionals should have most of the power in organizational policy making, and from this perspective a board member can contribute little to the agency except perhaps legitimation. On the other hand, a democratic ideology regards as a norm the professional obligation to educate citizen volunteers to enable them to develop their leadership abilities. There is some impressionistic evidence that although the democratic ideology is officially promulgated, the technocratic ideology is widespread even if it is not publicly acknowledged (Kramer, 1981).

As reported in one of few surveys of board members of nonprofit organizations:

> Although in theory both director (in profit-making organizations) and trustee board members of nonprofits should make policy decisions, chief executive

officers and executive directors have control of strategic management even though their power is derived differently.... Many trustees ignore the task of discussing policy and accept the de facto decisions of the executive director, though such neglect and acceptance seems to vary with the size of the organization (Unterman & Davis, 1982, p. 36).

While board-executive relationships are influenced by the attributes of the actors and the situation in which they find themselves, they are also shaped by the organizational context in which the interaction takes place (Mintzberg, 1983). The extent to which one or the other may prevail is affected by such structural factors as the size, degree of complexity, bureaucratization, professionalization, or decentralization of the organization. One could hypothesize that the more these variables are optimized, and affect the distribution of authority and power, the more dependent will board members be on the executive for information and assistance (see Table 3). The agency's fiscal system will also operate in favor of one or the other. In organizations dependent on many small donors rather than on a few large donors, or where there is reliance on governmental contracts and grants, the executive may be less dependent on the board members' fundraising abilities. Also, the stage of development of the organization, whether it is new, old, growing, or declining may also have differential effects on the power of the board or the executive, with the board more influential in the early rather than in the later stages of an organizational career (Perlmutter, 1970; Senor, 1964; Zald, 1969).

The ways in which people use power can be arranged on a continuum from authoritarian to leader, catalyst, supporter/enabler, interpreter/in-formant, submissive, and servant (Bolan, 1971). These types of behaviors can be collapsed into a three-point scale of controlling, facilitating, or *laissez-faire* behaviors. Each end of the continuum represents an extreme, and it is rarely the case that executives are authoritarians or merely note takers at meetings, scurrying servants who do whatever the board wishes. At the same time, it is not unheard of that by means of a very careful facade and appropriate posture, the clever professional can maintain a democratic form but really run the entire organization. Contributing to this is the lack of agreement on the roles of the executive except that s/he should be "helpful." There are dozens of somewhat diffuse, often conflicting, and ambiguous roles. The following is a list of the most frequently cited roles of the executive:

activator	developer	grants person	organizer
administrator	director	guide	planner
advocate	educator	initiator	resource person
analyst	enabler	interpreter	staff
catalyst	entrepreneur	leader	stimulator
consultant	expert	manager	synthesizer
coordinator	facilitator	mediator	"technipol"

Given this diversity, and the absence of guidelines regarding when to perform which role, it is not surprising that there is considerable confusion, lack of consensus, and a high potential for role strain and conflict. For example, a sharp divergence of opinion regarding the major responsibilities of executives was found in a 1974 study of over two hundred executives, presidents, and over sixteen hundred board members of United Way agencies in New York City (Schoderbek, 1979). Presidents and board members saw the primary role of the executive much more as an administrator rather than someone responsible for policy. While presidents and board members regarded the hiring and firing of staff as the highest ranking executive responsibility, it was ranked as ninth of thirty functions for the executives. Policy recommendations to the board was the second most frequently role cited by executives. The findings of this study are summarized in Table 3.

Conditions Conducive to Greater Power for the Executive

To the extent that these variables are optimized, there is a greater likelihood that the executive will have relatively more power than board members:

Organization	large size complexity bureaucratization decentralization	professionalization technical knowledge base many small donors reliance on government funds
Board Members	large number high turnover infrequent meetings little service utilization/benefit multiple community loyalties shared welfare ideology relatively low knowledge, experience, status, prestige & access to resources weak agency identification low degree of financial support	
Situation	severe time constraints routine, absence of crisis	
Issue	substantively clinical, technical, professional or inter-organizational less tangible, non-fiscal or community-related non-precedent setting, less policy low salience non-controversial programmatic	

Who Dominates When?

Actually, we have very little research evidence regarding the conditions under which one or the other dominates. In the past, some sociologists have made broad generalizations, claiming that most of the time the professional dominates the board, while others claim that the opposite is the case (Gouldner, 1963; Wilensky & Lebeaux, 1965). A recent exploratory study concluded that the more effective nonprofit organizations may be those with "strong" executive directors, and that the influence of the board of directors is not very important (Tulipana & Herman, 1983).

In one of the few empirical studies, four different patterns of power distribution were identified in the governing boards of 15 Israeli agencies. They were arranged on a continuum at one end of which power was concentrated in a single person, either the executive or the president, and at the other end, power was dispersed with varying forms of professional leadership (Kramer, 1981). The agencies were almost equally distributed between the patterns of concentrated and dispersed power, but these patterns did not seem to be associated with any particular set of interests, issues, or values. For example, the type of power distribution was not related consistently to the degree of active participation on the board or the rate of turnover. Attempts to carry the analysis beyond this point were not productive because the concentration of power in the executive or the board does not tell us when and how it will be used, and on behalf of what interests, values, and issues. It is, therefore, difficult to avoid the pitfalls that have plagued studies of community decision-making which assume a stable, consistent, and fixed distribution of power that persists despite the issue and particular situation.

Consequently, the power/dependency relationship between board and executive is neither constant, nor a zero-sum game; rather, "it depends," i.e., it is contingent on the factors that have been previously identified and which are summarized in Table 3.

A Contingency Model of Board-Executive Relationships

Table 3, which identifies some of the leading factors affecting the potential distribution of power between board and executive, shows the limitations of the partnership metaphor, and underscores the need for a more comprehensive and realistic model of the relationship which will take into account its more political aspects. Such a model would view the organization as a political economy in which individuals and interest groups seek to influence decision-making and compete for control of resources as they try to promote their self-interests which are shaped by their respective roles, status, authority, and responsibility in the agency hierarchy.

While it would be possible to consider such a power-politics model (Gummer, 1980) as an alternative, or at least as a supplement to the traditional notion of partnership, it is possible to integrate them into a new, more dynamic and realistic contingency model reflecting the broader range of possibilities. Board members and executive are conceived as interest groups with distinctive resources to influence decision-making and who, depending principally on the nature of the issue, may collaborate or engage in political maneuvering or conflict. These three processes can be conceived as part of a consensus-difference-dissensus continuum in which the board-executive relationship may involve all three types and may move back and forth between them (Derr, 1978; Torczyner, 1978).

While other organizational, situational, and personal factors, which have been summarized in Tables 2 and 3, influence the type of relationship and outcome as predisposing or mediating elements, the particular place on the continuum and the specific character of the roles, strategies, and tactics depend mainly on the nature of the issue with which they are involved and the extent to which agreement between board member and executive is possible (Warren, 1975).

Among the critical dimensions of an issue are: (1) its substantive character (program, finance, personnel, etc.); (2) its controversial nature, which is usually related to the values and interests of board member and executive; and (3) the degree of change involved (scope, depth, duration, irreversibility, and such costs).

To the extent that these elements are minimized and/or there is consensus between board and executive, then the partnership model is appropriate and will prevail with its power sharing, open communication, and primary reliance on information, education, and problem-solving as rational means of persuasion (Connors, 1980). Under these collaborative conditions in which a debate, rather than a game or light (Rapoport, 1961) is the outcome, the executive's role is primarily that of an enabler, facilitator or catalyst, quite similar to the Model II behavior described by Argyris and Schon (1974).

Occasionally there are, however, important, controversial issues where there is a clash between the values and interests of board and executive which may involve major changes in organizational goals, policies, programs, structure, or allocation of resources, or which may pertain to the unacceptable role behavior of the executive. Or there may be substantial differences in opinion which greatly reduce the possibilities of agreement; e.g., the board may not recognize the condition which the executive has defined as a problem, or they do not understand the substance and the implications of a proposal. Incidentally, it should be noted that because of the asymmetry of their power, a compromise is not necessary when the views of the board and executive are at odds. Essentially, it is a one-way street because the board does not need to convince the executive of its position, while the reverse is true. Of course, the board may be reluctant to utilize its authority, knowing that the executive and staff may covertly sabotage an unpopular decision.

If, in the absence of consensus and despite opposition, the executive decides to persist in trying to overcome the resistance to his/her proposal on the part of one or more board members, then the executive must draw on other resources to exert sufficient pressures appropriate to a "campaign" strategy in which hard persuasion, political maneuvering, and manipulation may be required (Warren, 1975). The latter might involve giving the appearance of sharing, but exercising covert influence by omitting certain facts and deliberately selecting the best or the worst possible case. Because most boards are not monolithic and the executive has no vote, one may seek to develop alliances with various factions on the board which might support his/her position and at the same time try to avoid taking public accountability for the campaign (Brager & Holloway, 1978). If there is a major division within the board on the substance of an issue, on the means of resolving the problem, or even whether there is an issue, the executive may try to encourage some bargaining and negotiation between the factions and serve as a mediator rather than risk being an advocate for one's own position.

Under these conditions of disagreement, the executive's role is much less a partner or enabler, and more a promoter or advocate trying to strengthen certain coalitions of board members and to weaken others that do not support his/her position. (Note that this analysis does not take into account the particular merits of the executive's position, nor the extent to which one is primarily serving one's own interests, those of the clientele or the organization.) Although the professional literature has no legitimate place for such roles, rejecting them pejoratively as unprofessional, manipulative, unethical, or "Model I," political behavior by executives is more prevalent than is generally acknowledged. A concern with power would seem to be appropriate when there is a serious controversy and clash between the respective values and interest of board and executive. At the very least, a model of board-executive relationships should recognize the existence of power-politics and not treat consensus and a partnership as the only state of affairs (Katz, 1981).

There is still a third possibility on this continuum, although it may be more hypothetical than real because of its infrequent occurrence. Between difference and dissensus is a matter of degree pertaining to the likelihood of agreement which has diminished almost to the vanishing point because of strong antagonism between the values and interests of the board and executive. Among the possibilities for this condition to occur are: when there is unequivocal or unanimous rejection of the issue; when the proposed solution or bargaining may have broken down completely; when there is a sharp polarization of the perceived goals and demands of the parties in a major attempt to change the power distribution as part of a struggle for control of the organization; or when there is a move to fire the executive. Because of the win-lose or zero-sum character of a contest in which only the executive can lose, the objective of the executive is to try to move the conflict back to a campaign and ultimately to a stage of collaboration. A conflict relationship between board and executive is most unstable because the executive has few if any resources with which to coerce the board or to force an agreement because of one's dependency on them for his position. Unless s/he is prepared to risk the job, it is untenable for the executive to maintain an adversarial relationship with his board for any length of time. Even though the executive might have the potential power to wage a fight against one or more board members, the possible costs would probably be too great.

The continuum of the relationships between the degree of agreement on an issue and the subsequent strategy and roles of the executive are summarized in Table 4 (Warren, 1975; Derr, 1978).

Relationships between the Degree of Agreement and Subsequent Strategy

Type of issue (based on possibility of agreement)	consensus	difference	dissensus
Strategy	collaboration (debate)	campaign (game)	contest/conflict (fight)
Role	partner	advocate/mediator	adversary
Use of information	openly shared	strategically shared	secrecy or distortion
Power relationship	parity	struggle for parity	unequal

Conclusions: Conflict or Resource Exchange

A contingency model of board-executive relationships involving collaboration, difference, and dissensus is therefore proposed as a countervailing corrective to the prevailing view limiting the relationship primarily to a shared partnership. It is true, however, that in practice the system of board-executive relationships, particularly in middle-class boards, tends to suppress conflict. Despite the significant disparity in their respective authority, responsibility and power, as well as in their status and roles, values, and interests, the system of board-executive relationships in most middle-class boards operates in an equilibrium based on interdependence and exchange of resources (Greer, 1982). Why is this so?

Each party has resources and incentives to minimize conflict. Under the conditions of lay policy control and professional guidance, controversial items likely to cause undesirable conflict can be screened out through the executive's control over the agenda so that only safe issues are presented for consideration. This helps explain why so many boards are almost exclusively policy ratifying or policy adopting bodies, a phenomenon which has been described as "non-decision-making" in which many meetings characteristically consist of reports that serve to "educate" or "bring along" the board.

Other built-in factors from the standpoint of the board which tend to minimize conflict include the lower saliency of goals; i.e., the multiple community loyalties and the marginal attachment of most board members mean that some issues are simply not worth fighting about. Apart from the wish to avoid unpleasant strife and embittered social relations, board members are also hindered in some conflict situations by the absence in the social services of objective measures of organizational effectiveness and executive and professional staff performance.

Another view, of course, is that conflict is not necessarily dysfunctional, and there can be a "creative tension" between board and executive which can work to the advantage of the organization. Indeed, this is what seems to be the case. Analysis of the structure and dynamics of the board-executive relationship suggests that they are dependent on each other but for different resources: they both "need" each other to carry out their respective responsibilities and to derive the necessary satisfactions. There is a functional necessity for complementary collaboration between these two sets of self-interests in which resources are exchanged. The executive requires the sanction and support of the board for one's authority and responsibility, which includes technical assistance to them, and in turn, the board legitimates the agency. In return for the resources they bring to the agency, the board members receive from the executive prestige and validation of their corporate status as trustees and as community leaders. In the governance and policy making of the organization, both functional and hierarchical authority are needed and complement each other. The board has both legal and hierarchical authority, and the executive has a delegated hierarchical authority as well as the authority of expertise. The board presumably attends to certain aspects of the external environment which they share with the executive, while the latter is more responsible for internal management of the organization.

The input system also contributes to the equilibrium. The process of selective recruitment and socialization, nurtured by the self-perpetuating character of the board of directors of most voluntary organizations, means that new members tend to be chosen because of their similarity in values and status to the continuing board members, so there tends to be little disruption of the ongoing pattern of board-executive relationships.

Using the language of social exchange theory, we could conclude that board members and executives generally interact in a patterned series of transactions to exchange resources for their mutual benefit; i.e., they seek to optimize their respective interests and to avoid or minimize perceived costs. The behavioral and decisional outcomes of this interaction depend upon the power/dependency relationship between them and their relative power depends upon the importance of the resources they control (Emerson, 1975; Foa & Foa, 1980). Most of the time there is a balance of power which may, of course, be tilted in the direction of one or the other when the relevant variables are in place.

References

Argyris, C., & Schon, D. *Theory in practice: Increasing professional effectiveness.* San Francisco: Jossey-Bass, 1974.

Bolan, R.S. The practitioner as theorist. *Journal of the American Planning Association,* July 1980, 46, 261-274.

Bolan, R.S. The social relations of the planner. *Journal of the American Institute of Planners,* November 1971, 386-396.

Brager, G., & Holloway, S. *Changing human service organizations: Politics and practice.* New York: The Free Press, 1978.

Brager. G., & Specht, H. *Community organizing.* New York: Columbia University Press. 1973.

Connors, T.D. *The nonprofit organization handbook.* Englewood Cliffs, NJ: Prentice Hall. Inc., 1980).

Conrad, W., & Glen, W. *The effective voluntary board of directors.* Boulder, CO: National Center for Voluntary Action. 1976.

Derr, C.B. Managing organizational conflict: Collaboration, bargaining and power approaches. *California Management Review,* Winter 1978, 21, 78-83.

Emerson, R.M. Social exchange theory. In A. Inkeles (Ed.). *Annual review of sociology.* Palo Alto, CA: Annual Reviews, Inc., 1975.

Fayence, M. *Citizen Participation in Planning.* New York: Pergamon. 1977.

Feldstein, D. Democratic governance and professional role in agency policy. Unpublished paper, 1982.

Foa, E.G., & Foa, O.G. Resource theory: Interpersonal behavior as exchange. In K.J. Gergen, et al. (Eds.). *Social exchange: Advances in theory and research.* New York: Plenum Press, 1980.

Forester, J. Planning in the face of power. *Journal of the American Planning Association*, Winter 1982, 67-80.

Gouldner, A.W. The secrets of organizations. In *The Social Welfare Forum*, 1963. New York: Columbia University Press, 1963.

Greer, S. Citizens voluntary governing boards: waiting for the quorum. *Policy Sciences*, 1982, 14, 165-178.

Gross, B.M. *Organizations and their managing.* New York: The Free Press. 1968.

Gummer, B. Organization theory for social administration. In F. Perlmutter & S. Slavin (Eds.). *Leadership in social administration.* Philadelphia: Temple University Press, 1980.

Hasenfeld, Y. *Voluntary service organizations.* Englewood Cliffs. NJ: Prentice-Hall, Inc., 1983.

Kahn, W. On working with the agency board: A sometime neglected skill. *Journal of Jewish Communal Service*, Summer 1978, 54, 309-313.

Katz, A. Self-help and mutual aid: An emerging social movement? *Annual Review of Sociology*, 1981, 7, 129-155.

Knight, B.M. The professional and the board. *Canadian Welfare*, July-August 1968, 8-9 and 16.

Kramer, R.M. Ideologies, status and power in board-executive relationships. *Social Work*, 1965, 10, 108-14.

Kramer, R.M. *Voluntary agencies in the welfare state.* Berkeley: University of California Press, 1981.

Lew, C.S. *Guide to ethical decisions and actions for social service administrators.* New York: The Haworth Press. 1982.

Marmor, T.R ... & Marone. J.A. Representing consumer interests: Imbalanced markets. health planning and the HSAS. *Milbank Memorial Fund Quarterly*, 1980, 58, 125-165.

Mintzberg, H. *Power in and around organizations.* Englewood Cliffs, NJ: Prentice-Hall, Inc., 1983.

Nettler, G. Ideology and welfare policy. *Social Problems,* 1958-59, 6, 203-211.

O'Connell, B. *Effective leadership in voluntary organizations.* New York: Association Press, 1976.

Provan, K.G. Board power and organizational effectiveness in human service agencies. *Academy of Management Journal,* June 1980, 23, 221-236.

Rapoport, A. *Fights, games and debates.* Ann Arbor: University of Michigan Press, 1961.

Robins, A.J. & Blackburn, C. Governing boards in mental health: Roles and training needs. *Administration in Mental Health,* Summer 1974, 37-45.

Schoderbek, P.P. *Volunteer and staff responsibilities.* New York: United Way of America, 1979.

Schon, D. *The reflective practitioner.* New York: Basic Books, 1982.

Senor, J.M. Another look at the executive-board relationship. *Social Work,* April 1963, 8,19-25.

Specht, H. Professional interpersonal interaction. Unpublished manuscript, 1983.

Steckler, A.B., & Herzog, W.T. How to keep your mandated citizen board out of your hair and off your back. *American Journal of Public Health,* August 1979, 69, 809-812.

Stein, I.I. Some observations on board-executive relationships in voluntary agencies. *Journal of Jewish Communal Service,* 1961, 38, 390-396.

Torezyner, J. Dynamics of strategic relationships. *Social Work,* November 1978, 6, 467-474.

Trecker, H. *Citizen boards at work: New challenges to effective action.* New York: Association Press, 1970.

Tucker, H., & Zeigler, H. *Professional vs. the public: Attitudes, communication and response in school districts.* New York: Longman. 1980.

Tulipana, F.P., & Herman, R. Board-staff relations and perceived effectiveness in nonprofit organizations. A paper presented at the Conference on Nonprofit Leadership & Management. Boston. November 3-4. 1983.

Unterman, I. & Davis, R.H. The strategy gap in not-for-profits. *Harvard Business Review*, May-June 1982, 60, 30-32, 34, 36, and 40.

Warren, R.L. Types of purposive social change at the community level. In R. Kramer & H. Specht. (Eds.). *Readings in community organization practice.* 2nd ed. Englewood Cliffs, NJ: Prentice-Hall. Inc., 1975.

Weber, J. *Managing the board of directors.* New York: Greater New York Fund. 1976.

Wilensky, I. & Lebeaux, C.N. *Industrial society and social welfare.* New York: The Free Press, 1965.

Young, D. *If not for profit, for what?* Lexington, MA: D.C. Heath, 1983.

Zald, M.N. Political economy: A framework for comparative analysis. In M.N. Zald (Ed.), *Power in organizations.* Nashville: Vanderbilt University Press. 1971.

Zald, M.N. The power and functions of boards of directors: A theoretical synthesis. *American Journal of Sociology.* 1965, 75, 97-111.

Lessons for Successful Nonprofit Governance

Peter F. Drucker

Boards of nonprofit organizations malfunction as often as they function effectively. As the best-managed nonprofit organizations demonstrate, both the board and the executive are essential to the proper functioning of a nonprofit organization. These administrative organs must work as equal members of a team rather than one subordinate to the other. Moreover, the work of the executive and the board does not divide neatly into policy-making versus execution of policy. Boards and executives must be involved in both functions and must coordinate their work accordingly. In a well-functioning nonprofit organization, the executive will take responsibility for assuring that the governance function is properly organized and maintained.

Despite the almost limitless diversity in their mission and size, the majority of American nonprofits have the same governance structure. They have an unpaid; outside, part-time board. And, they have a paid full-time executive officer, called variously *president, executive director, executive secretary, senior pastor, administrator, executive vice-president, or general manager.* Despite their almost limitless diversity, nonprofits are alike also in that in many—maybe the majority—this governance structure malfunctions often as it functions. Boards are criticized as being rubber stamps for the executive. But, the same boards also "meddle." Board members complain that the executive officer "usurps" the board's policymaking function. Executive officers in turn complain that the board wastes endless hours discussing operational trivia. Board members complain that they get no information. Executive officers and their staffs complain about the hours, days, and weeks wasted preparing resorts on matters well beyond the board's competence and ken. And, there is confusion across the nonprofit spectrum—in churches and trade associations, hospitals, universities, community services, learned societies, and foundations—as to what governance the institution needs, what the task of each organ of governance should be, and how they should work together. Indeed, no subject provokes more heated debate in the nonprofit world than that of governance.

Yet, we know the answers—or at least enough of them to do the job. A small but growing number of nonprofits are truly well managed (Drucker, 1989). For many nonprofits, it is probably true—at least their board members so believe—that they are a good deal less well managed than the average business. However, the small but rapidly growing group of nonprofits that have organized their governance is beyond doubt better managed than some businesses with a reputation for first-rate management. These institutions have both a functioning board and a functioning executive. Some of these leaders in the nonprofit sector are colleges and universities, some are community services, some are churches, and some are hospitals. Some are very large national or international organizations; others are local and at best middle sized. Yet, all have reached pretty much the same conclusions in regard to nonprofit governance. Their solutions are thus generic and should apply across the nonprofit spectrum.

Clear and Functioning Governance Structure

The first lesson to be learned is that nonprofits need a clear and functioning governance structure. They have to take their governance seriously, and they have to work hard on it. They need effective leadership and management a good deal more than even businesses do—for three reasons.

First, they lack the bottom line that a business has. They must therefore have a clear mission that translates into operational goals and that provides guides for effective action. Of course, businesses also deteriorate if they do not have a clear mission; they become diffuse, and their efforts splinter. But, in good times a business can muddle through for a while with no other lodestar than the financial bottom line. A nonprofit institution will start to flounder almost immediately unless it clearly defines its mission and emphasizes that mission again and again. This is doubly true for the nonprofit that relies on donors, volunteers, or both.

Second, the nonprofit needs a clear definition of the "results" that it seeks to obtain. Again, a business can, though only for a few short years steer by the financial bottom line alone.

Last, a business earns its money for its performance; the money is its own. In contrast, the money of the nonprofit, whether obtained from donors or from the taxpayer, is given against promises. Nonprofits are not owners; they are trustees of the money that they spend.

Nonprofits thus need both strong organs of accountability—for mission, for results, for allocation of resources and their productivity—and a clear process for discharging these responsibilities. They need effective, strong, directed governance and a clear governance structure.

These are truisms. Everyone nods and says *of course,* but far too few nonprofits listen, let alone act.

Effective Board and Effective Executive

Nonprofits need both an effective board and an effective executive. Practically every nonprofit will accept one or the other half of this assertion. But a good many will not accept that both are needed. Yet, neither the board-dominated nor the executive-dominated nonprofit is likely to work well, let alone succeed in perpetuating itself beyond the tenure of an autocrat, whether that individual be board chairperson or executive officer.

In a good many businesses, especially in large publicly held ones, boards have become slumber parties. They only wake up when there is a serious crisis and usually when it is way too late. In the large and successful petroleum companies that grew out of Rockefeller's Standard Oil Trust, but also in companies in Europe and Japan, boards have traditionally been a legal fiction. Some nonprofits, too—large private universities or large churches dominated by a powerful, charismatic pastor—have reduced their boards to a purely ceremonial role. And, boards as a part of governance are not known altogether in the canon law of the Catholic church (although American Catholic dioceses are increasingly setting up lay committees that in effect are governing boards), in the Salvation Army, and in the typical labor union (which is surely also a nonprofit institution).

But, most nonprofits could not emasculate the board even if they wanted to. One reason is that the board often actively leads in raising money. Another, more important one is that board members are committed to the nonprofit's cause. If they have no legitimate function and no real job to do, they will do mischief; they will "meddle." The nonprofit has no choice but to work on making its board an effective organ of governance. Only an effective board composed of independent but committed outside people can give the nonprofit the clear focus on mission, the definition of results, and the accountability for the money entrusted to it that it needs. Without these, any nonprofit will soon decline into nonperformance.

At the same time, every nonprofit, except maybe the very small and purely local one, must also have an effective executive officer. Its success in this century has made the American nonprofit too big, too complex, too important to be managed by its board.

The community hospital in the small New England town where I lived in the 1940s was still run by its board. It did not even have a chief medical officer or a nursing supervisor. But, it also had no emergency room, no ambulance service, no X-ray department, no physical therapy unit, no clinical lab, no social worker, and not even a well-baby clinic. To be sure, it was no longer simply a place where the poor could die in a little dignity, as it had been two decades before. But, its job was still primarily to provide private physicians with beds for their patients, not to be a health care center. Similarly, none of the churches in the town at that time tried to provide anything but two services on Sunday mornings and Sunday school to go with them. And, it was not until World War Two that the American Red Cross—the world's largest volunteer organization—went beyond disaster relief and took on blood banks and health and safety education.

Indeed, the most noteworthy feature of the American nonprofit institution is not its size. It is the explosive growth in the scope of nonprofit work and the parallel growth in the demands placed on the competence of the nonprofit institution. These demands go way beyond what good intentions and generosity can supply. Increasingly, they demand professionalism of a high order. The more a nonprofit institution relies on volunteers, the more professional its management has to be. An organization has far too many things to do for it to be able to operate without professional, full-time staff. Furthermore, if performance standards are to have any results, they must be coupled with executive accountability.

Board and Executive Officer as Colleagues

Nonprofits waste uncounted hours debating who is superior and who is subordinate—board or executive officer. The answer is that they must be colleagues. Each has a different part, but together they share the play. Their tasks are complementary. Thus, each has to ask, What do I owe the other?, not—as board and executive officers still tend to do—What does the other one owe me? The two have to work as one team of equals.

Double-Bridge Team

The double-bridge team is a model for the board-executive team in nonprofit institutions. In the double-bridge team, neither player is more important; they are equals, and they are equally indispensable. The job for the stronger player is to adjust to the style, strengths, and personality of the weaker partner. The executive officers in nonprofit organizations are the stronger players. It is their job to adjust both what they do and how they do it to the personalities and strengths of their chairpersons.

In more than eleven years with one of the country's largest community services organizations, the chief executive has worked with four board chairpersons, each of whom served for three years. The first was strongly outside focused, a good speaker and skillful in public relations. The successor was inside focused, effective with local chapters and happy working with them but somewhat publicity-shy and awkward on the platform. The next chairperson saw her main task as one of raising money, and she worked hard on getting much-needed business support. The fourth and last chairperson—still in the job today—is concerned primarily with the recruiting, training, and motivating of volunteers. Each chairperson's priority was a legitimate one, and each brought enthusiasm and considerable skill to the tasks on which he or she concentrated. All, in other words, deployed themselves properly. But, each had results only because the executive officer positioned herself in the areas in which her partner, the board chair was weak or had little interest—the inside during the tenure of the first chairperson; the outside during the tenure of the second one; operations during the third chairperson's term; programs, outside relations, and money raising during the last years.

Tasks of Board and Executive Officer

What are the respective tasks of the board and the executive officer? The conventional answer is that the board makes policy and the executive officer executes it. The trouble with this elegant answer is that no one knows (or has ever known) what policy is, let alone where its boundaries lie. As a result, there is constant wrangling, constant turf battles, constant friction.

Effective nonprofits do not talk much about policy. They talk about work. They define what work each organ is expected to perform and what results each organ is expected to achieve. One work assignment for the board may be to raise so many dollars in contributions in the coming year. Conversely, it may be the work assignment of the executive officer to recruit a given number of new volunteers the next year and to introduce two new programs successfully. Or, the board may commit itself to a certain number of community appearances by each of its members—one of the work assignments of the board members of a major rural cooperative. The board's work assignment may include a specified number of board-conducted, in-depth audits of individual hospital functions and of intensive meetings with major department heads. For the vestry in a large and rapidly growing evangelical church or the lay board in a Catholic diocese, the work assignment may be to specify, design, supervise, and edit the materials that the church uses to recruit and train volunteer workers. For the board of a theological seminary, it may be a half-day at each of its bi-monthly meetings spent reviewing one of the school's educational programs. In the effective nonprofit institution, every board committee—indeed, every board member—accepts a work program with specific achievement goals. So, too, does the executive officer.

This has two implications, both still anathema to many non profits and their boards. First, the performance of the entire board, each board committee, and each board member and the performance of the executive officer and all key people on the staff are regularly appraised against pre-established performance goals. (This appraisal is best done by a small group of former board members.) Second, board members and executives whose performance consistently falls below goals and expectations will resign or at least not stand for reelection.

Boards Should Meddle

Boards should meddle. To begin with, there is no way to stop them, and if you can't lick them, you had better join them. Board members of a nonprofit organization should be committed to the cause. They should be deeply interested and involved in it, they should know the programs and the people who work on them, and they should *care*. But also, nonprofit boards are usually organized in such a way that 'meddling" is part of their job. They work in committees, each with a specific mandate, such as fundraising, or physical facilities, or youth activities. This forces them to work directly—that is, without going through the executive officer—with people working in the particular area of the committee's concern. It thus forces them to "meddle." They had therefore better be organized so as to meddle constructively.

In one of the country's oldest nonprofit boards, the Board of Overseers of Harvard University, which was set up more than four hundred years ago, members act as visitors to one of the university's academic departments or schools. They meet regularly with the department, interview faculty and students, and appraise the department's performance. A good many people in academe consider the Harvard board the most effective, if not the only effective, American university board.

However, the board's meddling must strengthen rather than divide the institution. This requires first that there be no restrictions on contacts between board members and staff members. Restrictions are in any case ineffective, and they only make board members and staff members suspicious. They invite politicking. Nevertheless, the executive officer needs always to be informed of any contact between a board committee or board member and a staff member. The Harvard board achieves this by having each visitor submit a formal and written report, which is discussed first with the academic department and then presented to the president and the full board. Equally effective but simpler is a commitment—entered into by board and staff members alike—to have each staff member report any board contact immediately to the executive officer, preferably in writing and with a copy for the board member.

This may seem petty. It is. But the executive officer's fear of "meddling" and the resentment of board members at being "isolated" from the organization are, in my experience, the main cause of guerilla warfare between the two organs of governance in the nonprofit institution. It is almost impossible to cure. But, it can be prevented by a little elementary hygiene.

Who is Responsible?

Who should be responsible for an effective board, for the relationship between board and executive officer, and for the structure of governance in the nonprofit institution? The standard answer *is,* the board's chairperson. There is only one thing wrong with this: it does not work.

What works is to assign responsibility for the effective governance of the organization to the executive officer and to make it one of his or her key duties. I know the arguments against this: it is risky. There is a danger of the board's becoming the executive officer's creature and a *roi faineant,* a shadow king. It would indeed be greatly preferable if the board chairperson were to take on the duty.

Alas, I have not seen a single one who was willing to do so. It simply takes too much time. Wherever I have seen the job done, it required five years of hard, persistent work. And, that goes well beyond what a part-time outsider can spare, no matter how committed he or she may be. Making the organs of governance effective in the nonprofit institution and creating the proper relationship between them should therefore be considered a priority task of executive officers, and it should receive serious consideration when executive officers are hired and appraised.

Lessons

The lessons from nonprofits that have developed a working and effective governance structure will not come as a great surprise to many people in the nonprofit world, but they will still not be particularly popular. Indeed, they may be quite unpalatable to board members and executive officers alike. They clash with the widespread view that nonprofits are governed by good intentions. In fact, nonprofits have to be governed by performance.

At the same time, these lessons contradict the equally widespread belief that all a nonprofit institution needs is to be managed in a "more businesslike" way. No, nonprofits have to commit to a cause, they have to have a mission, and they have to be imbued with passion. Nevertheless, the growing number of nonprofits that have worked out an effective governance structure and the lessons they offer should come as a relief to the many dedicated people in the nonprofit world who complain—some to the point of despair—about the chasm between the good intentions and the performance of their institution, whether it is a church, university, hospital, or community service. It is indeed fairly simple to make nonprofits effective. It does not require miracles—it needs will and work.

Reference

Drucker, P. F. "What Business Can Learn from Nonprofits." *Harvard Business Review*, Sept.-Oct. 1989, pp. 88-93.

Charting the Territory of Nonprofit Boards

Richard P. Chait and Barbara E. Taylor

The board of trustees of a nonprofit organization has one responsibility: to keep the organization on a straight course for the long-term good of the whole. In other words, trustees exist to govern the organization—to monitor quality and to see to it that the organization fulfills its mission.

But many trustee boards do not govern. They get bogged down in operating details, matters that are best left to staff, while ignoring the very issues that could determine the enterprise's success or failure. The following two examples illustrate:

- The president of Perkins University (all names in the examples used in this article are fictitious) asked a trustee committee to advise him on a site for a sculpture donated by a professor of art. A week before the meeting of the board's physical-plant committee, the university maintenance crew put the statue on the proposed site and photographed it. The committee, whose members included top executives from major companies, carefully studied the pictures and concluded that the location was too prominent for such a "lascivious" work of art. So ultimately the university returned the statue to the artist along with the photographs. Later the artist informed the president that the committee had placed the sculpture upside down!

- Sheridan Hospital's board of trustees sat passively by as the annual operating deficit steadily mounted from $100,000 to $1 million, until the cumulative operating debt surpassed $10 million and long-term capital debt was nearly three times that. The trustees finally arranged for the state to buy the facility and lease it back at a nominal fee. During this critical period, the trustees also spent a couple of hours debating what to give board members as appropriate tokens of recognition.

These are not extreme examples of trustee behavior. It seems that otherwise intelligent individuals and astute businesspeople often toss aside the principles of good management, and sometimes even common sense, when they put on trustee hats. Why is it, asks Kenneth Dayton, former chairman and CEO of Dayton-Hudson, "that so many corporate directors grow horns when they become trustees? Why do they assume that they can do things as trustees that they would never think of doing as directors, interfering with management's role and making decisions or requests that no corporate director would think of making?

The Price of Managing and Not Governing

What's the harm if trustees are off placing statues instead of governing, especially if the administration is coping and the organization is surviving or even flourishing? Granted, costs in the short run may be minimal, but over time, this type of behavior can cause several kinds of damage.

The loss of perspective. Lay boards exist, in part, to ensure that nonprofit organizations (NPOs) do not become the captives of interest groups within the organization. Yet too often well-intentioned trustees become immersed in the operations, as opposed to the overall goals, of a particular program—whether it is the dialysis center, the Impressionist collection, or intercollegiate football. Such trustees can be indistinguishable from the most ardent administrative advocates.

Similarly, a board member actively engaged in the day-to-day matters of a certain office can develop personal ties that obscure institutional perspective. Arnold Edwards, a semi-retired trustee of the Wilkins Art Institute, visited almost daily with the institute's treasurer to offer advice, generally heeded, on various financial and investment decisions. When Wilkins new president recommended that the treasurer be replaced, Edwards protested vehemently. When the board affirmed the decision, Edwards praised the treasurer and in his speech violated board confidences; he was no longer a detached overseer.

The loss of talent. Some trustees thrive on involvement in operational affairs. But is such behavior really the best use of the board's time and talent? Trustees who believe the board's primary concern is the organization's long-term welfare will avoid getting involved in trivial, day-to-day matters. These can be the most talented board members and arguably the people the organization needs to cultivate most diligently. Often, however, such trustees don't speak up when the board strays from governing; they just stop coming to meetings and beg off committee assignments. Or they resign. As one corporate chairman and college trustee told us, "If I have to sit through another meeting taken up with student campus violations, I'll drop out. I'll put my talents elsewhere. I've got a hundred other things to devote my time to!"

Similarly, when trustees regularly intrude in administrative matters, the most competent administrators feel undermined and discouraged. When boards continue to meddle, some administrators resign.

The loss of institutional vitality. The biggest cost to the institution is enervation. An Ivy League college or a great metropolitan hospital won't necessarily experience severe or immediate erosion in quality because of an administration-oriented board. But trustee time is a limited commodity, and if it's frittered away on operations, it cannot be spent on policy and strategy. Trustees mired in administrative minutiae become less knowledgeable about the organization as a whole, less enthusiastic, and less effective. As a result, the institution may miss an opportunity to reel in a big donor, seize a strategic opportunity, or ratchet to a higher plateau of performance.

Some boards have successfully relied on an experienced CEO to set the course and single-handedly lead the institution. But when such a CEO finally departs or when the board tries to reassert its primacy in governing the organization, its earlier neglect of issues of purpose, direction, and strategy will show. The skills and structure necessary for it to govern effectively will have atrophied. And the board may have lost the credibility it needs to exercise its authority in a way that others will willingly accept.

Why Do Boards Administer Rather than Govern?

If the damage to the institution is so obvious, why do so many boards become operations oriented or worse, meddlesome, and thus shirk their governance responsibilities? The causes for trustee preoccupation with management are varied—some good, some bad. Inappropriate trustee involvement, moreover, may be transient or it may be persistent, growing out of a condition endemic to the particular NPO. We've found at least five reasons that may draw boards into chronic involvement with operational activities.

Trustees may have specialized knowledge. Smaller, less affluent NPOs with limited resources and few staff specialists tend to seek trustee involvement in daily operations. Often the NPO will deliberately choose as board members people with a particular expertise and will expect them to advise and help the organization on legal, financial, and real estate matters, for example. In these instances, drawing a sharp line between policy and administration would limit the board's value to the organization. The Crandall School was such an institution. Plagued by financial problems, it had a historic campus building that the town had closed as a fire hazard. Without even consulting the administration, a small group of trustees formed a private foundation and raised enough funds for the building's restoration and maintenance. The administration was delighted.

As a rule, however, the board's authority should not rest on a foundation of technical competence. This is especially true of larger, more sophisticated NPOs, which are our chief concern here.

Trustees may have a special interest. At universities, it's common to find trustees who are interested in a particular sport or academic program. Hospital trustees may immerse themselves in programs treating a specific medical condition, especially if their own families have had direct experience with that illness. At a museum, trustees may be interested in the art of a particular country because of their own national origin. Naturally, trustees gravitate toward what interests them and tend to become involved in the operational details of those select programs.

Trustees who donate money for a particular project or chair often concentrate their attention on the beneficiaries rather than on the institution as a whole. They may see their donation as forging a special bond with the head of the project or the chairholder. Organizations frequently encourage such ties by arranging, for example, for the donor and the chairholder to meet once a year.

Institutions often regard such relationships as carrying more benefits than detriments, even though trustees are compromising their detached perspective. For example, the president of an orchestra told us, "You can be sure that the donor for the first oboist's chair will regularly make an impassioned plea for an oboe solo in the repertoire. That's not too difficult to handle."

Some trustees would rather act than delegate. As senior managers of corporations or senior partners in professional firms, many trustees are accustomed to making decisions and taking action. In fact, they are stimulated by it. Such trustees are reluctant to delegate authority to administrators, even where capable management and effective traditions of self-regulation exist. David Nyquist, a veteran trustee of Adams Hospital, was new to the board of Chase College. He was convinced that a joint degree program in nursing would be immensely beneficial to both institutions. Without telling either administration, he enthusiastically arranged a meeting of college faculty and hospital personnel to discuss the topic—alarming the able managers of both institutions. Like many well-meaning trustees, Nyquist was insensitive to the concept of shared governance, where the professional staff resists the imposition of authority, especially by lay persons knowing much less about its organization's mission.

Trustees tend to manage during an internal transition or crisis. The more a board trusts the CEOs judgments and abilities, the less likely that trustees will feel a need to intrude on management's prerogatives. Usually a relationship of confidence and trust develops over time as the board (specifically the chairperson) and the CEO cope successfully with problems. The former CEO of Garfield Museum gradually won the complete trust of the board, which, during his eight-year tenure, withdrew entirely from administrative affairs. By contrast, the museum's new CEO, not as highly regarded by the trustees, still chafes under the board's close supervision after two years in office.

When the CEO fails to earn the trustees' confidence, the board may ask one or more trustees to assume greater responsibility for day-to-day operations. "I have been utterly amazed over the years to observe how (nonprofit) boards always tend to fill management voids," writes Kenneth Dayton. "If management is weak in an aspect of its operation, a strong board or board member will move in and take over"—often quite literally. More than a few trustees have occupied an office adjacent to the CEOs and assumed control, as if the board had placed the organization into receivership.

The board's fundamental responsibility in such cases is to save the institution. The second responsibility, however, is to restore the institution to normalcy. So when the crisis is over, the board should pull back and enable the professionals to run the organization.

Trustees may manage in periods of external turbulence and crisis. As conditions in an organization's external environment shift from normal to turbulent and then to acute, the board will almost certainly become more involved in administrative operations. Trustees are often knowledgeable about technical, political, and economic details of the environment. Frequently, they're in a position to influence that environment. For instance, board members may be asked to lobby to affect legislation, to raise money, or to sway public opinion. When Vale College, a 150-year-old women's college, decided to admit men, its trustees embarked on an alumnae relations campaign aimed at minimizing anticipated resistance to the idea. The administration considered the trustees, as alumnae, best suited to sell the idea of coeducation to other Vale graduates. Vale's trustees served as external representatives for the college, however, which is very different from running a business.

Levels of Policy

As we have seen, trustees can have very good reasons to be involved in policy matters. Circumstances can require it. Too often, however, trustee preoccupation with operations is reflexive, with little thought given to the institution's long-term goals. That's when problems arise. Since trustees cannot and should not make all policy decisions, the board must decide *which* levels deserve what degree of consideration.

Choosing the right policy level is like picking the right pitch in baseball. Ted Williams adhered to one cardinal principle at the plate: know the strike zone. To get a better look at the pitcher, he would sometimes take a pitch right down the middle, and to protect a runner he would occasionally have to swing at a bad pitch. But most of the time, he swung only at pitches he would most likely hit. He let the rest go by. Similarly a board of trustees should concentrate its talent and energies on policy levels that have the most impact on the organization's future and let the rest of the issues go. Remember, the board's role is to govern to keep the organization on a straight course over the long term.

Richard M. Hodgetts and Max S. Wortman, Jr. have developed an administrative model that identifies six policy levels, ranging from major policies concerned with fundamental issues of mission to "rules" that guide everyday conduct:

1. *Major policies.* Fundamental issues of mission or business definition, typically involving questions of institutional direction, values, priorities, and principles that guide other decisions.

2. *Secondary policies.* Questions of primary clientele, types of services, delivery systems, which may focus on relationship of programs and departments to the overall mission. These issues often entail significant decisions about human, financial, and physical resources.

3. *Functional policies.* Concerns of major functional operations, such as planning, budgeting, finance, marketing, and personnel.

4. *Minor policies.* Decisions that govern day-to-day practices. They may be important as a pet project of an individual or of a special interest group.

5. *Standard operating procedures.* Mechanisms and procedures to handle routine transactions and normal operations—matters of form, process, method, and application of other policies.

6. *Rules.* Regulations that guide or prescribe everyday conduct.

Taken together, these policy levels comprise the "policy structure" of an organization. For the most part, the board should devote little energy to lower level
policies such as operating procedures and rules; they usually fall too far outside its
appropriate sphere of concern. But this hierarchy is not rigid. Rather, we suggest
that boards view the levels as a spectrum. Compensation policy, for example,
affects the entire range of institutional goals and values. Should compensation
reward merit only? Ensure equity? Motivate performance? Mid-level policies concern criteria and process. What defines merit? Who makes the decisions? How
much information should be disclosed? Finally, there are operational questions.
How often should paychecks be issued? Should local banks have direct deposit?

When a policy question arises, the board should at least be aware of its place
on the policy spectrum. Is this a higher level policy matter? If not, why is the matter before the board? The answer may well be that the issue has implications for
higher level policies. If so, what are they?

Blaine College's board of trustees faced such a policy consideration in the
guise of a "minor" administrative matter. The academic affairs committee was
debating a faculty proposal to create an honors program for superior students.
The administration had specifically recommended a 3.8 grade point average to
qualify for summa cum laude and a 3.5 GPA for magna cum laude. The trustees
were earnestly asking questions like, why not have thresholds of 3.7 and 3.4, and
what are comparable schools' standards?

The discussion continued until one trustee asked *why* the college wanted to
establish such a policy after 100 years without one. The dean of faculty explained
that the policy was part of a larger strategy to recruit more academically gifted
students. Other possible elements included a Phi Beta Kappa chapter, summer
fellowships for the brightest undergraduates and a special seminar series for honors students. In short order, the committee's discussion shifted from decile differences in GPAs to the strategic objective of a stronger student profile. Both issues
were matters of policy but it's clear which one was a proper consideration for the
trustees.

A Policy's Four Development Phases

A policy—a course of action—doesn't exist in a vacuum. It should be developed
in pursuit of the ultimate goals of the institution or the complementary objectives
of a particular department. The four phases of policy development are: establish
policy objectives, formulate a policy statement, implement the policy, and evaluate the policy. The board has a different role to play at each stage of development
and so too does the administration.

1. *Define policy objectives.* NPOs frequently draft policy *statements* without connecting them to policy *objectives.* Administrations propose and boards enact policies on salaries, promotions, professional development, and affirmative action, to name a few, without consideration at the outset of the ultimate purposes of the policy.

One hospital board, for example, may develop a policy of merit pay for professional staff to fulfill its objective of ending automatic increments for marginal performers. Another hospital board may view merit pay as the most effective means to neutralize competition and stem turnover. While both objectives are reasonable, specific policy provisions and measure of success will differ markedly. For this reason, the trustees and the CEO should discuss, determine, and enunciate policy objectives or purposes before the administration proceeds further.

As a practical matter, management has more information and greater expertise than trustees, so the CEO and other senior managers should be intimate partners with the board when formulating policy objectives. The CEO has the duty to provide a context for policy formulation by keeping the board informed about the important issues that will affect the long-term life of the institution. If there is no regular procedure to do so, the board can ask the CEO for a "memorandum of strategy" that answers the question: "What is your vision for this institution (or department) and how do you expect to achieve it?" Once reviewed and accepted by the board, the memorandum provides a strategic perspective on organizational direction and serves as a basis for trustees and management to develop together a work plan for the board and its committees.

2. *Formulate the policy statement.* Once the objectives have been determined, management can draft the policy. Because most NPOs are "bottom heavy" organizations, dominated by professionals such as social workers, academics, or physicians, the process will probably entail broad consultation and a search for consensus. The administration, not the board, must manage the process and draft the policy statement.

Now and then, however, senior administrators should inform the board of the tenor and direction of discussions. As preferred options emerge, these might be previewed for the board. Such an "early warning" system reduces the chance that trustees will be surprised by the administration's formal proposal and reject it. Failure to update the board as policies are drafted, especially on controversial issues like divestment of South African holdings, for example, often produces equally objectionable alternatives: either the CEO sheepishly retreats from a public position or the board reluctantly approves a policy in order to spare the president embarrassment.

The trustees' responsibility is to ensure that the policy statement meets the policy objectives, the process of consultation was suitable, and the criteria for policy evaluation are appropriate. While trustees may raise questions or express reservations, the board should resist the temptation to rewrite policy recommendations. Boards are more affective as questioners than as editors. State the objection, articulate the concern, offer the suggestion, then direct the administration to craft the proper language, either immediately if the board's reservations are comparatively minor or at another time if qualms are substantial.

3. *Implement the policy.* As a rule, the board should be involved in policy execution only as a facilitator, and individual trustees should participate very selectively. Under normal conditions, there are only a few situations when individual trustees might properly be involved in policy execution.

First, the chairman *and* the CEO may decide that one or more trustees can best handle a task. As we said earlier the decision to involve trustees depends greatly on the breadth and depth of staff expertise, though this practice does not excuse the board from ensuring that administrators acquire and develop necessary management skills.

Second, participation in policy implementation can teach a board member about the nature of the enterprise or improve communication between the board and key internal or external constituencies. With those goals in mind, board members are invited from time to time to serve on various broad-based committees.

Finally, trustee involvement may be warranted when the board or the executive committee wants to conduct an occasional spot check or performance audit to ensure quality control or conformity with organizational policy.

In all cases, trustees should be involved in policy execution for only a limited purpose and time. Board members have a crucial role to play in governance but they are not appointed to perform the NPOs day-to-day tasks. So rather than acting as surrogate administrators, trustees should allow managers to manage. Rather than *do* more, boards would be better advised to *demand* more.

Trustees, however, tend to ask less of management in part because many administrators are modestly compensated, especially by for-profit standards, and in part because board members are lulled into a dysfunctional politeness due to the nature, character, and culture of the organization. It is difficult to be "hard" when the organization is "soft." After all, some trustees reason, how much can one ask of an art historian turned college president, of a cleric turned hospital administrator, of a social worker turned agency executive? The answer is, at a minimum, ask enough to ensure that the board does not routinely have to implement policy.

4. *Evaluate the policy.* Among the many trustees we have interviewed and advised, most can recite the organization's goals for the next five years. Far fewer can recount the goals for the last five years, and fewer still can articulate whether those aims have been realized.

The same proposition applies to policies. Boards approve apparently momentous policies, often after protracted debate, then never revisit the matter to evaluate the results. Has the new credentialing policy improved the quality of patient care? Has the new incentive structure stimulated faculty interest in teaching? Has the sabbatical leave policy strengthened the museum's scholarship? Very often trustees—and CEOs—do not know.

The board does not have to exercise constant oversight or demand monthly reports. For higher level policies, the CEO and the board should agree on an appropriate time frame for evaluation. When the time arrives, the CEO should brief the board thoroughly about the policy's consequences, both intended and unintended. For mid-level policies, the CEO should occasionally report on the policy's impact. And for lower level policies, the CEO may simply assure the board that evaluations occur.

In all cases, management should design and conduct the assessment, analyze the results, and suggest any policy changes. Through reminders, questions, and directives, the board should make certain that management discharges these responsibilities.

Board Focus

How do the six policy levels and four stages of policy development work together to define the board's role? In the main, the board's attention—its most critical resource—should be concentrated on developing higher level policy objectives and statements and then, on a selective basis, on executing and monitoring important policies. The board should pay peripheral attention to developing mid-level policy objectives and statements but expend little energy on their implementation. Trustees should devote almost no attention to any phase of lower level policy development.

Within these general guidelines, the board has flexibility to act. Trustees should not spend a great deal of time trying to precisely categorize every policy issue. They simply need to be sensitive to the various levels of policy and to apply common sense to defining their role, with the understanding that it changes with each phase of policy development.

Keeping Informed

Speaking at a seminar, Robert Mueller, former board chairman of Arthur D. Little, Inc., observed that "the scope of board action is greatest when the knowledge is least complete. And the scope of board action is least when the knowledge is great." To govern knowledgeably, boards need information—but of the right kind and in the right amount. This they rarely get. Trustees commonly lament that they are inundated with irrelevant reports and data and deprived of the information they really need to be knowledgeable about their organization.

Many NPO managers provide trustees with *management* information, not *governance* information. In some cases, the CEOs motives are pure: they simply want their boards to have the same information they have. But what happens is that a board, equipped with management information, delves into administrative matters. Why would anyone expect these trustees to behave differently?

For many years, the academic affairs committee of the Porter State College board received the resumes and publications of candidates for tenure. Naturally enough, but much to the chagrin of the academic vice president and the faculty, the committee examined the data and assessed the candidates individual qualifications for permanent positions. If, instead, the committee had received the administration's assurance of the candidates professional qualifications plus data showing the relationship between the candidates talents and the college's needs, then the committee would more likely have focused on questions of institutional strategy and alternative uses of resources, which are more appropriate issues for trustees. The new data would have shifted the trustees' threshold question from "Are these candidates qualified for tenure?" to "How will these appointments advance the institution's strategy?"

Some CEOs motives are more Machiavellian. Either as a matter of management style or due to deep-seated doubts about the board's ability to make sound decisions, some CEOs deliberately divert the board from important policy matters. In general, the more complex the organization, the more readily the CEO can control the information the board receives. And because some CEOs presuppose that trustees who know a great deal will interfere in matters the administration would prefer to handle alone, both the temptation and the opportunity to bury the board beneath a mountain of insignificant information can be substantial. Many CEOs who are eager to avoid board participation learn to deflect board attention from crucial questions artfully with a steady barrage of paperwork and show-and-tell sessions.

Trustees and senior managers can adopt a governance information system to increase the probability that the board will be well informed on consequential matters but spared volumes of data on insignificant items. The procedure for creating such a system is fairly simple: the trustees and senior managers decide together what information the board needs, how often, and in what format. A retreat, preferably with an outside expert or consultant, provides a good opportunity for trustees to ask the rarely asked question, "Why do we need this information?" After the board agrees on what information it needs, management translates that decision into data requirements—content, format, and frequency of reports the administration must provide to the trustees.

Indeed, just developing such a system should stimulate discussion among trustees and staff about appropriate divisions of authority, responsibility, and accountability. Furthermore, with a governance information system there usually are fewer occasions when some board members are in the know and others aren't, a common problem that hinders cohesiveness among trustees. And the system should eliminate, or at least reduce, requests by individual trustees for information unrelated to the board's role.

Trustees would also profit by getting feedback on their own performance. Unfortunately, this seldom happens. The board meets, adjourns, and then meets again, sometimes three or six months later. Maybe once a year, at best, the chairman conducts an informal evaluation or the board devotes an hour or so to self-assessment. With few structured occasions to offer feedback, trustees swallow constructive criticisms, the board meanders into trivial discussions, and the level of collective yet silent exasperation increases.

Some good methods to get feedback are:

1. Board members can set aside time toward the end of each meeting to review, for instance, the magnitude of the issues, the quality of the discussion, and the patterns of participation. Any tendencies to dwell on lower level policies or to emphasize less significant trustee roles can be spotted quickly. Going once around the boardroom at the end of each meeting so everyone can comment provides fast feedback—or board members can comment anonymously on an index card.

2. The board can undertake a self-evaluation once a year. Such a meeting, devoted exclusively to board performance, offers a means to socialize new trustees and re-socialize long-rime trustees to the board's established norms—the (often unwritten, unspoken) rules of the game.

3. The board can seek comments from senior managers and other key internal and external constituencies.

Having the Odds in Your Favor

No approach to governance can guarantee that boards will always be effective. On the other hand, we believe that the probability of success will increase significantly if trustees recognize that the board's role varies depending on the level of policy under consideration and its development phase.

We have described circumstances in which a board might venture more deeply into the realm of lower level policies or participate more directly in later stages of policy development. In that sense, we have presented a dynamic and contingent model. The board, in effect, must be elastic, able to stretch and adapt as circumstances warrant. Yet at the same rime, it must be sufficiently resilient, disciplined, and self-aware to snap back into shape when more normal conditions return.

Trustees who are alert to the general level and phase of policy development will be better able to determine whether, why, and to what extent a particular matter merits their attention. A board will be less prone to drift into an extensive consideration of a low-level issue merely because information was available or the CEO placed the matter on its agenda. And trustees will be better able to focus their thinking on questions truly crucial to the organization's future.

Notes

1. Kenneth Dayton, "Governance Is Governance," in *Proceedings,* Professional Forum II (Washington, D.C.: Independent Sector, 1985), p. 9.

2. Richard M. Hodgetts and Max S. Wortman, Jr., *Administrative Policy: Text and Cases in the Policy Sciences* (New York: John Wiley & Sons, Inc., 1975).

3. Miriam Mason Wood, "Guidelines for an Academic Affairs Committee," *Trustee Responsibility for Academic Affairs,* ed. Richard P. Chait (Washington, D.C.: Association of Governing Boards, 1984), p. 19.

4. Alvin Zander, *Making Groups Effective* (San Francisco: Jossey-Bass, 1982), p. 113.

The Governing Board's Existential Quandary: An Empirical Analysis of Board Behavior in the Charitable Sector

Miriam M. Wood

Introduction

In the play *Rosencrantz and Guildenstern Are Dead,* Rosencrantz and Guildenstern are the main characters, not merely minor players binding together the plot of *Hamlet.* A similar reversal occurs in organization research when volunteer board members, usually portrayed as minor actors in the institutional drama, are placed stage-center. There, like Rosencrantz and Guildenstern, they find themselves facing the questions, "Where are you going?" and "What are you going to do when you get there?" Hence the existential quandary.

When I spoke personally in this vein with board members and executive directors from eight 501(c)(3) agencies, they often described a board "in transition." But they did not feel overwhelmed. Instead, many of the more influential and, most especially, the newer board members spoke enthusiastically of clarifying an agency's mission or, as some put it, "our goals and objectives." Of particular significance in these conversations was evidence that boards typically—although not invariably—pass through distinctive developmental phases. In this process, the values espoused by the board evolve from dedication to the "cause" represented by the organization's mission to a "professional" interest in the agency's outward success. Using this knowledge, enterprising board members and staff executives can manage processes of change that heretofore may have seemed puzzling or unique to one particular agency.

The eight participating agencies have been in existence from ten to thirty-four years. Each has one or more programs serving young people in the junior and senior high age group and has no more than twenty paid staff. Included were agencies with programs intended to enhance normal development, such as scouting, as well as agencies with programs designed to remediate problems such as drug abuse. The sample was selected from fifty-three local social service agencies, twenty-six cultural agencies, and a plethora of civic and character-building organizations located in a grain belt metropolitan area, here called Midwest City-County, which has a population of about three hundred thousand. Fourteen percent of the city population is black and 2 percent of Spanish-speaking origin, primarily Mexican. In the county, blacks account for 8.5 percent and Spanish-origin for 1.5 percent of the population.

The agencies include two serving youth only (Economic Education for Youth, Part-time Parent), three for which youth is the primary but not sole clientele (Ballet of Midwest City, Hotline, Prevent Child Abuse), and three which serve youth secondarily to other age groups (United Hispanics, Appalachian Community Center, Women's Board). At each agency a conversation was first held with the executive director, who provided the names of the chair of the board, the chair of an important committee, a new member of the board, and a member who "marches to a different drummer"—presumably two insiders and two outsiders in the boardroom sub-culture. Each of these individuals was then interviewed at his or her home or office or, occasionally, at a restaurant. The conversations lasted about an hour, with assurances given to participants that their identities and that of each agency would be disguised in the report of the findings.

Of the thirty-two board members interviewed, fourteen are women, including one black and one of Spanish-speaking origin, and eighteen are men, including one black and two of Spanish-speaking origin. Four of the executive directors are men, including one of Spanish-speaking origin, and four are women. Also interviewed were two members of a group intending to establish a ghetto-based youth agency; these two proto-board members are black. In size, the eight boards range from ten to sixty-one members.

Part I of this report recapitulates the findings, while Part II places the results in theoretical context and relates them to selected prior research on nonprofit governing boards. A bibliography appears at the end of the text.

Part I

The Professionalization of Zeal

Nothing about a volunteer board is more striking than the changes in attitude it typically undergoes during its early history. These changes may occur within a shorter or longer time frame depending upon circumstances, but the outcomes are roughly—if not precisely—predictable and can best be defined as the professionalization of zeal. That is, board members of new agencies become progressively less committed to pursuing a "mission" and more committed to achieving "goals"; they become less committed to the cause around which the agency was organized and more committed to the bureaucratic procedures they believe will assure the success of the agency as an on-going entity. The diagram below illustrates this changing value-orientation of a board by highlighting key phases and events.

As the model indicates, founding board members are dedicated to the cause their agency is designed to forward, or the principle it will advocate, or the social ill it will remediate. For example, a member of the organizing committee for a ghetto-based youth center has little interest in the formalities of the board of which she will be a member but speaks passionately of methods for reducing the influence of street gangs:

> I'm interested in a program to deal with young people's minds. All the recreation centers in the world won't help if people's minds aren't dealt with. We want to give the children more resistance to joining street clubs. We want to give them a shoulder to lean on so they don't feel left out. All we have to do is to cause the young people [to think to themselves], "There's more in me than what I'm doing on the streets now."

Founding board members often exude fervor, and their conversation implies that the overarching purpose of their agency is not simply a corporate goal, but is a socially redeeming quest. There is a moral tinge to their remarks and a willingness to contribute considerable time and effort. It is not surprising, therefore, that the soon-to-be board member quoted above anticipates being on duty at the youth center during nighttime hours, when gangs are active:

> When the building opens, I intend to be there; I'll have a bed there and my German shepherd [for protection].

Mission as cause/principles; Goal as procedures/success.1

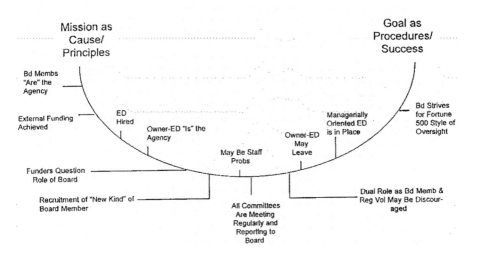

However, as the agency matures, its success as perceived by the community becomes more important to board members than the content of its programs. For heuristic purposes, the diagram expresses this change of values as the polar opposite of the board's views at the outset of an agency's history, a contrast that is evident in these remarks of the board chair at an established agency:

> We do not design programs. The executive director makes the decisions and uses us as a sounding board.... Our job is basically to open the door. Most board members give only a couple of hours a year to open a door or make an appearance, but not to work.

Although the model describes the evolution between these two contrasting points of view, it is intended only to suggest typical phases in a board's history, not inevitable stages. Key events and circumstances are placed on a curve that marks a progression in the value orientation of the collective mind of the board, but the curve is not itself a measure of time; it can only be said that the boards of older agencies have typically passed through more phases than have younger organizations.

Earliest Phases

In the earliest days, months, or years of a 501(c)(3)'s history—until a forceful executive is in place—the board "is" the agency in the sense of representing the agency's mission in the community. During this period, one or two board members may appear especially interested and dedicated, may become more strongly identified by the agency's publics with the agency's mission than are other board members, and often one such individual will function as the de facto, unpaid executive director. Board members and others may make donations to defray costs of operating on this marginal basis, but stable funding sources external to the board—the United Way, government agencies, and so on—are usually required if a part—or full-time staff person is to be hired. At this point, it is not unusual for the most active person on the board, the de facto executive director, to be given the position formally. At several agencies in Midwest City, a de facto executive wrote the proposal that first funded his or her salary.

Presence of a paid executive does not always signal a change in the board's role. Until there is a paid executive who becomes an influential presence within the boardroom and has some visibility in the community, the board will continue to "be" the agency. Just such a situation exists at one Midwest City agency where, although there is a paid executive—marginally qualified according to certain board members—the board continues as the locus of important activity, as this board member's ruminations reveal:

> I got a call yesterday about [an opportunity for] funding, and this guy called us his favorite organization. I told him Shirley [the board chair] and I wrote a proposal [for his type of program] a while ago, and so we're going to see him at 7:30 next Monday morning. With Shirley and me, it sometimes feels like we do all the work. People say if you or Shirley dropped out, things wouldn't be the same, and I hate to think that. Last night for example I was on the phone for two hours. I would say that not a day goes by that I don't have some contact with the agency—ten or fifteen hours a week, maybe, more when there are special events.

But at some point an executive director, who may or may not be the first or second incumbent, will gain the board's confidence as the perpetuator of the agency's redemptive work, and ownership of that motive force and of the programs designed to exemplify it will pass from the board itself to the executive director, here called the Owner-ED because of the personal commitment and proprietary attitudes characterizing his or her administrative style.

With an Owner-ED in place, board members soon come to feel that the executive director can take care of things, and in the community there is recognition of the executive as the principal—and often the sole—spokesperson for the agency. Board members, some of them exhausted from the fervor of the earlier period, or perhaps more interested in hands-on volunteer work for the agency than in boardroom issues, may spend board meetings "socializing." A disciplined approach to their role seems unimportant since the agency has become, in effect, the Owner-ED's "baby." As one Owner-ED puts it, "The meetings are a pep session and nothing happens and I'm left with it." And being "left with it," apart from occasional moments of ambivalence, is the situation most Owner-EDs prefer.

A turning point in the board's history occurs when—as is happening now at one Midwest City agency in its tenth year, at another in its sixteenth, at a third in its twentieth, and a fourth in its thirty-first—some event causes the board to reassess its role. In several of the Midwest City instances, reassessment has been prompted by outside funders who have implied that the board is not meeting its responsibilities and has let itself rely too much on the knowledge and energy of the executive director. "What would the board do," they are asked, "if something happened to the executive director?"

The implied threat of substantially reduced funding, together with a feeling that the substance of the question is at least worth considering, galvanizes a volunteer board, as this chairperson explains:

> Until this year the board was not active; we met four times a year, but our funders became unhappy with the board, saying we should play a more active role. We get our direction from Louisa [the executive director]. She's a strong personality, plays no games, and tells you what's on her mind in no uncertain terms. She's highly effective, but not scientific. For example, she's not one to keep unduplicated lists of clients and our funders called me and expressed those concerns. So now the board meets once a month and we have restructured things somewhat.

"Restructuring" generally implies two, often concurrent, changes in the board room, the first being the recruitment of a "new kind" of board member.

MAPs: The New Kind of Board Member

This new kind of board member has a perspective on organizational life that is typically, but not exclusively, manifested by Middle-Aged Professionals (MAPs) in the age group 35-50. Three attitudes of this ideal type distinguish their activities on a volunteer board. First, their approaches to problems and solutions tend to be expressed in bureaucratic terms and to rely on the rationality implied by bureaucratic structure and process, as this MAP board chair observes:

> We're trying to upgrade the committees so the board is responding as a ruling, decision-making body and so committees are doing their end of it.

Furthermore, problems and their solutions are brought together through a rational process that results in the definition of the agency's goals; the rhetoric of "goals," "objectives," and "results" is apt to supersede the notion of "mission." This frame of mind leads a recently appointed board member to conceive of the agency as a business in a competitive environment where the best strategy is to have a differentiated product:

> I don't know if the board has a problem but the agency has a problem and that is, what is its function in relation to other agencies that deal in the same area? Apparently there is overlap and I'd like to see this agency doing something different, filling a need, but I don't have a real good handle on what makes us distinctive.

And third, a board member who is a MAP conceives of his or her board activities as altruistic, civically valuable, and at the same time a form of self-enhancement. These motivations exemplify the psychologist Abraham Maslow's description of "self-actualizers," who seek opportunities for "character growth, character expression, maturation, and development." (Maslow 1970:159) The Maslowian mix of values is exemplified by a 40-year-old lawyer's explanation of why he was interested in joining the board of a youth-serving agency:

> I do child custody work, and it has a horrible effect on kids, and this was an opportunity to help on the other end. In a sense I'm creating a problem, and [the youth agency] is an attempt to offset it.... I guess I'd have to say some are on the board for their resume, but most of us have heard how successful the agency is and know it's a board that does something. You're out in the community doing things, and it was an opportunity for me to do something.

The MAP conception of what it means to be "a board that does something" may give pause to an Owner-ED who has developed a feeling of ownership for the agency and its programs. He or she may be ambivalent about the board's changing expectations:

I'm nervous. We've not been an agency that was focused on meeting board needs, not like the board of_____—I'm on that board, it's a much bigger agency, where the director serves the board as well as the agency itself. I serve this agency and want the board to help me and that will mean committees that involve staff time. The board can be a powerful partner, but it can get out of control. On the other hand, growth requires committees for personnel, finance, and so forth, which are all connected.

A member of this Owner-ED's board describes these same issues from the perspective of comfort that MAPs feel with the popular conception of a Fortune 500 board of directors:

A lot of the newer board members have had experience with more structure, a more traditional kind of board operation that you would see, like the board of a big corporation. Like with the finance and long-range planning committees, two board members are normally assigned to work with the staff and are active along familiar lines.

Another MAP implies that an Owner-ED's management style is simply incompatible with his own more bureaucratically oriented views:

Our executive director is not a believer in long-range planning. He's a trouble-shooter, and I really think the fun of his life is putting out fires. I think he feels his job would be boring if everything was predictable, and that's one of his few failings.

With the threat of reduced funding in prospect, board members feel they cannot indulge the administrative proclivities of even the best Owner-EDs. By the same token, not all executive directors can, or will, adjust to the new procedural demands and to the changing attitude toward social problems that the MAP perspective seems to imply. As this Owner-ED with a board in transition over the past year explains,

I don't have ownership in this agency. It's not my own small business.... It used to be I wanted to make a difference. But a lot of the board didn't want to get involved in these new programs, and the staff didn't like them particularly. But I thought if those new programs for innocent children don't survive, then we none of us survive. That was the kind of impact I wanted to have.

The Impact of Committees

As committees begin meeting regularly with the ED and other staff and reporting regularly to the board, new board members and veteran members who feel that the MAP influence is timely experience a collective feeling of exhilaration. Their increasing understanding of one another's views, their growing knowledge of the agency, and a newfound sense that the board is in control give them a sense of accomplishment.

Such confidence may be put to the test in short order by the "staff problems" likely to arise at this juncture. That is, as staff members other than the executive director begin to meet regularly in committee settings with several board members and feel freer to talk frankly, festering problems may erupt in a way they usually do not when the board appears to respond according to the Owner-ED's bidding. Just how such a personnel issue may come to the board is described by a committee chair at an agency where, in recent months, committees have become increasingly independent of the Owner-Executive:

> I have recently been approached by staff and asked to solve a problem [concerning the Executive Director]. A key staff person called me to ask for a reference—she's leaving—and in my opinion for staff to come to a board member, things at the agency have to have gone [down] a long way. So I called the president of the board to find out if there was something going on that I didn't know about. He knew there were some staff problems, but not that they are as widespread as I have been told.

The processes set in motion by an active committee system help to produce and reinforce other, more subtle changes, especially within the boardroom itself. For example, as committees become more independent of the Owner-ED, board members have occasion to reflect that their responsibilities place them at the top of the organization's managerial hierarchy. Then too, as they become more knowledgeable about the agency, the information coming to them informally from board members serving as "regular volunteers" begins to seem illegitimate; such dual service is viewed by MAPs as putting the board in a compromising position because regular volunteers are supervised by agency staff. In addition, board member-volunteers may be viewed as a threat by an Owner-Executive who no longer feels that the board is under the proverbial thumb. This situation is described by a long-time volunteer, now a board member:

I have more contact with the agency than most members of the board because I'm a volunteer. But the board just passed a resolution that you can't be in a dual position on the theory that it creates a problem for staff members who can say, technically, here is my boss the board member being a volunteer.... Anyway, I had a long talk with the executive director and the chairman of the board, and I gave my word I would go off the board at the end of next year. I think they'd of been happier if I'd been willing to give up my volunteerism right now.

Often the tension is palpable between the old kind of board member, who is willing to be hands-on in the agency's programs, and the MAPs, who have a more disinterested, managerial approach:

There's a big division on the board. Half of us want people [on the board] who are interested in the programs and can work in them; others want chief executives who don't have time to work but who can raise funds, which they do.

At this point, pressures inside and outside the organization may be intense. Within the board, there may be tensions between the old and new points of view about the nature of board stewardship; external funders may have the agency under scrutiny; and problems within the staff, perhaps heretofore unknown, unexpressed, or unacknowledged, may have come to the surface. The focus of these simultaneous events is usually the Owner-ED, who may or may not be able, or willing, to cope with the staff problems and funding questions at the same time that that board is asserting its authority. And so the ED may resign. Perhaps the reason given is a lack of "security," an expression of the loss of control an ED can feel when a formerly quiescent board becomes active. Sometimes there is a showdown period in which the Owner-ED fights for her or his views and for the allegiance of the board and only resigns when requested to do so. In any event, either through a conscious change in the management style of the Owner-ED or through recruitment of a Managerially-oriented ED, the board enters a phase in which board behavior is guided by its members' conceptions of the activities of the board of a Fortune 500 corporation.

Routinizing the Fortune 500 Style

Although many details of this particular phase are unique to each agency, one commonality among boards involves the passing of an unambiguous signal to the ED that he or she must assist the board in mimicking the Fortune 500 model of oversight. Specifically, board committees are to meet regularly and discuss pertinent issues based on information and data provided by the ED or other staff members; decisions regarding policy matters are to be made by the board; and these decisions are to be implemented by the ED, who will make progress reports to the committees from time to time. Implicit in this message are two key assumptions, first, that the board has an important, substantive role to play in the agency and second, that faithfully executed bureaucratic procedure at the board level will contribute to the agency's success.

Of course, no matrix of expectations and behavior patterns is static, and an undercurrent of change is continuous in the corporate style processes of oversight. Over time, usually a period of years, a slow reduction occurs in the quotient of independence displayed by a corporate-style board. An Executive Director who works with a board that has become more dependent describes what happens from her point of view as the Fortune 500 style of oversight becomes highly routinized:

> Any board makes decisions based on what is inputted by the Executive Director. If you're smart, you give information in a way to mold their thinking, but also if you're smart, you don't want to sway them too much. The people on my board are used to making decisions based on data, and they expect that data to be correct, and if you aren't bright enough to provide that ...

Such a situation is good for the board and good for the agency, it is firmly believed, but it leaves some board members a bit wistful for the good old days. One board member, an experienced CEO in the Fortune 500 context, observes:

> The board has a problem stimulating itself to continuing carrying out the objectives that the Executive Director has set up. Once you're so successful, it's sort of a question what else is new, and it's a problem to get people motivated. The board feels its primary objective is to raise funds, and it is, and after a while, they really don't like that. There really isn't much you can do other than supply money.

This civic-minded volunteer, faithful as he is to this board, derives greater satisfaction from his activities on another volunteer board which "can develop what it wants to do and decide on its ten most important goals and programs."

More generally, what seems to occur with boards operating in the Fortune 500 pattern is a gradual settling back into a state of dependence and inertia similar to the situation when an Owner-ED was in charge—except that now the

Executive Director is managerially-oriented and views himself or herself as a professional rather than a moral agent identified with the mission of the agency. At this point, a savvy, managerially-oriented ED may be conscious that if the board chose to do so, it could assert that the ED is exceeding the bounds of administrative authority; the board could, in other words, rise up in a declaration of independence—much as it did in the past when under the sway of an Owner-ED. To avoid that showdown requires prudence and restraint, as this managerially-oriented ED has learned:

> So many times an Executive Director will not listen to the danger signals and try to get a project done no matter what the cost. The other end of that is if you go to a board committee and say you have a problem, what shall we do about this?—someone may say, "Here's what I would do." And sometimes it's a solution from their business and if they offer it, you're stuck doing it. My philosophy is never to ask a question without an answer.... It's a thin line keeping a board together and active. You have to involve them enough to give them a sense of purpose, but if it's too much and takes too much time [that's bad]. I don't think we've ever found it, that thin line.

Clearly, finding the Golden Mean of board involvement is as challenging for executive directors as it is for conscientious board members.

Part II

Applying the Model

The foregoing description offers a perspective for viewing the behavior of boards before they reach "maturity," here defined as the initial establishment of a Fortune 500 style of oversight. Although some readers may be troubled that the principal criteria for board maturity are active committees, bureaucratic procedures, and the appearance that the agency is successful, the fact remains that this is the judgment implied by those interviewed. The model as presented is nothing more than a systematic rendering of the perceptions of board members and executive directors. The phases are typical if not, scientifically speaking, predictable.

Mission as cause/principles; Goal as procedures/success. II

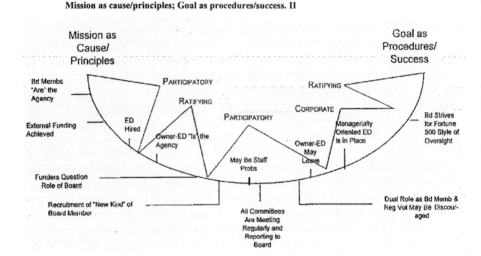

In this context, the model suggests that embedded in the proprietary attitudes which a dedicated executive may harbor towards a new agency are the seeds of a "crisis"—a crisis that could perhaps be averted if the typical developmental pattern could be anticipated. Then too, board members can use the model to discuss analytically the differing values of new and old board members. More generally, the value-orientation of the model responds to the assumption among some citizens and scholars that nonprofit board members have a set of responsibilities which are, broadly speaking, moral in nature. As Herslinger and Krasker (1987: 104) observe recently in *Harvard Business Review,* "managers and directors represent the voice of society in nonprofit organizations."

Extending the Model

Obviously, the notion that a board has reached maturity when it first succeeds in mimicking the Fortune 500 style of oversight raises the question, "What happens next?"

By chance, my own inquiries in another sub-sector of the nonprofit universe suggest a possible answer (Wood 1985). In research on private college boards using an interview methodology similar to the methodology here, the trustees and presidents of ten institutions in existence from eighty to two-hundred years were found to have three operating styles: (1) ratifying, in which the board serves as the president's sounding board but is his or her "rubber stamp" in formal decision-making; (2) corporate, in which the board plays a substantive role in framing financial and managerial issues in concert with the president and may thereby change the timing and outcome of decisions; and, (3) participatory, in which the board continually gathers information independent of the president, intermittently makes formal decisions contrary to the president's advice, and occasionally overrides a prior presidential decision.

These so-called operating styles, which differ according to the degree to which the board will (or will not) substitute its judgment for that of the president, can be usefully superimposed upon the model of board phases of development from founding to maturity with results as shown on the diagram above.

Briefly put, the board of a nonprofit exercises its collective judgment most independently during that early period when there is no paid executive and later when it reestablishes its authority over a dominant Owner-Executive Director. At these times, the board is functioning in the participatory operating style. The interpersonal and group dynamics resulting in the ascendance of an operating style can be obvious, as in response to a crisis, or more subtle, as when founding board members, exhausted from trying to run the agency themselves, engage in an unarticulated, perhaps unconscious, complicity with the Executive Director to relinquish ownership of the moral authority and programs of the agency; such a board quickly becomes a "rubber stamp." A similar complicity occurs later, when a board is working with a managerially-oriented, bureaucratically attuned individual who, responding to his or her own inclination or to cues from the board members, allows corporate-style oversight to become empty ritual. Today it is the corporate mode which, in the view of the participants, seems to provide the most satisfactory balance between the initiative properly exercised by the Executive Director and the legal authority reposing in the board.

Research on operating styles in absentee collegiate boards suggests that rubber stamp boards in that sector are rare, perhaps because of a societal climate in which members of most private college boards are aware of the wavelet of controversy over board effectiveness and most particularly, the rise in cost of directors' liability insurance. In collegiate boards at present, there seems to be a pendulum movement between the corporate and participatory styles. In locally-based 501(c)(3)s, however, my hunch is that members of corporate style boards, comforted psychologically by the proximity of the local agency and its ready visibility, may gradually lose their sharpness and discipline and slowly become ratifying. Then at some point an event internal or external to the agency-whether the addition of a new kind of board member, complaints from hands-on volunteers about the quality of the programs, the unexpected departure of the executive director, or the threat of reduced funding—catches the board up short and throws it into the highly independent participatory mode, from which it gradually declines into the more routinized corporate mode, as suggested by the following diagram:

The two prongs shown pictorially at the top left of the oval are intended to signify that a substantive reevaluation of mission at both the board and staff levels is most likely to occur when the board is in the participatory mode. A substantive reevaluation of purposes—in contrast to implementing a routine planning process, which may be a feature of the corporate mode—presumably involves deciding whether the agency will change its course, as opposed to broadening or narrowing it. The model suggests that 501(c)(3) boards continually progress from one phase to another at intervals unique to each agency.

These Findings in Theoretical Context

This broad perspective on nonprofits and their boardroom sub-culture over an indefinite period of time is more compatible with the "grand"—some would say grandiose—theories of Talcott Parsons than with more specific models of organization life offered by other theorists. Conversations with board members and executive directors are illuminated by Parsons view that social systems are dependent upon the symbols, values and norms of the broader culture and also on personality systems, which provide motivation (Mayhew 1982:6, 13). His structural-functional theory, involving the dynamic movement of social systems in search of equilibrium, corresponds with changes in board behavior emerging from a perceived need to re-establish a satisfactory balance between the board and the rest of the agency or between the agency and the external environment. Although Parsons has been criticized for failing to take adequate account of change and conflict, his framework readily encompasses the model here that correlates collective values with board behavior and posits a relationship between these two variables over time. Of course, the model here is also derivative of other models of organization life, notably those that conceptualize organizations as coalitions of powerful constituencies, information-processing units, open systems, closed systems, meaning-producing systems, and so on. Of these, the information-processing model is most useful in understanding governing boards over time, while the others highlight selected phenomena that seem to influence the board's behavior intermittently. For example, boards tend to function as relatively closed systems in the ratifying mode, as open ones in the participatory, and in a middle, or permeable, position in the corporate mode.

These Findings in Relation to Other Research on Nonprofits

Of the relatively few articles on board-executive relations, Ralph Kramer's contingency theory is among the more detailed and penetrating. Especially useful is his definition of power, taken from Hasenfeld (1983:178-185), as "a reciprocal relationship where the power of one derives from the dependency of the other" (Kramer 1984:191). Kramer identifies twenty-five factors "conducive to greater power for the executive" in relation to the board. Of these, eight are related to organization, nine to board members, two to situation, and six to the issue. Interestingly, the interviews in Midwest City provide a mixed commentary on the salience of this framework.

Kramer hypothesizes, for example, that greater executive power is associated with the organizational variables of large size, complexity, bureaucratization, professionalization, decentralization, technical knowledge base, many small donors, and reliance on governmental funds. In Midwest City, however, executive domination in the earliest phases of board development is the typical experience at smaller agencies where none of these variables applies. The distinction is significant because an estimated 60 percent of human service nonprofits (approximately two-hundred sixty-five thousand organizations) have twenty-five or less full-time staff (Gronbjerg et al.:28). High turnover in board membership is also said to be conducive to executive power; however, Midwest City offers examples of young and mature boards where a stable core of old members actively perpetuates executive domination of the board through its influence on the selection and socialization of new members.

On the other hand, the Midwest City interviews confirm Kramer's hypothesis that infrequent meetings tilt power in favor of the executive; indeed, the first step of the "new kind" of board member is to increase the frequency of meetings by activating the committee system so that all committees, instead of just the executive and finance committees, meet regularly and report to the board. Also confirmed is Kramer's assertion that the absence of crisis tends to favor executive domination. In fact, the Midwest City experience suggests that perception of a "crisis" is the key factor in moving the board from a rubber stamp posture to a highly activist mode.

Kramer's framework stipulates that board power tends to be reduced when programmatic issues are in high profile. However, the Midwest City research suggests that when a board in its early history first activates its committee system and is in the participatory mode, the board's authority over programs is increased by virtue of the board's better knowledge of the agency and the tendency of MAP-influenced boards to reduce program issues to bureaucratic decisions about finance or to specific performance goals. In mature boards operating in either the corporate or ratifying modes, there is a reversal of this dynamic. At that point, the managerially-oriented executive typically uses bureaucratic procedures to distance the board from the substance of policy.

Also of interest in light of the findings in Midwest City is Melissa Middleton's (1988) eight month study of the social ties and networks within the board of "East Coast Orchestra," a young arts organization that appears to be evolving from a founder-dominated board to the Fortune 500 style of oversight. Middleton describes an organization in which the transition from the founding board was sparked not by external funders, but by the departure of the first general manager, presumably an Owner-ED (170). The few remaining members of the founding group, who show up as the strongly-tied trustees, still exercise a "gate-keeping" role over the selection of new board members (171). In the meantime, moderately-tied trustees now occupy most of the formal leadership positions and are MAP-ish in being more task-focused and in speaking of their involvement as "an alternative to their daily occupational routines" (172)—in other words, they sound like Maslowian self-actualizers. Weakly-tied trustees also manifest this Maslowian attitude: "I get a helluva kick in seeing organizations grow" (175).

In general, the study of East Coast Orchestra confirms the main themes in the Midwest City data. One notable difference concerns the board's perception of "heavy-hitters," defined by the orchestra board as members with corporate connections or ties to wealth. Middleton found that such members were weakly-tied and not active, but also that they and their status were "invisible" to other board members, who continue to speak of the board's need for "heavy-hitters." In Midwest City, in contrast, wealth or corporate connections render a member highly visible. Corporate success is much admired, and local corporations and corporate divisions have a policy of making executives, especially in the upper middle corporate ranks, available to charitable boards. In practice, this seems to mean that the majority of such board members are "weakly-tied" not because the other board members, consciously or unconsciously, want to keep them at arm's length as "outsiders" (173), but because corporate executives assigned to the task of boardsmanship only periodically attend the board meetings where personal ties could begin to develop.

References

Gronbjerg, Kirsten A., Madeleine H. Kimmich, and Lester A. Salamon. *The Chicago Nonprofit Sector in a Time of Retrenchment.* Washington, D.C.: The Urban Institute Press, 1985.

Hasenfeld, Yeheskel. *Human Service Organizations.* Prentice Hall, 1983.

Herzlinger, Regina E. and William S. Krasker, "Who Profits from Nonprofits?" *Harvard Business Review,* January-February, 1987, pp. 93-106.

Kramer, Ralph. "A Framework for the Analysis of Board-Executive Relationships in Voluntary Agencies," in Florence S. Schwartz, ed., *Voluntarism and Social Work Practice.* University Press of America, 1984, pp. 179-201.

Maslow, Abraham. *Motivation and Personality,* 2nd ed. Harper and Row, 1970.

Mayhew, Leon H., ed. *Talcott Parsons: On Institutions and Social Evolution.* University of Chicago Press, 1982.

Middleton, Melissa. "The Characteristics and Influence of Intraboard Networks: A Study of a Nonprofit Board of Directors," in Robert Herman, ed., *Nonprofit Boards of Directors.* Transaction Books, 1988, pp. 160-192.

Stoppard, Tom. *Rosencrantz and Guildenstern are Dead.* New York: Grove Press, 1967.

Wood, Miriam M. *Trusteeship in the Private College.* Johns Hopkins University Press, 1985.

Beyond the Organizational Chart: Board-Staff Relations in Healthy Congregations

Rev. Stefan M. Jonasson

Congregational leaders, much like those of any other kind of institution, love organizational charts! They are especially fond of those diagrams that show "who's in charge here," particularly where their own position is close to the summit of a pyramid, while carefully delineating the roles and responsibilities and the key players. Unfortunately, human institutions are rarely characterized by such neatness and clarity. In fact, religious communities may well be among the messiest and most complex—let's say "most organic"—of all human organizations. The religious community, by whatever name we call it, is one where it is difficult and at times nearly impossible to distinguish between owner and customer, donor and recipient, member and participant, or leader and servant. Congregational life defies neatly constructed organizational charts, even as it requires a high degree of organization!

Short of drawing a three-dimensional diagram of overlapping circles, misshapen boxes and erratic lines, the most useful and accurate organizational chart, insofar as formal structure is concerned, will juxtapose the board and staff of the congregation alongside one another—in other words, it will show them in partnership. In most congregations, the clergy live and work on both sides of the chart, participating actively in the board's work and deliberations while also guiding the staff, serving as a link between board and staff while simultaneously maintaining the appropriate distance between them. The clergy are unique in congregational organization in that they have a direct relationship with the congregation itself, its board, and the remainder of the staff. (It goes without saying that, in most traditions, the clergy is also held to have a special relationship with God or whatever that tradition's source of authority may be.)

Perhaps the most obvious factor in defining how the board and staff of a congregation relate to one another is the polity of the denomination to which it
belongs. At one end of the spectrum are those congregations that are either fully
independent or part of one of the congregational traditions, at the other end are
those whose polities are Episcopal, while in between are those traditions that
blend these divergent tendencies. In the United States and Canada, the Episcopal
denominations have absorbed many of the assumptions of congregational polity,
so strong is the influence of the prevailing democratic values of the culture, not to
mention the impact of consumerism. Consequently, even advisory boards (as distinct from true governing boards) have considerable influence on what happens
in their congregations, although their polity may vest primary authority in other
places. The net result is that most North American congregations possess considerable autonomy and their boards wield real power in guiding their affairs.

Although structure and systems are important factors in the governance of
religious organizations, personalities will generally prove to be more significant.
Simply put, mature and faithful people can make almost any organizational
structure work, whereas the best structure will crumble if it is led by individuals
lacking in personal maturity and the gifts of leadership. When a particular individual fails to adhere to normal protocols or otherwise acts in ways that undermine healthy relationships, it is unhelpful for peers to ignore the behavior. In the
case of board members, it is a responsibility of the board as a whole to protect the
staff from board members acting on their own personal agendas. In the case of
staff, it is the responsibility of the staff member's supervisor or work group to
hold the staff member to professional standards of service.

Just as good fences make good neighbors, good boundaries between the organizational parts of a congregation do make for good relationships. However, it is
necessary to avoid excessive rigidity about these boundaries. Few of us would
choose to live in a neighborhood where the fences had no gates, so we should be
suspicious of any governance model that defines boundaries so neatly and tightly
that there are few opportunities for direct interaction between the parts. It would
be like building organizational fences without any gates, or with too few gates for
the length of the fence. Nowhere is this more important than when it comes to
the relationship between the board and the staff of a congregation. One often
hears the call for these two spheres to be kept neatly separated, a sentiment that is
expressed in many different ways: ministers and parishioners can never be friends,
the board has no business meddling in staff matters, the staff should stay out of
congregational politics, members should never be hired to fill staff positions, the
board should avoid micromanagement, the minister has no business talking to

the nominations committee, and so on. While some of these assertions may have limited usefulness, they are often rooted the congregational equivalent of urban legends and tend to promote turf protection rather than good boundaries and healthy relationships.

In practice, there's really no reason why socially competent people cannot cross the boundaries from time to time, especially when doing so promotes deeper understanding and more harmonious relationships, as long as they do so in a respectful manner and with the others' consent. It is undesirable to allow a congregation's relational etiquette to be determined by fears about the socially inept. It is far more productive to keep the relationally challenged individual off the board and out of the staff in the first place, something we seem loathe to do in religious organizations!

Staff members need to understand that one of the rewards that board members receive for their service is, in fact, the privilege of having a closer relationship to the staff of the congregation, who are usually perceived to be at the center of activities. While it's natural for staff members to want to keep board members at a distance from their day-to-day work, it is highly desirable for staff to nurture respectful and clear relationships with board members.

Board members should never exploit staff relationships to accomplish things for which they cannot get approval from their colleagues on the board. Similarly, individual staff members should not manipulate board members to implement through board action what they cannot get the senior staff to agree to.

In many traditions, ordained ministers are called to their positions by a vote of the congregation rather than named by denominational appointment or hired by the board. Where this is the case, it is essential to recognize that the minister (or ministers) have a direct relationship to the congregation as a whole and are ultimately accountable only to the congregation. While they may have a reporting relationship to the board, they are not directly accountable to the board for their ministry and its customary responsibilities—preaching and teaching, pastoral care and public witness. However, they may be held accountable by the board for board-delegated responsibilities, such as the supervision of other staff, management of congregational funds, and implementation of board policy.

The size of a congregation is an important variable in determining the appropriate relationship between the board and staff. In the family-sized congregation (those averaging fewer than fifty participants), the board *is,* for all intents and purposes, also the volunteer staff of the congregation! Since the board of such a congregation fills what amount to staff roles on a volunteer basis, the question of board-staff relations is pretty much an internal conversation. The board of a family-sized congregation will commonly focus its attention on recruiting and motivating a volunteer pool of which the board's own personnel will be the dominant number.

It is in those congregations that grow beyond family-sized systems that the question of board-staff relations takes on real importance. In a pastoral congregation (averaging fifty to one hundred fifty in attendance), so called because its relational system typically focuses on a minister (or pastor), board-staff relations are initially framed as a matter of communications and accountability between the board and a solo minister. In such a context, it is difficult not to "take things personally" in both the positive and negative senses of that expression. The most dangerous thing a board can do in this case is seek to supervise the daily work of the minister, while the most dangerous thing for the minister is to allow an adversarial relationship with the board to develop and fester.

As soon as a congregation reaches the size where it is able to hire a single paid staff member, its board must learn to relate to the staff in a single voice. It is neither appropriate nor helpful for individual board members—not even the chairperson—to arrogate to themselves the privilege of supervising the staff. This can be especially difficult in the pastoral congregation, since most board members will continue to function, in some way or other, as volunteer staff members.

In program churches (one hundred fifty to three hundred fifty in attendance) and large congregations (three hundred fifty plus), the board-staff relationship changes dramatically, since congregations of this size undergo an increase in organizational complexity, demand for specialization, program growth and autonomous groups, and evolve towards having multiple professional staff and a cadre of support staff. While the staff will typically adapt more easily to the trend toward specialization, the board needs to understand that its role also becomes more specialized, requiring greater focus and a more limited sphere of activity.

As congregations grow to the size where board members are no longer expected to double as volunteer staff, the board is left with six primary functions: visioning, policy-making, stewardship, sponsorship, advocacy, and consultancy. Visioning and policy-making should be its dominant focus, since a clear and compelling vision will set the stage for everything else that happens, while well-crafted policies extend the board's influence throughout the entire congregation. (If a congregation's bylaws are thought of as its skeleton, then its policy framework can be imagined as the regulatory system that keeps the vital organs in check!) Neither of these two functions can be effectively pursued without a close and trusting relationship between the board and the senior staff of the congregation. If the senior staff is isolated from the board, it will be effectively insulated from the results of the board's work in these areas. As stewards, the board holds the congregation's assets in trust, including moral and other intangible assets, while as sponsors, the board should collectively be among the most generous supporters of the congregation with both time and money. As advocates, the board represents interests of the congregation as an institution both to its own members and, more importantly, to the wider community. As consultants, board members are available to the staff—*at the staff's initiation*—to provide counsel and encouragement from their particular areas of expertise. It is the unfortunate tendency of many boards to neglect the first two functions and devote excessive energy to one or more of the remaining four. As stewards and consultants, in particular, board members can be very tempted to interfere in the staff domain, even when seeking to be genuinely helpful to the staff.

In multiple staff congregations, the board should generally restrict its involvement in staffing decisions to policy directives. The board should establish clear policies about retention and dismissal, employment standards, compensation and benefits. It should not, however, insert itself into matters involving the supervision of individual employees, save for situations involving grave ethical misconduct or legal peril to the institution—and even then, a sound policy structure will usually enable senior staff to do what needs to be done without direct board involvement. It is nevertheless helpful for the chief of staff, usually the senior minister, to involve the board in hiring and termination decisions involving other senior staff positions, if only as a courtesy.

When the professional staff of a congregation grows beyond three members, choices need to be made about which members of the staff will attend board meetings on a regular basis. Just as too many cooks spoil the broth, too many staff members at board meetings tend to spoil the board's process. In fact, boards can feel overwhelmed if too many staff members are present, which will lead to poor decision-making and poor board-staff relations. In larger multi-staff congregations, it is best that the staff presence at board meetings be limited to the senior minister (or co-ministers as the case may be) and perhaps the chief administrative officer, with other staff being invited to meetings on as "as needed" basis.

When a congregation is experiencing conflict or otherwise dealing with controversial issues, it can be very tempting for both the board and staff to withhold information from one another, or at least over-manage the flow of information. It is almost always counterproductive to do so. Naturally, there will sometimes be matters that must be handled with a high degree of confidentiality or respect for privacy—personnel matters, certain financial negotiations, litigation, and the like. But far too often, boards are asked to make governance decisions in the absence of vital information that the staff possesses, while staff members seek to implement programs as the board considers changes in funding or mandates.

At no time is the temptation to withhold information more tempting than when the information contains unpleasant news. Board members should never first hear about a financial shortfall from the congregation's auditor, after it is too late to do anything about it, and staff members should never first learn of a board decision from a board member's spouse! It is also important to avoid "spin" when presenting information, whether good or bad; any commentary on the information presented should include both positive and negative implications. Boards and staff both deserve information from one another that is forthright, accurate, and concise yet complete.

Much has been written on the perils and pitfalls, frustrations and failures of religious leadership, whether we're thinking about clergy, staff, lay leaders, or the large supporting cast that constitutes the modern religious community. The real news, though, is how *well* things usually go despite the perils and shortcomings. When the relationship between a congregation's board and its staff is working well, it will look like the organizational equivalent of a dance. The parts of the system will be clearly discernible and in close proximity to one another, moving through their environment with grace, if not quite in lock-step with one another. The quality of relationship between the board of a congregation and its staff looks no more like an organizational chart than dancing looks like those dance-step templates that get laid out on the ballroom floor. Much depends on goodwill and maturity, clarity and commitment. In the end, the real life of the congregation is lived beyond the organizational chart.

The Rabbinic Role in
Organizational Decision-Making

David A. Teutsch

The legitimation of decision-making in an organization rests on an agreement about who ought to have authority and what constitutes proper process. But how any group perceives legitimation will be deeply affected by how its leaders are perceived as carrying out their roles. Rabbis often have complex roles and multiple sources of authority, and these need to be examined to understand the legitimation of their roles in organizational decision-making. My ideological preference is for combining open discussion and democratic processes with serious Jewish learning, values exploration, and study of current information from the social and natural sciences. But I will set that aside here in order to examine the rabbinic role as a context for decision-making.

In thinking about the rabbis of old, most Jews in my experience rely on two images. The first is of the scholar sitting dressed in dark clothes and debating points of law in the yeshiva with large, dusty, incomprehensible tomes spread open on the table before him (always him!). The other is the wise adjudicator making pronouncements on the *kashrut (Jewish dietary laws)* of a chicken and settling fights between quarreling neighbors. These images conjure up an automatic power, authority, and claim to authenticity that most modern Jews find alternately comforting, and alienating. It provides much of the multivalent emotional backdrop, but not the contemporary context within which most contemporary rabbis function. In practice contemporary rabbis have evolved far past this picture of their roles even though they still frequently struggle with its emotional consequences, which often color issues surrounding decision-making processes.

Without dwelling on the evolution of the rabbinate—a subject that has a growing literature of its own—I would like to propose a five-part typology of the contemporary rabbinic role. Within each part are options that are more traditional or less so, and more authoritarian or less so. Most rabbinic positions have varying amounts of all five elements, which are listed here in no particular order:

Pastor-Priest

From the magically transforming power of ritual actor to the healing and calming presence of the pastor at sickbed or counselor in times of trouble, rabbis have profound, personal relationships tying them to individuals whose lives they touch. In this role the rabbi often consults with the individuals but usually retains full control, and always retains veto power over decisions about what the rabbi will say or do. The rabbi's power here comes from his/her tie to key experiences in the lives of others, from control over transformative rituals, and from the intimate knowledge of their lives. This power, often experienced as parental, not only provides a critical source of role legitimation. It is often a two-edged sword that can make the rabbi an admired or resented symbol of authority depending upon the psyche of the beholder.

This is particularly the case for those rabbis who maximize the more dramatic, awe-inspiring aspect of their role as priest rather than the more consultative, personal aspect of their role as pastor. When rabbis internalize the priestly role, they sometimes understand themselves as *klei kodesh,* holy vessels. This not only legitimates their uniqueness and power in the community; it implies they are always above reproach. That claim creates resentments around the issues of power and blame as well as a belief that rabbis do not understand what "real life" is about because they do not participate in it.

Administrator-Facilitator

The title of the position and the job description will vary depending upon the congregation or organization, but usually the rabbi is an important professional with responsibilities for overseeing and coordinating with other staff, planning and executing programs, serving as a liaison with various committees, and performing a broad variety of other organizational functions. In many of these functions the rabbi makes large numbers of routine decisions unilaterally and often unselfconsciously. The rabbi may also be a key facilitator, communicator, and/or strategic planner. In matters involving policy or innovation, the balance among unilateral action, advice and consent, and group decision-making varies widely, but there is always a balance, and there are always disagreements and gray areas regarding where that balance is. When the rabbi is an effective administrator and communicator, the rabbi's presence can pervade every organizational activity and decision even when the rabbi is not physically present. This often enriches and improves leaders perspectives and helps to break down the rabbi-for-ritual and board-for-money model in which the rabbi (and hence Judaism) is seen as irrelevant for anything practical. But it also can bring out in some laypeople the sense that they are not being trusted and given the freedom necessary to do their jobs.

Scholar-Adjudicator

In most settings the rabbi is a major source of Jewish knowledge and teaching. This root of rabbinic power and function may be expressed in ways that are more authoritarian (e.g., *halakhic—Jewish law*—decisor) or more supportive of individual choice ("Let's look at sources that show how and why traditional practice does it and then look at some contemporary alternatives so that you can decide what you want to do"), more aimed at empowering through transferring skills and motivation or at retaining traditional roles by handing down pronouncements. All rabbis necessarily do some of each in the course of their function as repositories of Jewish learning, but once again the balance shifts from rabbi to rabbi and organization to organization. If the rabbi retains the sole right to be the repository of tradition, this may well result in a reluctance to share power in areas perceived as historically lay-controlled.

Maggid-Teacher-Prophet

Providing inspiration and motivation, giving *divrei torah (lessons on the weekly bible portions),* teaching in the classroom and leading informal learning sessions are part of most rabbinic positions either regularly or more occasionally. Depending upon the rabbi's position, message, charisma, and personal relationships with students, teaching may be a powerful and centrally important, even commanding aspect of the rabbinic role, or it can be one of only minor significance. Through it the rabbi can expound tradition, champion innovation, or stress social action. This can be done through prophetic (and hence authoritarian) demand, through exhortation to discussion and, action, or through providing emotional support, interesting material, and challenging questions. With the maggid-teacher-prophet too the balance among these elements will reflect rabbi and organization as well as the relationship between them. When the rabbi tends to the more authoritarian as teacher and preacher, this will often increase resistance to the spread of the rabbi's influence in venues that are not traditionally those of the rabbi.

One aspect of the role is teaching by example. It is inevitably the case that the rabbi is a role model. I remember my astonishment as a young rabbi when I found a congregant staring into my home pantry. Responding to my confusion, she said without embarrassment that this was her chance to see what foods were okay to buy for her newly kosher kitchen. Functioning as a role model gives the rabbi the claustrophobic feeling of always being on duty. Should rabbis aspire to serving as role models of extraordinary holiness and commitment, or of blending Jewish commitment with lives that otherwise are not so different from those of the people around us? How will this affect rabbinic authority and power?

Beneficiary-Supervisee

The rabbi generally depends upon the organization for a livelihood. Rabbinic compensation is a large budget item, reflecting the central importance of a high level of rabbinic function to the success of the organization. Controversies abound over how to supervise rabbis and evaluate their performance, and how to determine appropriate compensation. While there are legitimate reasons that rabbis want to avoid using the term, from this vantage point they are employees. Whether tough and demanding or flexible and soft-spoken in matters involving supervision and compensation, the rabbi inevitably struggles over this aspect of leadership, which is an inevitable result of serving as a professional communal leader.

A painful dissonance can exist for the rabbi as a result of the power that flows from the first four rabbinic roles and the relative powerlessness often experienced as a result of the fifth role. When resentments have built up over the extent of the rabbi's exercise of power and authority in some of the first four rabbinic roles, this is often acted out in the fifth. Sometimes this is appropriate, but often it revolves around lay leaders who have not worked out their own problems with authority or with the Jewish tradition. It is most difficult to handle when the appropriate and inappropriate elements are mixed together, as they all too often are. In my experience the only way to avoid this is to maintain an ongoing dialogue regarding the way that power and authority can best be exercised in the organization. Often this is a conversation that the rabbi and organization do not foster with the result that it takes place in stressful and destructive ways.

A rabbi I talked with recently could not understand why congregants seemed angry with him so often just as he began his new contract. After all, he told me, they had just given him the full increase he had demanded if he was to continue with the congregation. I asked what the budget consequences were, and he noted dues increases, expanded fundraising, and a serious deficit. I pointed out that the way he had obtained his increased compensation had been experienced by at least some of his congregants as blackmail and asked whether that might explain the new feelings he had encountered. This is an uncommon situation. More often when the negotiation turns sharply adversarial, it is the rabbis who capitulate and must then deal with their feelings of frustration, anger, and impotence. These feelings too have powerful implications for the distribution of power and authority in the congregation. They will often show up later in situations unconnected to the original conflict. As a rabbi I saw at a *shiva minyan (prayer service for mourners)* several months ago put it bitterly, "I am their paid Jew."

The interaction among the various aspects of rabbinic leadership has a profound impact on the nature of the rabbinic role in organizational decision-making. The division of authority in the many areas of rabbinic and organizational life, the relative powers of rabbi and organization, the complex of feelings and attitudes between them, and the degree of self-consciousness that exists about the relationship all deeply influence the nature and smoothness of the decision-making process.

Rabbis who are highly present and powerful in all of the aspects of leadership may dwarf the other professionals and lay leaders with whom they work. This domination may result in weak leaders being attracted to the organizational hierarchy. It may also result in unstated anger and frustration gradually building up toward the rabbi. Sometimes rabbis persuade and build consensus, thereby creating a cooperative commitment to change. Other times rabbis force change or block it through a coercive exercise of personal will. Bending a resistant organization to the rabbi's will is like bending back a tree branch further and further. If it doesn't crack, it will unleash a dangerous amount of uncontrolled energy the moment the rabbi's grip loosens. Rabbis who are particularly strong in one or more areas and less so in others sometimes effectively compensate by inviting volunteers or other professionals to fill the gaps. This diffusion of power and responsibility often results in an increased sense of partnership and mutual worth. On the other hand, when the rabbi resists acknowledging areas of weakness and avoids getting help from others, this can result in conflict, negative evaluations regarding the rabbi's performance, and sometimes (particularly when traditional attitudes toward the rabbi are present) an institutionally dangerous version of the-emperor-has-no-clothes or elephant-on-the-table. When the weaknesses are acknowledged but not compensated for, the result can be institutional weakness.

Agreements about power and authority are essential to any successful decision-making process because cooperation is needed to implement decisions. Sharing power requires that the rabbi not exceed the amount of authority that the organization is willing to accept. In the roles of priest, counselor, prophet, teacher, administrator, adjudicator, scholar, and teacher, the rabbi can exercise an enormous amount of both power and authority outside the narrow confines of the official decision-making process. Unless the rabbi and organization are willing to allow the rabbi to become the dominant center of the organization with the rest of its members pushed into entirely subordinate roles, the rabbi cannot exercise sole authority in all these areas. Most rabbis, by virtue of their own predilections, will choose to specialize in one area or a few.

Some rabbis will avoid being authoritarian even in their areas of greatest involvement and specialization, but that takes enormous strength of character because the effect of people looking up to the rabbi—putting the rabbi on a pedestal or treating the rabbi as a parent-figure or as someone special—is that the rabbi develops the expectation that the rabbi should always be treated as an authority figure. Given that many go into the rabbinate partly because they find the public role attractive, there is a particularly strong tendency for rabbis to delight in being at the center of attention and authority. (What person doesn't?) This can create a complicated dynamic in which discussing decision-making processes becomes unexpectedly tense and even explosive.

Those who are unhappy with the overall division of power and authority between rabbi and other organization members or who are unhappy with the division regarding any one of the five basic rabbinic roles will fight for a re-division or, feeling unable to do that, act out their resistance in other ways such as undermining the rabbi elsewhere or pulling back from the organization. This provides a pressing reason for becoming self-conscious about the division of power and authority, placing questions about decision-making processes in that context, and taking care in designing the decision-making process to develop a consensus around power issues and methods of decision-making. I have observed that in the life of most groups, agreement about the method of decision-making is more important to achieving a positive outcome than what the method is.

Decision-making methods also necessarily differ depending upon the size and nature of the organization. A *havurah (friendship circle)* can operate with the entire group participating in making all decisions of any consequence. Small congregations necessarily require some representative decision-making. Large congregations need highly differentiated committee structures and delegate many more operational decisions to paid professionals. Congregations can be ideologically committed more to centralized authority as illustrated in the Reform *Temple Management Manual,* to a broader democracy on the Reconstructionist model, to rabbi as *moreh d'atra* on the Conservative model in which often the rabbi has relatively little involvement in financial affairs, or to rabbi as ultimate authority in all matters, as in the *haredi (ultra-fundamentalist)* Orthodox world.

Different kinds of organizations also have different modes of decision-making. The Federation of Reconstructionist Congregations and Havurot, for example, is deeply committed to a democratic system in which all significant decisions are made by lay leaders. The Reconstructionist Rabbinical College, following the methods laid out by its accrediting agency for colleges and universities, takes only broad questions of policy and finance to its board, relegating other decisions to complex staff-driven procedures involving administrators, faculty, and in some cases students. Hillel directors have the responsibilities exercised by executive directors in small to mid-size not-for-profit agencies. Chaplains often form an independent administrative unit that is only lightly supervised by the hospital, nursing home, prison, or other facility.

What can be deduced from this diverse list of models? That decision-making processes should be designed in light of many variables. The most central of these variables include:

- the nature, purpose, and structure of the organization;

- institutional history and ideology;

- the skills, style, personality, and preferences of the rabbi;

- the history and status of the relationship between the rabbi and the organization;

- and the personalities and histories of leaders and opinion makers within the organization.

All of these ought to shape decision-making structures more than preset universal blueprints of processes and divisions of powers. Particularly important are having clarity about what the rabbi is good at and interested in. Since rabbis occasionally change jobs and many other organizational changes occur from time to time, frequent review of decision-making processes is highly important. This is one of the important functions of bylaws committees.

Some universal comments about decision-making are needed to fulfill the purpose of this essay. These will of necessity reflect my Reconstructionist views. My first assumption is that individuals ought to be as free as possible to follow the dictates of their own consciences. Rabbis as individuals—like anyone else—should not be required to violate their own consciences regarding what they themselves will or will not do. Second, the community has the right to determine its own direction. It can delegate decisions to the rabbi, but it is the community as a whole that has the right to determine its own good. Third, that maximizing input is most likely to result in the best decision, but that less significant decisions should be made in the smallest appropriate group after the shortest appropriate discussion in order to avoid squandering the time and energy of the group. Boards should expect committees to formulate full proposals and present reasons for and against them.

Rabbis tend to focus most on issues of ritual and individual status, areas primarily of concern in their priest/pastor function. While these are the areas most directly affecting their own activities, they are not the only critical places in need of substantial input regarding Jewish precedents and values. For example, the most powerful assertion of the congregation's priorities and values is evidenced in its budget and program, yet most rabbis spend little time exploring how the budget can be shaped to reflect most fully the organization's values and priorities. Decisions regarding health insurance for secretaries and the elaborateness of interior decoration also embody powerful moral choices.

Participating in planning processes and providing Jewish input to the broadest possible series of decisions provides the rabbi with critical opportunities to educate organizational stakeholders and shape the overall organizational direction. For some congregational rabbis this suggests too great an involvement in the administrator role, but I suggest that this function can as easily be understood under the rubrics of scholar and teacher since it shapes the organization through Jewish education. This mode of intervention will not be resented if it is not undertaken in a coercive or authoritarian way provided and if resentments about rabbinic power or adversarial style have not built up already in ways I described earlier in this essay. I would argue that the rabbi should have substantial input in every matter that is in any sense Jewish. I know few rabbis who have superb opinions about which heating company should get the contract, but I hope that they develop Jewishly informed opinions about issues like the environmental impact of synagogue consumption or the interaction between the nature of architecture and the character of Jewish prayer.

The rabbi will have the greatest influence in decision-making processes in the least grating way if the rabbi builds consensus by using opportunities for one-on-one discussion and for teaching rather than relying on strong assertions during large meetings. While taking strong stands during decision-making meetings may occasionally be necessary, it strains relations and uses a great deal of political capital so that doing so should be understood as a tactic of last resort. The demystification of the rabbinic role results in a greater reliance on persuasion and facilitation. Especially in congregations and clusters of havurot, the rabbi more than any other single person has the opportunity to talk with people and feel the pulse of the organization. This provides the opportunity to shape views in a way that builds consensus and trust. If the rabbi can convince the leadership that major decisions should be accompanied by relevant Jewish study that will not only improve the organization's direction. It will also serve as a decision-making model for organization members in their own lives.

The model in which one side wins an argument and the other side loses is destructive to everyone. We need to remind all the organization's members including the rabbi that we are struggling to make decisions *l'shem shamayim (in the name of heaven)*. Keeping score is bad for everyone because it encourages decision makers to give ego needs precedence over thoughtful listening and compromise. In my experience, the roots of lay-rabbinic conflicts about decision-making lie in the basic roles of the rabbi. Conflicts and tensions result from the way that power and authority balance there. That becomes amplified if there is a breakdown of listening skills in the decision-making process or if the professionals do not put enough time and energy into facilitating the dialogue in advance of meetings where decisions will be made. By virtue of their presence, knowledge and role, rabbis are usually the most influential people in their organizations. They need to learn to use that influence. If they don't, before blaming anyone else regarding poor decisions or hostility toward the rabbi, they should consider their own responsibility. It is true that occasionally an emotionally disturbed or vindictive or obtuse organization member will upset the decision-making process. In my experience, however, it is much more difficult to do that when the professionals are doing their homework.

I don't believe that a rabbi who fully develops and vigorously uses the interrelated skills needed to function as Jewish resource, teacher, and facilitator will suffer from an inability to move the organization on issues of importance. The organization will be powerfully influenced by where the rabbi stands. Furthermore, when the rabbi is fulfilling well the tasks needed by the organization but not demanding the right to make decisions, it is my experience that often the right to make a sensible mix of decisions is generally naturally and gracefully given. This, however, may take years. Most organizational theorists agree that it takes five years to make successful changes in areas of an organization that are deeply embedded. It takes another five years for those changes to become fully institutionalized. Rabbis, like other organizational leaders, need to learn patience!

We are in the business of teaching Torah. Often we are most effective teaching one Jew at a time. Teaching does not mean that our students will arrive precisely at our conclusions. But if we trust them, we know that as at Yavneh once we are done teaching and discussing, it is up to them to cast their votes with the most learned voting last.

The ideological statements in this essay are for the most part not different from those propounded by some of our colleagues as long as twenty years ago. What has changed in the interim is our awareness of the impediments to their implementation, some of which I have discussed here. As our awareness of the difficulties in carrying out our vision of the rabbinic role has increased, so has our understanding of the skills, insights, and motivations needed to surmount those difficulties. The reshaping of seminary curricula should increasingly reflect these considerations. Even when the curricula are optimal, however, substantial experience is needed to fully comprehend their implications. Thus these concerns should be revisited frequently through continued professional training for rabbis in the field.

The Endangered Rabbi

Arthur Gross Schaefer and Eric Weiss

Behind the smiles, the warm handshakes and even the embracing hugs, rabbis are sometimes sad, exhausted human beings feeling empty and disillusioned. Many are burning out, consumed by emotions of anger, frustration and loneliness. This mood of despair does not affect all rabbis to the same degree or at the same time. Nor is it necessarily persistent or irrevocable. There are wonderfully giving rabbis whose perspective and experience will be radically different from that offered in this article. However, the phenomenon of clergy burnout is pervasive, affecting veteran and new clergy alike, cutting across all religious movements.

There are varied and enriching opportunities afforded to rabbis. A rabbi's life is often full of wonderful and precious experiences and exciting challenges. And yet, all the worthy activities a rabbi does may not fully ameliorate feelings of isolation and silent desperation. For some there is a sensation of being trapped in a situation that is overwhelming and from which there is no easy escape. Clergy often believe that no one really wants to listen to their pain or that they should not burden congregants with their problems. Many become numb and bury feelings of frustration deep inside over-scheduled lives while trying to help ease the pain of others.

Rabbis need to be role models of a spiritually-balanced life rather than yet another example of a stressed out professional. In many ways, the future of the Jewish people is at risk when rabbis, the front line teachers and facilitators, endure excessive stress and debilitating loneliness. While many careers exact endless hours, few demand that one always be a role model whose actions, and those of the family, are closely and incessantly scrutinized.

In addition, a game of deception is being played as the rabbi preaches the values of family, study and prayer. Look behind the sermons that implore the congregants to place their families first and their careers second, and you will find that often the sermonizers' actions betray their own words. Ask rabbis how often they take time for personal prayer or study and you will frequently hear only sad-

146

ness in their responses. When rabbis believe that they must neglect core values of family and study in order to be "effective," they dilute the quality of their lives.

Rabbi burnout has not been a subject of sufficient discussion in public nor even among the clergy. Rabbis don't like to admit, even to themselves, that they are unhappy and "stressed out." Rather, most clergy, like most other professionals in our culture, take the macho approach and try to tough it out themselves. Rabbis generally believe that they are like other successful people in our society who are able to take on difficult problems stoically and find solutions independently. The rabbi uses whatever support is available (colleagues, family, therapist, selected friends) to learn how to "personally" cope with the given and seemingly unchanging realities. Similarly, lay communities generally treat the situation as "personal to the particular rabbi." If the clergy does not fulfill their expectations or is not feeling fulfilled, then it is that particular rabbi's problem to work out.

This current climate of taking the problem as personal creates a mood of confusion, anger and inadequacy. Most rabbis believe that if only they were better speakers, worked longer hours, were more visible, more politically astute, more efficient managers, they could master the problems and feel happier. This situation of clergy burnout will not be solved by focusing on the individual cleric or particular congregations. There is a critical need to view all of these individual instances of stress and burnout as symptoms of a systemic crisis that is affecting the Jewish community. It is important to realize that the pain each rabbi and congregation is feeling is just a little piece of the anguish that is being experienced by the religious leaders and communities as a whole.

Much of this growing sense of frustration and disillusionment is generated by conflicting expectation on the part of the rabbi, the synagogue's board and the congregation. A good place to begin the analysis is to create a discourse where each constituency can voice expectations of the religious leader.

Expectations of the Rabbi

An old rabbinic handbook provides a definition of the rabbi's function which many who enter into the rabbinate still believe:

- The rabbi has a general knowledge of Judaica.

- The rabbi has techniques for passing on knowledge of Judaica, i.e., can teach and give sermons.

- The rabbi can officiate at life cycle events.

- The rabbi has a sense of mission, i.e., feels that the Jewish people have a destiny that will be manifested through the individual synagogues and through the movement into which those synagogues are organized.

Today's rabbinic curriculum follows this basic agenda as it provides the students with tools to be teachers of Jewish tradition. There is virtually no significant focus on synagogue administration, fund raising or counseling. The role of the rabbi is usually seen through the prism of the texts students study, which cast the rabbi's function as a combination of a jurist, teacher, philosopher, healer, priest and prophet. Most aspiring rabbis construct and nourish their vision of their rabbinate on the basis of this understanding.

Furthermore, rabbinic students usually feel a deep religious calling. Their personal relationship with God, while perhaps mysterious and not completely formed is nonetheless of central importance for them. Many enter the rabbinate with a hope that they can share their religious and spiritual inspiration with others, to bring people together by focusing them on their primary relations to God and to God's covenant with the people.

Most students never fully consider or develop the tools, except in the most informal of circumstances, to deal with many of the actual demands that will be placed upon them. The student often does not realize the importance, or formulate a process, of creating a healthy relationship with a board of directors or trustees. Students almost never study the complex dynamics of congregational relations that they are expected to help manage. Rabbis need a more mature understanding of synagogues and their boards. They need to develop the ability to listen to the expectations of the board and the congregation which may differ front their own. They should have learned skills to help the board and the congregation listen to their vision. Consequently, they should be able to facilitate the building of a shared vision based on mutual understanding and partnership.

Expectations of the Board of Directors

It is the board of directors that usually interacts most directly and powerfully with the rabbi. The board ratifies the hire/fire decisions, evaluates performance and decides salary, benefits, convention allowances and other matters that dramatically affect time and focus.

As clergy often do not have a sophisticated understanding of boards, so boards often have no idea how to evaluate a rabbi's skills as a mentor of Jewish tradition. Rather, the directors may feel that they can only judge the rabbi's effectiveness based on the smooth running of the temple as a business organization. Issues of budget, membership numbers, fundraising, employee procedures can be their primary focus. Priorities that may be central to clergy such as prayer, study, observance, social action and covenant with God are too frequently not shared by board members or even considered relevant to the board's function. Accordingly, the board will tend to view clergy primarily in their role as supporting and maintaining the business needs of the operation. So clergy, like other business professionals, are expected to read budgets, direct the other employees, bring in sufficient capital to help the operation continue, and keep things running smoothly. In addition, it becomes assumed that the rabbi will attract and retain members so that there will be sufficient income from dues and donations to support the operation.

This view of the need to keep and attract membership usually translates into many things for the rabbi. The religious leader must be popular. So the rabbi is strongly encouraged to avoid doing things that could lose members and their financial support. The rabbi is forced into a continual popularity contest not only by the concerns of the board, but also by self-interest.

A rabbi's compensation and benefits package is likely to be one of the largest and most conspicuous items in the temple budget. If membership falls off, and revenues decline, board members may eye that seemingly large number in a most critical way. While the board attends to the bottom line out of a sense of responsibility, the rabbi may watch the bottom line out of a need for survival arid financial security.

Excessive concern for holding onto congregants for financial reasons will mean trying to retain all the congregants, no matter how superficial their commitment to the institution or how unceasing their demands. The rabbi may be forced to focus time and energy on those least committed, often least appreciative and least understanding of the role of a congregation and a religious movement. Such members may leave if the wrong thing is said, if someone else is given a desired honor, or if the rabbi does not cater to their whims. Rather than strengthening the core of committed members, a rabbi must often devote an inordinate amount of attention to the periphery of the congregation. And yet, the board expects the rabbi to do what is necessary to keep them as members. If they leave, it is often viewed as the rabbi's failure.

The rabbi may get so caught up in the demands of congregational life that it becomes a continual whirlwind of exhausting activity trying to be successful in all situations and satisfy everyone's expectations. Moreover, the rabbi may be placed in a classic double bind situation. The board needs the rabbi to become sufficiently powerful to accomplish its expectations. However, should the rabbi actually become popular and powerful the lay leaders may become uncomfortable and start to compete with the rabbi for the very power the rabbi thought the board wanted him/her to garner. It is at this point that the rabbi's own needs and vision suffer and are often positioned at such a low priority that they can eventually become lost.

Expectations of Congregants

Perhaps the least definable group of expectations is that of the congregants. Because a congregation is comprised of diverse individuals from varied backgrounds, their expectations will reflect this diversity. It is important to appreciate that many of their expectations were formed by previous experiences. Congregants will often draw uncritically from memories of a previous rabbi to create a model by which the current rabbi will be judged. If their previous clergy person was a great sermonizer, then any "good" rabbi should give great sermons. If they remember their childhood religious leader as having the ability to instantly come up with a good story to fit any occasion, they believe that any decent rabbi should be a great storyteller.

The rabbi is expected to be a teacher, sermonizer, officiant, counselor, healer, advisor, visionary, ambassador, fundraiser and all around fix-it person. The rabbi must be a master teacher, but may not find eager students—either children or adults, the rabbi may end up pretty much alone, but be expected nonetheless to provide the intellectual and spiritual "juice" on which the congregation will run.

The rabbi is called into many families during their most chaotic periods to deal with the happy occasions of birth and marriage, and the grief and terror of divorce, disease and death. The rabbi comforts people, and helps them to struggle with the deep moral and spiritual questions that these radical events bring up. Some of a rabbi's deepest satisfaction may come from this aspect of the work. While this work can be gratifying, it can be enormously stressful. Rabbis both love and hate the potentially addicting drama of being continually on call as a central player to deal with significant life events.

The rabbi goes from a funeral to a baby-naming, from visiting someone who is in a hospital sick with cancer to a meeting with a family about a Bar/Bat Mitzvah. The rabbi is expected to be fully appropriate and empathic in each distinct situation and not carry the emotions from one event to the next, the rabbi who shows up for a Bat Mitzvah planning session is not expected to carry in the grief from a recent funeral. The rabbi presiding at a baby-naming is not expected to show depression over a congregant dying of cancer. The rabbi learns to "manage feelings" and thereby teaches that feelings are to be kept private and not shared by the larger community.

The rabbi does not move in a communal matrix, but rather travels from island to island and bears this burden alone the rabbi cannot focus the healing energies of the community because congregations don't actually function as communities. The members usually don't live in proximity to one another or work together. Many of them don't even socialize together. Rather than serving a function *within* a community, the rabbi begins to function as a paid substitute *for* community. When a family needs sympathy, they can't go to their neighbors (who may not even be friends) or to their extended families (who probably live far away). So they call the rabbi to represent the extended family.

The congregation can be a difficult taskmaster with its variety of demands. While most rabbis retain a deep love for their work and a caring for their congregants, they are frequently running just a bit scared as they try to meet the unending demands. The rabbi might begin to feel like a solitary vending machine dispensing comfort, spirituality, wisdom, as desired by the customer/congregant. The basic goal becomes keeping the congregants happy rather than moving the community to embrace concepts important to Judaism such as holiness, covenants and duty.

As the rabbi reaches back to the beginning, the sense of optimism is recalled, the belief that community could be built, that spirit could be raised, that the tradition could be imbued with richness. The rabbi who ran into the conflicting expectations of the board and the congregants may suffer a frustrated or failed vision.

The loneliness that descends on the clergy is reinforced in a number of ways. The rabbi has few peer relationships to sustain inspiration or in which to share confidences. The rabbi needs to respect the confidentiality of congregants. Unlike a psychotherapist who usually does not interact with patients socially, the rabbi must retain potentially disturbing truths about individuals. Also, unlike therapists who can confront their dysfunctional clients and refer them to another professional if the chemistry is not working, a clergy person knows that a particular difficult congregant may always remain a part of the congregation and be a constant source of irritation. In addition, private information about the rabbi or the family is fair game for gossip. This of course makes it difficult for the rabbi to cultivate trusting friendships with congregants, or with anyone who might associate with a congregant. Rabbis are generally advised against having confidential relationships with congregants or using congregants as accountants or for any business purpose. For many rabbis, it is only other clergy (Jewish and non-Jewish) and non-members that they feel comfortable enough with to not worry about what they say or how they act.

So the rabbi's original expectations of creating a supportive community, the sense of mission regarding the Jewish people and the covenant with God, all begin to be compromised. The idea of spirituality seems less and less relevant to the everyday demands of the job. Study becomes purely instrumental, a quick preparation for the next class to be taught, and the idea of study for its own sake becomes an unattainable luxury. The dreams begin to fade, the passion begins to diminish.

Where Do We Go from Here? The Larger Context

The starting point for this discussion was the way our rabbis are suffering and burning out, partially due to conflicting expectations. We believe that it is crucial to look clearly at the disabling situation in which our clergy work in order to gain an understanding of the malaise affecting our indispensable transmitters of Judaism.

The rabbis of yesteryear, at whom we may look with nostalgia, inhabited a world in which religion was not a matter of choice. As Rabbi Harold Schulweis put it; "My grandfather went to synagogue because he was Jewish. His grandchildren go to synagogue to become Jewish." The rabbis of today cannot rely on the "Jewishness" of their congregants. As Peter Berger puts it in *The Sacred Canopy:*

> [Religions] can no longer take for granted the allegiance of their client populations. Allegiance is voluntary and thus, by definition, less than certain. As a result, the religious tradition, which previously could be authoritatively imposed, now has to be *marketed.* It must be 'sold' to a clientele that is no longer constrained to buy. In this [situation] the religious institutions become marketing agencies and the religious traditions become consumer commodities. A good deal of religious activity in this situation comes to be dominated by the logic of market economics.

As Jewish professionals begin to realize the need to market the tradition to what had previously been a captive or eager audience, they begin to realize that the product is not that easy to sell. People appreciate the tradition in an abstract way, and feel a sentimental obligation to it. Nevertheless, many people, even affiliated Jews, are not integrating the tradition deeply into their lives. Congregants do not seem hungry for Jewish knowledge or living a Jewish lifestyle. In this situation, the rabbi takes on the ultimate burden, not only becoming the CEO and the chief salesperson, but also the main product as well. The rabbi begins to sell personal warmth, wisdom, presence and attentiveness. Thus the rabbi must be everywhere all the time to keep the institution going. In a sense, the rabbi becomes the community, responsible for everyone and responsible to everyone. Unless the rabbis, the lay leadership and the movements can move out of this rut, rabbi burnout will continue along with the further crippling of Judaism.

Where Do We Go from Here? Four Suggestions

Recognizing the presence and magnitude of the problem is one essential step towards resolving it. While there are rabbis who have made peace with and found healthy ways to deal with the many issues presented here, we assert that the problem is real and it will not solve itself. It is necessary to take a broader view and to consider a variety of remedies.

1. *Dialogues with rabbis, lay leadership, and other Jewish professionals.* Rabbis need to be willing to come down from their *bimahs,* take off their robes, and risk sharing their feelings in open dialogues with their lay communities and with each other. It would be important to bring in other Jewish professionals who work with rabbis, especially cantors, educators and administrators who can lend their insights into what is happening to our clergy and other Jewish professionals. All need to first listen to the pain, anger, frustration and dreams of one another before there is the ability to fully understand the other's expectations.

2. *Creation of a congregational Covenant Committee as a way to help generate a continuity of vision.* A Covenant Committee is intended to develop and safeguard an individual synagogue's stated mission. The committee's task is to become a path of continuity that helps connect the past to the future by giving active voice to the congregation's mission statement. While the Covenant Committee formed by a previous board would not overrule the current board, it would assist to balance a board's contemporary focus by contextualizing the present with their perspective of the past and a vision for the future.

3. *Rabbinic associations must take a leadership role by asserting and supporting models which allow rabbis to practice Jewish values of family, study, prayer and acts of religious action.* Rabbis need the support of their rabbinic associations to help receive the backing of boards and the congregations to live their lives in harmony with Jewish values. Rabbinic organizations must speak loudly of the rabbis need to live a life of commitment to the family, study, prayer and

actions in the community. As long as there is virtual silence in the face of the pressure being placed on our clergy to adopt secular standards of success, values of family and study will be viewed as not significant to advancing one's career. This silence results in rabbis being diminished and the Jewish future undermined.

4. *Rabbinic organizations must take leadership roles and support alternative models of congregational services.* Rabbinic seminaries, the rabbinic community and the placement systems appear to support the notion that the bigger a congregation a rabbi has, the more successful that rabbi has become. This bias continues as rabbis from the bigger pulpits are usually appointed to positions of power within rabbinic organizations. Moreover, if an individual decides to remain in a smaller pulpit for a long time, that is often viewed as being stuck. The rabbi is perceived as unable to move up the "corporate ladder" of congregation success rather than congratulated for having found a congregation which has become home. Rabbis are diminished and some creative and needed leaders feel alienated when it is blindly asserted that bigger must be better. Large congregations are needed for a variety of reasons, but too often their attainment has been given a disproportionately high prominence by the institutions that train and support the rabbis.

Those who choose to be chaplains, serve on college campuses, or serve as rabbis in other than the valued, successful, typical congregational format need to be honored as important and indispensable teachers of Israel and Torah.

Many rabbis place family as a high priority and find that a full-time congregation position may be in conflict with that goal. Movements and congregation organizations should view part-time and shared-rabbinates as creative and viable alternatives. There needs to be a rethinking of the common belief that two or more rabbis cannot successfully divide and share responsibilities and work out the other challenges to effectively serve a congregation.

Conclusion

The growing despair among rabbis is a pressing problem for the entire Jewish community. The suggestions advanced in this article can be helpful if they are addressed openly to rabbis, lay leaders, rabbinic training institutions and others. Ultimately, the issues will not be raised if the pain and despair are kept hidden. We hope that this article will inspire all to share spiritual pain and spiritual aspirations more publicly. Such a sharing can inspire deep and empowering dialogue. Such dialogues can transform our community.

Board-Staff Relations:
A Personal Reflection

Rev. Lee Barker

My experience in seminary was pretty much the same as that of every other student. In four years there, I learned nothing of value about Boards and how to work with them. It was my mother who gave me my first piece of advice I could use in the practical world of ministry and church. She didn't mean it to be advice, exactly. The truth is that it was an expression of her own exasperation and I picked it up from there. She was a social work administrator, the first woman in the state of Minnesota to head a county welfare department. She had worked with Boards all of her life. She could guide them with an expert touch and engender from them the most creative leadership. Good thing, too. Her territory was the in the most rural, conservative part of the state. When it came to women in authority, the men who were elected to serve on her Board were neither the most sophisticated nor the most hospitable. Even so, she was able to work her magic with them. Then, a decade into the job, she announced her retirement. When she did, she explained to me, "I knew it was time to quit because I began to talk to the Board as if they were four year old children."

Tucked into that confession are two lasting lessons for the professional whose work takes them into partnership with a Board. First, if one wants to work happily and effectively with a Board, its members will always be granted the greatest respect. And second, in a whole variety of ways, that respect is challenged and tested constantly. This is wisdom well worth integrating into one's religious leadership, an integration which one has no hope of achieving without drawing upon some of the bedrock principles of religion. Hope, honesty, authenticity, surrender, presence, service and spirituality—when these virtues are strong, one can do great work with Boards.

And when they are weak?

A most recent reminder of the ease with which one can come to underestimate a Board came just a few months ago when a well-intentioned and usually savvy colleague of mine found himself under some professional strain and, as a result, made a couple of miscalculations. He had been called to a congregation, which for many years had been burdened by internal conflicts that continued into his tenure. Even so, his ministry was productive and the church thrived. But then, a decade into his ministry, he sent out, inadvertently, a private email to his church's list serve. Eventually it found its way to most every member of his rather large congregation. The email contained some intemperate statements which may not have been obviously egregious, but which could have been perceived as crossing a confidence. A certain segment of the congregation was appalled by this email and, using it as a reason to resurrect old conflicts, took their concern to the Board. Many members of the Board took up the cause of the disgruntled. My friend viewed this as betrayal and told me his strategy was to outlast them, "It won't be long, terms will expire, new members will be elected and all will be forgotten." In the ensuring weeks the momentum gathered, the pressure on the Board became intense and, just a few months after the spark of the original incident, the Trustees negotiated his resignation.

I have no doubt my friend could have survived the mess created by the errant email. By far, most congregations do not ask the clergy to be perfect, only to demonstrate grace and growth in response to our human failings. Under usual circumstances my friend could have seen this. And now in retrospect he can. But once the strain of it all caused my friend to think of the Board as ancillary to his ministry, once he forgot that they were holding at least as many cards as he was, his ministry was over. It was as if he had dismissed them as if they were four-year-old children—all unintentionally. It can happen to the best of us.

My friend should not have been surprised. He had been in the ministry long enough to know even the most passive Boards have a power that can be roused. Best it is roused to move the church in a positive and bold new direction. Best it is roused by a vision that is rooted in religion and sweeps to greatness.

In order to stay motivated and focused the Board must have a sharp sense of where it is going and what it is aiming to do. The minister is called to foster that visionary leadership.

It has been my happy discovery that my own theology, and the theology of the congregations I have served, has lent itself perfectly to empowering effective Boards of Trustees. It is a theology that suggests there is a relationship between service and spirituality. The only reason to be engaged in the work of religion is to effect some positive transformation either in the private, spiritual self or in the public arena of the larger world. And the two are interwoven. I so much like the way Dag Hammarskjöld put it when he wrote, "In our era the road to holiness passes through the world of action." We cannot be content with leaving the world as it was when we were born into it. We will find our own spiritual fulfillment by serving both those who are known and unknown to us, those in our immediate circle and those of future generations. Nudge the world and its people out of their brokenness and usher them toward wholeness.

It is a theology of action, and if it is to be fully realized it cannot be fenced off from the work of the Board. The cleric who believes it is "unministerial" to be engaged in the affairs of a congregation's governance, who takes no interest in the Board's nominating process or who does not lend any help in training its members; that is a cleric whose Board runs the risk of falling to the forces of fragmentation and brokenness.

It could be that each situation requires its unique solution to guide its leaders to serving that vision of wholeness. On the other hand, there are some certain solutions that have merit no matter who the players are and what ground they occupy. I think about the first congregation I served and how those universal solutions manifest themselves.

> Even now, at age fifty, I am the owner of a youthful looking face. When I took that first pulpit at age twenty-five I appeared positively pubescent. Visitors would attend worship and, seeing me in the chancel, would assume that our little congregation was observing a special "Youth Sunday." My theory is that one reason my candidacy appealed to the search committee was that is that I was young. After all, the previous pastor was accused of possessing a rather controlling nature, one which led to all sorts of hurt feelings, disempowerment of the congregation and, in the end, a big church fight. The result was a church that had no functional Sunday school, a building that had been neglected and was in serious disrepair, and an under actualized social outreach program. In short, it was a seriously spiritually bereft church.

I knew that somewhere in its collective subconscious the congregation wanted their next minister to be one *they* could control. I also knew that there was no way I could be that easily controlled minister they sought. It just wasn't me. It is mandatory to be dead honest with oneself, to know in the most unvarnished way who one is and whom one is serving. One cannot afford to see it rosy. Obstacles that are not acknowledged are obstacles that can never be overcome.

One must also be able to see beyond the obstacles, to what the church may one day be and to bring that vision alive within the governing body.

In that first church I did two things at the outset. First, I persuaded the Board to go on a retreat, a kind of a get to know one another weekend that would allow us to do our human equivalent of sniffing and wagging so we could see how our working relationship might develop. Second, while waiting the several weeks for that retreat to take place, I cultivated a relationship with a few Board members who seemed to be impatient with the lack of forward motion in the church. There was one man in particular who I thought might serve as a willing partner in jump-starting the Board. He was born in our denomination and bred in our ways, something that is a bit unusual in our movement, but which often leads to the fiercest desire to see our churches succeed. He was a businessman who was used to aiming high and getting results from taking that high aim. We talked for hours, at downtown lunches, in the church parking lot after meetings, at dinners which would have otherwise been social occasions. Throughout I tired to lend him the kind of presence out of which his desires for the church could well up. The magic was kindled. In time he become quite effusive about his hopes for offer a better religious education for our children, for restoring our sorry building, and for extending our passion for justice so we could make a difference in people's lives. By the time the retreat opened with worship, he was ready to voice this new, revitalized direction for this church.

It didn't come from the minister. I had been called with both affection and suspicion. It came from one of their own. And he was a bulldog kind of guy who was unable to hear the hesitancy and reluctant response of his fellow Board members. They were dubious that their conflicted, anemic church could pull together and muscle up for such bold moves, but they could not so immediately figure out how to say that clearly to him. When the retreat came to its end on Saturday afternoon, there was a plan in place to move the church forward within three years. It was a beginning. And within a week, before other Trustees could find a way to naysay it, I took it to the congregation.

I remember what I said, almost to a word. It was in a sermon titled, "The State of the Church". I said, "I am in awe of the Board of Trustees of our church. They are such a spiritually strong group of men and women. They are the kind of leaders who feel so passionately about what this religion of ours has to offer, who believe so strongly in the transforming nature of the church, that they are willing to take the of risk articulating a vision for us that will serve as our guide for the years to come. And if I am impressed by them, I am doubly impressed by you, for you are the people who elected them to their positions. You took the courageous step of lifting up leaders who had the capacity to change your church and in doing so, alter your very religious lives." It seemed to do the trick. This was not disingenuous flattery. It was the attempt to hold each person accountable for the actions they took that got us to these new circumstances. And doing it in a flattering way! And it worked. After that, there was no turning back either for the Board or for most everyone else in the congregation.

Most everyone

In the spirit of full disclosure, I should add that our stronger, more visionary Board did not meet with unanimous approval. There were those who protested, decrying what they considered to be an undemocratic and authoritarian superstructure. These were enflaming words to religious liberals and I admit that the charges caused me to second-guess myself. As the few fell away, however, more mature Board members persuaded me that the church could not advance itself if it were to capitulate to the voices. They church had stumbled along with weak leadership, now it was time to try another way. The Board was clear. I got clearer. By the time I moved to my next ministry, the church was stronger than it ever had been in its entire 60-year history.

No institution moves forward without a shakeup in its power relationships. And when the shift takes place the fearful act out in ways that would drag it backwards. In responding to those people compassion is in order and so is patience. But the strength of the vision must hold. If my Board had a strategy for me in those days, it was teach me that lesson once and for all

As for my own strategy with the Board, I see the behind the scenes coaching and encouragement as a strategy of hope. It is a strategy that Erich Fromm might have endorsed. Fromm is the social philosopher who wrote in his book, *The Revolution of Hope*, "Hope is paradoxical. It is neither passive waiting nor is it the unrealistic forcing of circumstances that cannot occur. It is like the crouched tiger which will jump only when the moment for jumping has come … to hope means to be ready at any moment for that which is not yet born … those whose hope is strong see and cherish all sign of new life and are ready at every moment to help the birth of that which is ready to be born."

A minister's work with a Board is the world of hope. It is also the work of trust.

One colleague told me about the predicament he found himself with one Board president. The back-story is that for many years there had been in the church a commonly held fantasy that one day they would merge with another, nearby congregation. In recent years the other church had fallen on hard times and had dwindled to a couple dozen stalwarts. In one of their regular meetings, the president told the minister that she had been exploring the possibility of a merger with the president of the other congregation and, because of their vulnerability; they were prepared to enter into a negotiation with their church. She would like to bring it up at the next Board meeting. "Of course," he said, "How wonderful." But he did not mean it. He actually had no heart for the merger. But when it came before the Board, he publicly supported it and helped to construct a lengthy, complex process by which the congregation could consider it. He explained to me that he had no choice because the president of the church was a good friend of his and she had worked so hard to secure the negotiation that he did not wish to disappoint her. He then worked behind the scenes to defeat the measure. In the end, with the fallout of disappointment and heartache, it was defeated. And although the Board never caught on to truth of his opposition, they knew something was amiss. At the very least they knew that their minister was not totally invested in the merger. His enthusiastic words were not backed by any action. The whole effort took a huge amount of Board energy, detracted from other initiatives that would have enjoyed more ministerial favor, and ended with a big fizzle.

I love my dear colleague, but I cannot manufacture the excuse that would affirm such in authenticity, no matter how well intended. If a Board cannot count on their spiritual leader to tell them the truth, the whole truth, then we have no right to expect from them the truth, the whole truth. And that is no way to live, not professionally and not religiously.

I don't mean to make this last observation seem so obvious or easy to enact. It is neither. There are subtle ways to not tell the whole truth, so subtle that it can escape one's own detection. But it will always undermine one's effectiveness in working with Boards. The biggest mistake most ministers make fits into this category of deception. It might be called the cheerleader syndrome.

Earlier in my ministry, whenever I advanced a new idea, I did not allow myself to consider its downside. I was only a cheerleader for every good thing that would result from moving forward with a new plan or program. Of course there is always a downside, losses if you will, associated with any new way of doing things. Without admitting that to myself I could not admit it to the Board members and they, in turn, could not arrive at the conclusion that the potential gains outweighed the losses.

My best example of this is the way I introduced the possibility of going from one Sunday morning worship service to two. In both my second and third churches, due to surges in Sunday attendance, this was an issue that had to be faced by the lay leadership. In the first instance, I served as chief cheerleader for the idea of going to two services. I told the Board every good thing that would come from holding two worship services, most especially how it would allow us to grow in numbers and therefore in budget and program. I never identified some of the difficulties that would also come as a result of moving in that direction, the initial empty feeling in the sanctuary, the feelings of lost intimacy members of the community might experience, the pain of lunching a second Sunday School program. After the decision to move forward was made, and these obstacles arose, the Board was unprepared and a bit resentful. They even started to second-guess the decision.

I handled the situation much differently the next time around. In that instance I took every opportunity to point out the pains that would be incurred by moving to two sessions of worship. I also trumpeted my conviction that the innovation was worth it. The Board agreed with me and, when all my prognostications came true, they were not surprised at all. Indeed they had taken measures to soften the impact of the changes. Everyone was so much better off by my own newfound ability to voice the truth, the whole truth.

Life with a Board has so many hallmarks of the political arena that it is easy to be seduced into viewing ones relationship to it as a principally political relationship. But for those of us with a faith-based orientation, it is religion that links us to those folks. And that is something never to forget, even to the point of paying special attention to the spiritual lives of those who serve the church in that capacity.

My wife recently commented that I seem to take on a greater pastoral counseling role with members of the Board than I do with other members of the congregation. She was right. In a church our size, the senior minister could become too thinly spread in the pastoral role. It is essential to delegate much of that work to other staff members. But not when it comes to members of the Board. They give so much to their church, most often at great sacrifice. The level of service required of them is greater than other lay leadership positions. The pressures on them are unique. They always have the possibility of burning out and feeling as if their church takes more from them than it returns. It is important for them to know otherwise. So I make myself available to them. Indeed, I try to initiate pastoral calls on Board members, just to see how they are doing, and if there is anything their church (aka, me) can do for them, to boost them through the demanding period of their term. I make sure to articulate the religious dimension of their service during Board meetings, to acknowledge the spiritual growth that they demonstrate collectively and as individuals through their time on the Board. First and foremost this work with the Board is a ministry. In order for the Board members to guide the larger congregation in the ways of service, it is essential that they be in touch with the ways they have been transformed by service themselves. When they exhibit that awareness, they emit a gravity of purpose and meaning that will keep even the most burned out minister from ever talking to them as if they were four-year-old children.

In the course of writing these reflections, I was approached by one of our denomination's seminaries about the possibility of taking up its presidency. I was honored by the overture, but not at all certain I wanted to accept it. It so happened, at the time of the invitation, I was slated to begin a term as a member of the school's Board of Trustees. Still uncertain, I went off to my first meeting where I took witness of the hopes that body had for the school. They were clear about what they wanted. They wanted to double the size of the student body. They wanted to revitalize its program for public ministry. They wanted their school to be widely regarded as one of the three or four anchor institutions of our denomination, making its voice heard on the most consequential issues of contemporary religion. They wanted to build a new campus that could host all who would take advantage of a growing continuing education program. And yet the school had a recent history of failing to pull off plans of such magnitude. Like every educational institution it has been the focus for people of competing interests and, not wanting to promote one interest over another, it allowed itself to be stymied in its own efforts to move forward.

As the meeting continued I took note of a Board that was both talented and commitment. They lacked a necessary ingredient that could allow them to turn around the history of failure: they laced the ability to say why they wanted to grow their school so dramatically. If I were president, I thought, I would round them up and sequester them ion a retreat. I would offer them a bit of guidance and experience, a little inspiration too, and I would try to kindle within each and every one of them the ability to say, "Here is the religious reason to grow our school…." Then would be time to tap that reservoir of talent, to help them plan the strategies by which they could shape that school of their dreams. When I caught myself thinking that way, I knew I was hooked. I accepted the invitation and in just a few weeks, we will join together in retreat.

The members of the Board are not thinking this way, I am sure, but if they will let me, I am about to become a principle ministerial presence in their lives. I'll pay attention to their spiritual lives. I will help them more strongly link their service to the school and their own religious lives. In some sense, this new calling just begun, I feel as if I am starting in the ministry all over again.

My final official act at the church I served for the past nine years was one that I did not have to perform. There was a final meeting of the Trustees. I didn't have to attend. Not really. I had already said my tearful goodbyes many times. I had heard the expressions of love that been bestowed on me, enough to warm my heart for the next years. There was no more official business over which I could have any influence. But I attended the meeting anyway. How could I not? All the success that church and I enjoyed emanated most directly from my work with that Board. I had to say goodbye and tell them one more time how grateful I was for all they had given to our church and our liberal religion. To not do that would have been to disregard all that my mother taught me so many years ago. My last words to them were words of the deepest gratitude:

Thank you for allowing me to do this work with you as we have lifted this church to a greater plain.
Thank you for bringing out my best and most creative self in my work with you.
Thank you for allowing my ministry to be one, which was focused on possibility and hope.
Thank you for always articulating a far-reaching vision for our church and the world.
Thank you for demonstrating the unbreakable connection between service and spirit.
Thank you for reciprocating my great wellspring of love for you.

Oh please, when my time with the seminary is completed, let me be able to say the exact same words to the Board of that institution. Oh, please.

Reference

Fromm E. (1968) *The Revolution of Hope: Towards a Humanized Technology* New York, Harper and Row.

Scenarios from Real Life

These scenarios are selected from among hundreds I have collected over the years. While I have disguised the city and/or the organization, they are all from real life. They were shared with me by board and staff members, clergy, and educators (the latter not too frequently represented here), in the course of seminars, courses, consultations, and correspondence.

They reflect complications, which reflect a number of issues. Power-sharing concerns, unclear role clarification, status issues, insensitivity on the part of the board members, and personality tensions are but some of the real life happenings captured here.

They are cast in different forms, thus allowing differential use. Some can be discussed between two staff people; yet others between staff and board members. Some are set up to allow for small groups and/or individuals acting them out for larger group discussions. In most instances, questions have been raised for consideration. They are by no means comprehensive and the reader will undoubtedly add even more.

Most importantly, they reflect the concerns of hundreds and keep popping up in one form or another in organizations throughout the world.

New Leader Wants to Make Changes

A new president of a youth organization has been elected primarily because of her family connections and great wealth. The executive director had some qualms when her name was suggested for consideration. While she had been on the board for two years, her major activities had been with other organizations. The nominating committee had reservations but felt that a high-status, visible president could play an important role in the United Way, as a member of its executive committee and as one who knew many members of the United Way's allocation committee.

After her election, the director suggests they meet together to review her agenda for her term and to begin a planning process vis-à-vis choosing committee chairs, reviewing programs more seriously than she had previously, and the like.

She announces to the director that while she herself had no experience as a youth in the organization, the organization's mission had to be the community's highest priority and was too important to be left to the professionals.

She previously had indicated how much respect she had for the director, even though she notified him that serious administrative changes would have to be initiated.

As a self-designated change agent, she was taking strong action to implement her goals because she only had two years.

As the director, what would you feel your agenda with her would have to be at this first meeting? Do you view her as a greater or lesser asset than the nominating committee had hoped for? Can you identify strengths you would work on with her? What would you try to do to strengthen a relationship with her grounded in mutual trust?

Should an Executive Participate in By-Law Revision Committee Meetings?

The chairperson of a business and professional women's organization has charged an ad hoc committee with the task of revising their by-laws. The executive director (staff) wants to be a participating member of the committee. The volunteer leadership wants to develop their own by-laws without his participation, knowing they will have to obtain board approval, at which time the executive director can input ideas.

The director feels very strongly that he should be at the meetings in order to give his input into the revision process and to help assure acceptance of the by-laws by the executive committee and the board of directors.

Prepare a scenario, which leads to the inclusion of the director in the process. Include reasoning as to the appropriateness of the director being involved.

Prepare a second scenario, which keeps the executive out of the process until the ad hoc committee presents their findings to the executive committee. In this scenario, first deal with the reasoning for keeping the director out of the process. Then include a presentation to the executive committee where the director hears the new by-laws for the first time. Indicate what you feel the director might do at this point.

Assign people roles to present this scenario in a skit lasting no more than 6 minutes for both parts of the presentation.

Volunteer Leader Wants the Title but Does Not Do the Work

An executive is the professional head of a human service agency with very high status. It has long been a tradition for certain families to be involved in the agency's governance. They proudly played significant roles in governance, learning as much as possible about the agency's services through reading reports, observing those services which were not confidential in their nature, even serving as service volunteers as a way to give of themselves, and see the agency in action from that vantage point.

One of the family members, because of his family ties, was brought on the board a few years ago. He indicated his desire to be named president-elect after three years as a board member, even though he took no volunteer service role and observed no programs, as was evident by his participation on the board over the three-year period. The nominating committee felt it had no choice but to name the person president-elect and did so with the director's acquiescence.

He is still in his first year and makes no effort to educate himself. He chairs some key committees but asks the executive to prepare the agendas and then, in effect, turns the meetings over to be run by the executive director. There is one more year before he will ascend to the presidency.

Should the director make peace with having an essentially non-functioning president? To whom can she turn for help? What are some specific steps to be taken if the answer to the first question is "no"? What would you need to know that you have not learned from this scenario to help you as director to act?

Staff Member Mediates between Wealthy President & Young Adults' Group

The young adults' group at the YMCA is interested in community affairs and also is committed to serving the "Y". The group's leadership is having a board meeting with a staff person when the president appears unannounced. She is a very prominent person with great wealth who, together with her husband, is a very generous giver. The young adults are clearly awed by the unexpected appearance of the president. The chairperson stops the meeting to welcome the president and also asks her if she wishes to say anything to the group. The president thanks the chairperson for the opportunity and proceeds to ask the group to sponsor a major fundraiser for the YMCA—a concert which would have to be held in six weeks because a famous entertainer would be available on that date.

Just watching the group's faces, the staff person realizes that the undertaking could not be successfully implemented in the time required. He waits for the chairperson to say something but he does not. The staff person decides to intervene and turns to the president, pointing out that while the idea was a great one, there is no possibility of successfully planning and implementing the event in the requested time frame. The president continues to press the group while totally ignoring the staff person.

Once again, the staff person intervenes after no member says anything, repeating what he had said before. Twice more the cycle is repeated with pressure from the president, silence from the members, and interpretation from the staff as to why the request could not be fulfilled. After the third request, and the third attempted intervention by the staff person, the YMCA president turns to the staff person, angrily pointing out that at no time had she addressed her remarks to the staff person, and asks the staff person to be quiet. The president then voices her strong expectation of receiving a positive response to her request, and leaves the room.

Prepare a group to act this out with three people taking the roles of the president, the young adult chairperson, and the staff person. Decide on what the staff person should do after the president leaves. If you wish to have the staff person play a different role in the room, do so. In any case, be prepared to explain your decision.

What would you have done?

Power of a Wealthy Donor

You are the director of the women's division of a fundraising organization. You receive a call from a volunteer leader whose connections are integral to the upcoming fundraiser. She wants to know why her best friend, Anne, cannot go on a special fundraising trip to New York. Anne donates $2,000 each year. The volunteer's husband donates $10,000. You explain that the minimum gift for the trip is $5,000. The volunteer leader states that she is covered by her family gift and her friend should be as well.

What do you do? What do you say to the volunteer leader? How would you react if the volunteer leader stated that she would withdraw her assistance to the upcoming fund-raiser unless her friend was invited on the trip?

Clarification of Roles: Staff vs. Board

A women's division director (staff) puts herself into all planning activities for women's events/programs, and performs activities for implementation that are usually completed by volunteers on committees. She also makes some major decisions on her own, without consulting with volunteer leadership.

The chairperson (volunteer) of the women's division is new and has heard complaints by the members of her division. She feels she must get clarification from the women as to what they expect of staff and in turn clarify with the staff person what roles are appropriate.

The staff person feels that the committee has never understood the roles which staff can perform and should play in helping the division achieve its goals. She is eager to meet with the new chairperson.

The two meet. Have each person deal with the issue from her respective perspective. Then stage a presentation that lasts no more than five minutes. Be prepared to discuss the issues that this scenario personifies.

Minister *Emeritus* is Still Attached

New Faith Church, a small but diverse congregation, is the only Protestant church in town. Pastor George Olsen was hired by the congregation immediately following his ordination some fifteen years ago. Each of his contract renewal negotiations over the years was difficult and stressful; each time, his contract renewal was passed by a scant majority on the board. He was perceived to be a "divisive figure" because congregants were either strongly attached to him or profoundly alienated from him. He was never accused of unethical behavior, though his views were not always popular and he tended to express his opinions in strong language. In his fifteenth year, the board carried out a protracted and painful performance review of the minister, which involved polling the congregants by mail. Following the performance review, a congregational meeting was called to vote on renewing Pastor Olsen's contract. After a stormy debate, those present voted not to renew his contract. At the minister's request, and as a means of affording him a more dignified departure, the board agreed to designate him as minister *emeritus* of the congregation. Pastor Olsen was awarded a generous severance package and, after several months, accepted a position in a community about two hundred miles away.

While the church searches for a new minister, they are being served part-time by Pastor Smith on an interim basis. Meanwhile, many families remain attached to Pastor Olsen and are unhappy that he was "forced out" of the congregation. Several have asked Pastor Olsen to officiate at weddings and funerals. The board president and interim minister both feel that Pastor Olsen's presence at events of this type is likely to further polarize the church members. On the other hand, they are concerned that if they forbid his participation (he is, after all, minister *emeritus*), they will further alienate, and possibly even lose, some of their membership.

You are the board president for New Faith Church. Pastor Olsen performed your wedding, but you recognize that these problems are potentially destructive if they continue. What can you say or do to help mitigate the exacerbation of Pastor Olsen's continuing activities?

In the second scenario, you are Pastor Smith. Your concerns as interim minister have led you to ask for a meeting with your predecessor. You are respectful of all he did, and yet are sensitive to what it means to be an emeritus minister. Still, you are convinced that polarizing has already taken place and will be irreversible if steps are not taken soon to have Pastor Olsen become inactive in the congregation

You are Pastor Olsen. You have been called in to meet with the congregational president to discuss the next steps regarding the president and Pastor Smith's feelings. Play your role out in a responsible and dignified way. You know of their concerns, but feel you have earned the "right" to continue your activities.

The Assigned Seating Dilemma: Rewarding Generosity vs. Egalitarianism

A petition has been presented to the board of directors to eliminate assigned seating at a charity fundraising concert. Your three largest givers (third generation) from the same family notify you as a staff professional that they will stop supporting the organization if assigned seats are eliminated.

The members insist on meeting with the board of directors to resolve this, knowing they have a majority lined up on the board. The president has called the meeting even though you have counseled otherwise.

What would you do before the meeting?

Volunteer/Staff Differences over Fundraising Policy

Conflict resulted when co-chairs of a community campaign decided that a minimum gift to a fundraising event should be $100 even though the previous year's minimum was $250. The staff person and her supervisor met with the co-chairs and convinced them that the gift should be at least the same as the previous year. Through further discussion with the committee, the end result was the arrangement of a two-part event where those who attended the cocktail hour and dessert buffet were asked for $250 and those who attended only the dessert buffet were asked for a minimum of $100. A program, including a speaker and tribute to the community's clergy, was scheduled between the cocktail hour and dessert, thereby permitting all attendees to take part in that portion of the overall program.

What was the staff's goal? What was the hope of the volunteers? When are they incompatible? If there is a policy issue involved, what is it?

Co-Chairs have Personality Conflict

A young women's division of an organization was co-chaired by two women who were supposed to have equal responsibility. However, the second year co-chair felt that she deserved more seniority, while the first year co-chair did not like how the division had functioned in the past and wanted to take charge of the situation. The two of them had very different personalities and leadership styles as well as very different ideas about the direction of the division. They did not enjoy working together, and they tried to have as little contact as possible with one another.

The staff person used several intervention approaches. She involved the overall women's division leadership (their advisors) to impress upon them the importance of cohesiveness for the good of the division. She also served as the facilitator and intermediary. Before every meeting and whenever a decision had to be made, she either initiated a conference call for all three of them, or she talked to each co-chair individually and reported back to them on the other's opinion.

How does this approach affect the leadership of the co-chairs? As staff, could the situation have been handled differently?

Role play a meeting between the staff person and the co-chairs to discuss the leadership of the young women's division.

What would you do?

An Executive [staff] Deals with a Powerful New President

A Community Center executive director (staff) has been in the city for four years. He has established sound and positive relations with colleagues in and out of the agency and with all Center board members and most United Way board members.

The Community Center is a high status agency and has a number of third generation leaders. One of these in particular was "fast-tracked" into the presidency by his peers, though he is known to be impetuous, competitive, self-centered, tough, yet a creative, visionary, and charismatic person. His status with the power structure is unparalleled.

Before the first board meeting he and the executive met. The director urged the new president to spend five or ten minutes at the beginning of the meeting to outline his hopes for his incumbency. There was other business to conduct and a mutually arrived at agenda was developed with appropriate time as agreed upon allocated to each issue or report on the agenda.

At the meeting the new president spoke for forty-five minutes without interruption. He juggled the balance of the meeting's agenda on the spot.

Before the next meeting a number of key board members called the director, voicing their displeasure and concern. Two announced their readiness to resign.

What would you do as the executive director? List the advantages and disadvantages of discussing the meeting with the president alone? List the advantages and disadvantages of involving other officers in that meeting?

Are there variables you can think of which would guide your role, immediately and in the long run, in the kind of relationship you would like to have with this very powerful person?

Accountability of Volunteers

A frequent source of tension between professionals and volunteers is the fact that volunteers cannot be held accountable to the same degree as those who are being paid by an organization. In some instances, professional organizations, which rely heavily upon volunteers, may find that their investment in training the volunteers is not sufficiently repaid.

A rape crisis hotline was staffed entirely by volunteers who had undergone an intensive, forty-hour training by professional staff members of the local rape crisis center. The training sessions were a great investment of time and energy for the professional staff, involving the dedication of evenings and weekends beyond their regular hours. However, the "payoff" was equally great, for without volunteers to staff the hotline and to volunteer a few hours each month, the valuable social services could not have continued to function.

Participating in rape crisis training became a popular extra-curricular activity for many local students, providing a chance to engage in a worthwhile cause while meeting interesting fellow classmates. The training sessions were usually filled to capacity, with many students put on a waiting list for the following semester. At the start of each session, the professional staff made it clear that the training was not to be viewed as an end in itself, but as the first step in an ongoing commitment to the rape crisis center. However, at the end of each semester, the number of students who chose to begin working for the hotline was small. The professionals were unable to prevent this pattern from continuing. Finally, they made an inevitable decision to discontinue the training sessions.

Do you agree with this decision to discontinue the training sessions? What are the job expectations for the staff and for the volunteers? Who is accountable for the lack of commitment beyond training? What could have been done to produce a different outcome?

Choosing a Good Volunteer Leader

The campaign chair of the country club division is a very successful businessman, yet his role as a volunteer was marked by limited organizational ability, poor follow-through, and indecisiveness. The professional's attempts to help him calendar events, create and follow an agenda, and review pledge cards were in vain. While his peers viewed him as amiable, he was not a leader. The campaign was in danger, so the professional, the general campaign chair, and the executive stepped in and took action to plan a huge event that was very successful. They virtually bypassed the chair, although they gave him many opportunities to participate.

When choosing a leader, what needs to be included in the selection process? What attributes are essential to being a successful leader? What are the responsibilities of the board members and of the volunteer leaders?

List some of the effects of the decision of the professional, general campaign chair, and executive to plan the event themselves around the division chair.

Preparation of Volunteer Leaders and Staff People for New Program

Sarah, a staff person, was assigned to a new program. She was to work with a volunteer leader assigned to be the chair, to convince this volunteer of the worth of the program, and then have the lay leader present the program to a committee, which would further develop the program.

Sarah had several meetings with the volunteer leader. However, Sarah did not seem completely invested in the project. She did not know all the facts of the program since it was still in its beginning stages and many of the major decisions had not been made because they were to be made by the committee. Despite this, Sarah prepared the volunteer leader to the best of her ability. This was Sarah's first time preparing a chair, and neither of her supervisors was able to meet with her beforehand. The volunteer chairperson felt inadequately prepared for the meeting. During the meeting, the program was completely redone upon suggestion of the committee, but the volunteer leader felt out of control of the meeting. She brought this issue to Sarah's supervisor and complained about Sarah.

How do you imagine that this scenario ended?

Role play the meeting between the volunteer leader and the supervisor. Next, role play the meeting between Sarah and the supervisor, and finally, between Sarah and the volunteer leader.

How could Sarah and her supervisor have directed the process more efficiently?

Who Decides Fundraising Policy at Community Events?

A conflict arose regarding card calling at a community event. It was pre-determined by community leadership that there would be no card calling. Area campaign and board chairs decided at the last minute there should be. They put much pressure on staff to prepare the cards. The outcome was there was no card calling at the event, as it was deemed unnecessary and was contradictory to the wishes and plans of community leadership.

How, where, and when are decisions best made? Are these policy or practice issues? How should the decision-making process best be clarified?

A Job Poorly Done: The Tactful Solution

The outreach coordinator for a fundraising organization headed the prospect development effort. Her chair was one of the top volunteer leaders. He had a very strong personality and many captivating ideas. He was also very difficult to work with. The professional neglected to arrange for an initial meeting where the two of them would discuss a "general agenda" for the committee. Unfortunately, he arranged a committee structure inappropriate for the overall mission of prospect development and proceeded to take the prospect development effort on a different course than where the organization wanted it.

Specifically, he arranged a committee of many top leaders where they met and discussed current donors and how to upgrade their gifts. Originally, prospect development was to concentrate on non-donors and how to obtain new gifts. What actually occurred was not the best use of leadership time nor was it financially productive for the organization.

Due to inexperience on the professional's part, she was unable to redirect the efforts of this volunteer leader. What transpired was the development of files on individuals whom they already knew in the community. This information on major donors was valuable and it was passed to the director of major gifts. However, it was not what the committee was established to do and the committee did not accomplish the goals it had gone in with.

What steps could the staff person have taken to curtail this situation? What are the underlying issues between the staff person and the volunteer leaders? What potential problems may arise between the two and how can they be solved?

President Makes Promises He Cannot Keep

A large city planning organization is coordinating a capital campaign. The process of making this decision is through a task force specifically established to analyze the potential impact on the regular annual campaign as well as the overall capital needs of the community. The committee questions whether it would be best to let each institution raise money independently or through a comprehensive capital campaign.

Throughout the process the staff person supporting the committee feels that, in the long term, the community will not derive the greatest benefit from a coordinated campaign. This opinion is reinforced by information he has received from colleagues in other communities. During this period, though, the president has had discussions with many of the significant volunteer leaders in the various institutions and promised them that the organization will "come through." The president insists that a decision must be reached prior to the end of his term of office. During the final week of his term, an announcement is made that there will be a coordinated capital campaign. The staff is certain that this is the wrong decision.

A new president comes in and reverses this decision—there will not be a coordinated campaign. The organizers of the institutions are angry and feel that the organization has let them down. Each is now encouraging their constituencies not to support the annual campaign.

What is the responsibility of the organization in question to these institutions? Who should be involved in the decision-making process? How does the reversal of this decision affect the institutions? How does it affect how staff and volunteer leaders perceive the new president?

What are short-term and long-term implications of this decision?

Choosing a Committee Chair

A young aspiring tax lawyer wants to be the chairman of the endowment committee. The president and the professional who staffs the committee confer on it and agree that a more veteran leader, with great prestige in the community, would be a better choice. The young lawyer is angry with the staff person and blames him for the action.

What is the source of the conflict? Where does the power lie in this situation? Role play a brief scenario between the young lawyer and the staff person.

Allocation Formula When Funds Fall Short

In advance of the campaign, the board has established a pre-campaign budgeting formula, which sets percentages for overseas, national, and local agencies. This has been announced to the community as part of campaign interpretation.

The campaign raises only a little more money than last year and the preliminary budget figures indicate that local agencies will have to reduce services in order to stay within the budget. Advocates of local needs argue that the formula should be changed because no one anticipated the requirement to cut local services and people in real need will be hurt if the formula is maintained. Advocates of overseas and the campaign leadership argue against a change in the formula for the following reasons: some major gifts were made in consideration of the announced division for the funds, and it is unethical and unwise for the organization to renege on its stated policy. Additionally, they feel that many supporters will be offended.

Prepare a scenario detailing a debate of the issue. What is the outcome? Be prepared to defend a position.

Changing a Policy to Accommodate a Volunteer Leader

A volunteer leader wanted to alter the schedule for a public event that had already been decided upon and handed to the staff person by her supervisor. The volunteer leader was very angry and adamant about the desired change. The staff person explained the process that led up to the current program and why it was too late—process-wise and practically—to alter it now. The volunteer leader was still upset, so the staff person referred him to her supervisor for further discussion on the matter.

Who sets the policy? Who is involved in the decision-making? What are the staff and volunteers' responsibilities to each other? Role play a scenario between the volunteer leader and the supervisor. How would you handle this situation?

Too Much Power for a Wealthy Donor

There is a small community center in a rural area whose members are mostly working and middle class. Due mostly to the efforts of a committed and creative program director, the center has vibrant programming, cutting-edge pre-school, and excellent adult education.

Most of the administration is handled by volunteers, including bookkeeping. A new treasurer has just been elected and it will be her responsibility to pay the bills and make monthly financial reports to the board. When the treasurer receives the checkbooks and bank statements from the previous treasurer, she finds that nothing has been entered into the checkbook register in three years. After reviewing the bank statements, she finds the community center is $40,000 overdrawn from the bank and there is no money to make payroll.

The president of the board approaches a wealthy member of the community to bail out the center. The wealthy member says he will cover the $40,000 and help the community center through the year, if they fire the program director.

What would you do? What are the principles involved? Who holds the power? Develop a five-minute scenario that highlights the issues raised here.

Director of Education and Board President Clash

The director of education at a community outreach center felt that there was ongoing tension with the board president. The president never said "yes" to a single request, as if her job was to keep the professional in line and to be tough. The director felt very unsupported and uncared for by the center. As a result, she did not say anything but decided not to renew her contract after a year.

What steps could the director have taken to attempt to improve her situation? How does the staff person view her role? Does the president view it the same way?

How Volunteer Leader Sees Staff Person and Vice Versa

A volunteer leader for a budgetary layout project disagreed with the professional's chosen forms and labeled her figures incorrect when in fact the numbers worked. In the end, the professional's format won because it was in keeping with the department format and her supervisor stepped in.

Does the staff person see the volunteer as a puppet? Does the volunteer see the staff person as a secretary? Do they take each other's ideas seriously? Role play a scenario attempting to resolve the dispute between the staff person and the volunteer.

Tension between Volunteer Chairperson and Staff Person

The chairperson for a fundraising project did not have a good working relationship with his staff person, which led to frequent tension-filled telephone conversations and meetings. He was distrusting of the staff person from the beginning, questioning everything that she did and holding her accountable for circumstances beyond her control. She responded to him by trying to reason through each situation. This approach only made him more upset and, consequently, the relationship became a negative one.

How does the volunteer leader see his role? How does the staff person see her own role? Do they view one another's roles similarly? How would you—as a staff person—intervene in this situation? How would you as a board member deal with this?

Enthusiasm and Immaturity in a Leader

Ed, a minimally involved volunteer leader, had returned from a leadership development conference very enthusiastic about what he had seen and the volunteer leaders he had met.

A staff person was starting a new assignment and looking for leadership. She contacted the three local participants of this conference. Aside from Ed, the other two were not very receptive to meeting to discuss their experiences. Ed could not wait to talk about what he learned at the conference. The professional told Ed about her plans and his response was "tell me what I can do."

They worked together for the following two years to develop a new leadership group and involved many new people due in no small part to Ed's enthusiasm and hard work. In the process, Ed's self-confidence grew to the point where he was able to suggest new projects and expect them expedited. Although these ideas sometimes demonstrated his immaturity both personally as well as in relation to the organization, he took the staff person's criticism, pouted a bit, and went on from there.

He seemed to have learned something about working with others, was respected by his peers, and gained recognition from the United Way, rising to a leadership position. However, his working relationship with other staff had left something to be desired. Many found him stubborn, immature, demanding, and inflexible. The professional believed that she might have helped Ed more if she were not so understanding and supportive initially since he grew to expect this from everyone. The staff person also felt that it might have been better in the long-run had she explained the impossibilities of certain requests and demands on staff time instead of having been so sympathetic.

What are Ed's responsibilities as a volunteer leader? What are the responsibilities of the staff person? Is each person in this scenario aware of his role? Who is responsible for cultivating and developing new leadership?

How would you intervene as a staff person? Role play a brief scenario.

What could a board member do? Who could be that person?

Role of Staff when Volunteer Chairperson is Not "On Task"

A chairperson does not spend an adequate amount of time in preparing for meetings, nor respect the use of an agenda to sequence ideas. This problem stems from the leader's busy schedule, inability to separate the social process from running a well-focused business meeting, and an inability to sort out the relevant elements of a complex problem.

In response, the professional has found that preparing a "cheat" sheet for a chairman on complicated issues has helped to make the chairman feel that he is in control. Even if the chairman has expressed hesitancy about bothering with an agenda, the professional prepares a tentative agenda ahead of the meeting and sends it to the chairman. He then telephones to review the material. He has also suggested that an agenda might help committee members to sort out the issues to be discussed.

Do the staff person's actions undermine the chairman's role? Does this intervention produce successful results? What else can the staff person do in this situation?

Development Director and Division Chair Compete

A very active volunteer in the community for many years assumed the role of campaign associate, then campaign director (staff). The chairman of the women's division was an old friend and, in fact, the two looked forward to working together. That did not work out as presumed!

The working relationship became a competition. Campaign meetings were held and the director was not informed. Agendas for meetings were not done ahead of time and there were always "surprises." The chair circumvented the professional's office as much as she could and always negated her input. She asked the professional not to talk at meetings. Most recommendations or suggestions that the professional made were rejected, and she was delegated to the role of secretary instead of partner. The chair called the organization's regional and national offices on her own without the staff person's knowledge. She complained about the professional to the organization's president and the executive director. A great deal of anger arose on both sides.

Meetings were held with the chair, the executive director, the president, and the professional. Process was explained and disagreements were brought to the surface and discussed. There were several such meetings. The professional personally called the chair and set up a meeting outside of the office so that they could discuss their differences and make changes in their working relationship. For a while it seemed to help, but the chair soon reverted to her old habits. It made the professional's job very difficult. She had no trouble with other volunteers, or they with her.

How could the staff person have directed the process more effectively? What steps were overlooked? What kind of behavior did the volunteer leader model? Did the staff person model? What was appropriate?

How can personal relationships be beneficial to a working relationship? How can they be detrimental?

An Issue of Consideration, Accommodation, and "Who's in Charge"

Two groups from a local United Way are returning to their home city from the airport after attending a national conference in Washington, DC. One group is made up of volunteer leaders, the other of professionals drawn from many local agencies. Each group has a chairperson drawn from their number, and each group also has a United Way staff person assigned to them. While in the Washington, DC, the two groups shared some experiences together, but in general they attended separate workshops.

There is a bad snow storm. On the bus, the person who had staffed the professionals' group asks the bus driver to make a stop at the United Way building, which is where all the professionals have left their vehicles. The stop would entail having the bus leave the highway and delay the volunteer leaders' arrivals by ten or fifteen minutes. They plan to be dropped off at a mall close to where most volunteers live and a further twenty to thirty minutes beyond the United Way building.

The volunteer chairperson overhears the request to the bus driver and specifically forbids the driver to meet the request. The staff person tries to reason with the volunteer leader. The volunteer leader, a powerful member of the community, threatens to have the staff fired if she is countermanded.

Prepare a scenario involving your colleagues. Give each a role to play. As you prepare, think of what you would want to teach the rest of your colleagues. How would you have the scenario end?

Volunteer Chairpeople "Drop the Ball"

A married couple agreed to chair a campaign event for the leadership division, a cocktail reception at a $500 minimum. The first meeting was to discuss who they were targeting, how they should recruit, who the speaker should be, and develop the appropriate lists and the fundraising component of the evening. When the meeting ended, the staff person thought they had a consensus on the plan.

The couple was updated on the progress and faxed copies of the invitation for their input before it went to print. Thus far, everything met with their approval. The problem began when it came time for them to begin recruiting and making follow up calls. Both complained that they were very busy at the office and would try to make calls if they could. The staff person tried to encourage them by suggesting several ideas:

1. They farm out some of the calls to other members of the executive committee already committed to attending the event.

2. Plan into their day several phone calls a day over a period of time, so that the task would not be too burdensome.

3. She reminded them about the importance of the event for the leadership council and the overall organization.

They agreed to make calls, and the staff person followed up every few days to check on their progress and update them on attendance. They seemed to be getting frustrated because many people were declining for a variety of reasons, but the one they focused on was the eliteness of a $500 minimum. The staff person continued to try to encourage them, reminding them that the event was elitist by design and that there are other opportunities for people contributing lower dollar amounts. She then asked to meet with them to review the agenda. Both complained about their workload and avoided setting a meeting time. Finally, the week before the event, the staff person pushed again for a meeting. They agreed to meet tentatively two days before the event. That day, one of the spouses canceled. The staff person told them that she would fax them a copy of the agenda and they would discuss it over the phone later that day.

When the conference call came, one chairman was irate. Included on the agenda was time for a caucus, which was agreed upon at the first meeting. The other spouse feigned ignorance, thus creating a conflict between the staff person and the vocal spouse. The staff person asked her what she had envisioned for the event and she stated that she had expected no fundraising to take place, that anyone who came to the event whose pledge had not yet been recorded would be solicited following the event. The staff person reminded her of a discussion at the first meeting in which they spoke about distributing cards and taking time to caucus. It became the chair's word against the staff's, as the other spouse stated that he could not remember.

In order to resolve the conflict, the staff person spoke to the campaign director, the president, and the campaign chair of the division. These volunteer leaders spoke with the chairmen several times. They eventually compromised, agreeing to distribute pledge cards but not to caucus. The reception went well, but the staff person felt that they missed a golden opportunity to raise additional dollars for the campaign.

Did the rift between the staff person and the co-chairs affect the agency? What is the source of the conflict? What can be done about it? Who should solicit funds? Under what circumstances?

Chair is Too Passive

The chairman of the planning committee is very passive and accepts all the proposals that his staff make without question. The staff person would like him to be more involved in a leadership capacity.

Role play a scenario between the staff person and the chairman.

Setting Priorities

The United Way has conducted focus groups and distributed a leadership questionnaire. The focus groups confirm that the legitimate desire to honor givers and leaders is normal. The groups also confirm that people at all giving levels have the same needs. At the same time, the questionnaire reflects a sense of priorities that in some instances is not sufficiently related to long-term concerns, for example, the cost of housing is a barrier to home ownership, and the low level of concern for intensive services to young adults at a time in their lives when values, priorities, and friendships are being challenged more than ever. In other instances, priorities such as nationally based services lag far behind local concerns in budgeting. What should leadership do about this?

What are some short-term and long-term objectives? As leadership, how would you prioritize your actions?

Tactful Way to Say "Show Me the Money"

The staff person for a capital fund raising project for a community center recruited co-hosts on behalf of the volunteer leader who was spearheading the project. Written material provided to each co-host before they were asked to join the effort clearly stated that each co-host was expected to contribute at least $100,000. Three of the four co-hosts pledged their gifts at this level. Confirmation was needed for the fourth gift.

The leader who was spearheading the effort was unwilling to speak directly with this co-host and asked the staff person to speak to him on his behalf.

As requested, the professional called the co-host and told him that they were preparing the agenda for the fundraising event and needed to plan the order of gift announcements, higher gifts first. In that context, he asked him if he would be announcing a gift of $100,000.

The co-host was extremely angry that the professional had asked him about his gift. He replied that he would only give $10,000. He later called the staff person's boss to complain about this. The volunteer leader of the project was very pleased that the professional had called instead of himself.

Whose responsibility was it to contact the co-host? Were the expectations of the co-hosts clearly defined? Why did this dilemma arise? Should staff or volunteers solicit funds? Who is most effective? In what situations?

Failure to Communicate

A volunteer leader has reason to believe that one of the agency executives in his city has been hiding a growing deficit from his board and from the planning and allocation committee.

What steps should he take to find out what is happening? Who should he consult with? What is his relation to the executive in this situation?

Positive Changes without Negative Feelings

A volunteer leader in the community campaign (who has been active in the phy-
sician's and dentist's committee for many years) is not pleasant to work with, nar-
row-minded, and makes the staff person's job difficult. He seems, though, to
have many connections in the medical field, and does bring people to meetings.
His wife is also somewhat active on the dinner committee (she orders flowers,
music, etc.). He and his wife do not do solicitations nor do they encourage others
to do them. The volunteer leader is somewhat helpful in directing problem situations, and has helped secure honorees for the annual dinner. The professional's
problem is that she would like to move him out of the center of the picture into a
lesser role. She needs someone who is more cooperative and does solicitations.
New blood is needed. Out of respect for this leader, she does not want to push
him out completely. Remember, he is useful and does have contacts. The meetings are not widely attended.

*What steps would you take as a staff person to achieve your goal? As the volunteer
leader, how would you react? Role play a brief scenario depicting the interaction
between the volunteer leader and the staff person.*

Boundary between Volunteer and Professional is Blurred

A woman was a major volunteer leader in the community for fifteen years before
she became a professional. She works with some of the same people now as she
did then. Some of the people have been her friends since childhood, some are her
parent's friends, and others are her children's friends.

In working together she finds that the line between volunteer and professional
is difficult to discern.

*How much can she suggest? How much can she expect of her former friends? How
much can they expect of her? As a volunteer leader, other volunteers were her role models. She does not have a clear picture as to the separation between volunteer and professional.*

*Who can help to clarify the difference for this woman? What responsibilities does
she have? What changes can she expect?*

Overcoming a Reputation for Sexism

You are hired as the development officer (staff) for a large foundation. You are the first female to hold an executive position at the foundation since the former executive director was forced out of her position several years earlier following a series of newspaper articles, written by a board member, which ruined her reputation. There is a great deal of disagreement within the foundation about whether the former executive director was treated harshly and unfairly because of the fact that she was a woman.

Fundraising for this organization has been difficult since you began and was not successful in the years prior to your arrival. The organization now has a reputation for being sexist, and it is particularly difficult to raise money from funders concerned about women's rights. In recent years, the foundation has suffered a tremendous budget crisis that has resulted in numerous layoffs and shrinkage of many programs.

As a result of the devastating effects on the foundation, several board members want to remove the author of the articles from his position on the board. They ask you for your support.

How do you react? What roles and responsibilities define your position and the positions of the board members?

In small groups, discuss the reactions of the development officer, the board member who wrote the articles, and the board members who want him removed from the board. What issues influence your reactions to each character?

Sexual Harassment

You are the director of development (staff) for a large non—profit organization where you have served for a few years. The new campaign chairperson is a very prominent lawyer and large contributor to the organization. You are a woman and have been very successful over the years.

Your campaign chair asks you to meet with him in his office to review the coming year's campaign. As agreed, you arrive at his office at 4:00 p.m. He greets you, asks his secretary to hold all his calls, and you are ushered into his office promptly upon your arrival. The chairperson asks you to seat yourself and as you do, he locks his office door. After a few words of chit chat, he moves closer to you and begins to fondle you, while suggesting that the year would be fruitful on many levels for both of you and the community.

How would you handle this? Can you work out a scenario for this?

Female Staff at "Men Only" Fundraiser

You are the first woman to be hired as the director of development (staff) for a large nonprofit organization. You had been campaign director in a smaller city for a number of years prior to taking this job.

One of your first assignments is the major gifts dinner, which is held annually at the city's most prominent country club. The dinner's importance cannot be underestimated because historically sixty percent of the drive's total dollars are raised at the dinner. You have worked almost continually for months with the chairperson and the planning committee. You have had many luncheons at the club but have never been there during an evening. You arrive early on the evening of the event, elegantly dressed in an evening gown and anxious to partake in a successful fundraising event.

Your chairperson arrives shortly after, comments on his high hopes for the evening, and then comments on the fact that he had forgotten to mention to you that because this was a stag event (which you were aware of), the dinner never allowed women to attend. He apologizes for not having mentioned this to you but suggests that after you ate your dinner in the kitchen perhaps you could remain in the hall outside the dining room where you would be able to hear the program and keep track of giving when that part of the program began. This "rule" cannot be broken.

What do you do? What are the principles involved? Assign roles as needed to act out the scenario.

Rudeness between Volunteer and Professional

The campaign director (volunteer) asked the professional to follow up with him regarding his attendance at a meeting later in the week. The campaign director was in the agency's building for another meeting, so the professional waited for him after his meeting adjourned. He was engaged in conversation with another volunteer leader and a professional, so the professional waited until they were done speaking before she approached him. In a quiet tone of voice, she addressed him regarding his attendance at the upcoming meeting. He responded in a loud, derogatory way, "Don't bug me! You're being a nudge!" This was said loudly enough for the other professionals to hear. The professional felt completely embarrassed, thanked him courteously, went to her office and fumed.

How would you react at the moment? What would you do to follow-up your initial response?

Should Staff be Asked to Do Personal Errands for Board Members?

You are the new campaign staff person (six months). Your first assignment was to "staff" the annual country club luncheon for $10,000 to $25,000 givers. You have two Master's Degrees, so your assignment was a more complex one than usually given to a beginning worker.

You have worked with the luncheon chair almost from your first day on the job. You have also met together with the committee in planning the luncheon and preparing rating cards as to the potential giving—in short, all the actions needed to assure a successful fundraising event.

The day of the event you are seated at the table in the lobby before people have begun arriving. The campaign chair (a $75,000 giver) comes off the golf course where the lunch is to be held. He barely knows you, but will be attending the luncheon. The lunch chairperson is not yet at the club.

The campaign chairperson, still clad in golf clothes, walks over to you and says, "Hi, I'm George Gotmoney, this year's campaign chairperson, and I'm sure you know I'll be attending the lunch today. While I'm showering and changing clothes, I'd like you to do something for me: Wash my golf ball for me while I'm gone. Thanks. See you soon."

How would you handle the request?

Defining an Intern's Role

You are an unpaid graduate school intern at a large fundraising organization. At the beginning of the year you and your supervisor discuss your role in the agency. Your responsibilities are in conjunction with your developing an understanding of the fundraising (development) profession.

You are assigned to staff a committee and work closely with the chairperson. During the first semester the two of you work well together in setting goals and priorities, developing agendas, and planning events. During the second semester she begins to ask you to perform personal tasks for her, including packing the boxes for her upcoming house move and babysitting her son, on a regular basis.

You feel that your internship no longer holds academic value. You want to discuss this with your supervisor but you are unsure how to do so.

Role play the outcome to the scenario. What issues are raised? What do you base your decisions on?

New Executive Must Reassert His or Her Role

A large, private, nonprofit elementary school has spent many years searching for an executive director. Numerous people have been hired for the position without success. During this time, several board members have assumed certain professional roles that were not otherwise being fulfilled. Having become accustomed to their "professional" status, these board members insist that they be allowed to continue their roles even after the current executive director was hired. Although they are not professional educators, these board members believe they should be involved in most of the pedagogical and curricular issues that arise.

As the new executive director, how would you handle this situation? How does the past lack of delineation between volunteers and staff affect your decision?

Prominent Staff Executive has AIDS, Does Not Want Public to Know

You are a staff person at a large nonprofit organization with thousands of members and a large staff. The organization has a significant public profile to maintain. The group accomplishes its goals in large part, through its media campaigns and large-scale grass roots strategies. The image of the president (a staff member hired by the board), who is seen and heard regularly in the national media and on Capitol Hill, is a critical component to the organization's success.

In your third year at the organization you travel with the president extensively to arrange and assist in public liaison between the president and your constituents, sometimes media, and often staffers on the Hill.

The president contracted AIDS long before you began at the organization but began showing visible signs of the disease during your third year. He died one year later, but during that time a major conflict occurred between several members of the staff, the president, and the board. The conflict revolved around the president's desire to continue making public appearances in spite of his obviously deteriorating health. In addition, the president steadfastly refused any suggestion that he disclose his illness or his sexual orientation to the public. He stated that he did not want the organization's well-publicized battle with the Religious Right to focus on him, his disease, or his sexual orientation. Complicating matters was the fact that only a handful of the staff knew (but were not officially told because of the president's specifications) that he had AIDS. They were told he had cancer. The board included many high profile individuals in the entertainment and political communities.

The board requests a meeting with you (behind the president's back), asking how you think that the president is perceived by the staff, the organization's members, and the community.

How would you handle this situation? What are your responsibilities as a staff person? What are your responsibilities to the board? What are your responsibilities to the president?

Teamwork

The assistant director of an agency has been there a year and yet she and the executive, while working well together, are not a fully developed team. The executive does not consistently fully share issues with the assistant. Apparently, some volunteer leadership feels the same way about the executive. The assistant director begins to hear complaints about the executive.

What should she do? Does the situation differ if the executive is male or female? Role play a five-minute scenario between the assistant director and the executive.

Well-Qualified, Competent Staff Person is Not a Public Speaker

A well-trained, amiable person has been hired as planning director. She has research skills, writes well, is friendly, honest, and a real team player. She has one drawback: she speaks very poorly. She has developed a proposal for a key research project and goes to her supervisor for support. Her supervisor is convinced the plan is an excellent one but that it needs to be explained to the executive commit-tee. The president agrees that the plan is an excellent one, but that the plan will get little support if presented by the planning director.

What should the supervisor do? Please detail the specific steps that you believe the supervisor should follow.

Use of Unpaid Interns in Under-funded Magazine Work

The assistant editor at a popular nonprofit magazine managed the office's pool of interns, which had a consistently rapid turnover. During both summers that he was there, there were numerous interns, while during the school year there were typically only two or three.

The office was chronically and severely under-funded and under-staffed, a problem that required the paid staff people to put in many extra hours without compensation and to farm out important tasks to the unpaid interns. Precisely because he was doing much work with little recognition, his boss referred to the assistant editor as the "paid intern." The assistant editor felt it was incumbent upon him to protect the interns from being inundated with work for which they would not be paid. On the other hand, he soon became aware that the more he demanded of some interns, the better they responded because they felt that they were involved in office pressure and deadlines, and wanted to be depended upon. But when he became a more demanding intern coordinator, he quickly became frustrated by the lack of motivation that he saw in those interns who did not respond well to such demands, and by their lack of incentive to perform.

He handled the situation by feeling frustrated, not pressuring most of the interns and trying to give those who responded well to demands a lot of encour-agement and offers for recommendations. He also allowed an enormous pile of manuscripts to accumulate because he did not feel that he could further increase the interns' demanding workload.

What is the nature of the distribution of power and responsibility for staff and interns? Who sets the policy for interns or other volunteers? Who is responsible for fulfilling the duties of the interns? What is the most effective way for the assistant editor to delegate the responsibilities inherent in running a magazine, or any other business?

Canceling Under-funded Events

A program director budgets, so that all costs of an activity will be covered by fees. The economic situation has started to affect attendance at events. The director is going to cancel some of the events planned by members since the expected income from the event will not cover cost of the event. The director has to share his decision with the staff person who is in charge. The staff person identifies with the members and will be resistant to implementing the decision. The staff person believes that the members have worked very hard to plan the events and that there has to be a way to get more resources to continue the activities. The director believes that they *must* cancel the activities.

What should the staff person do? Who will this decision affect? What issues underlie the perspectives of the program director and the staff person? Role play a scenario detailing the interaction between these two characters.

Competing Student Groups on Campus

Alan works on a small college campus where he is responsible for working with vegetarian students to design activities that meet their needs and interests. In general, this has meant working with the student union, the college's administration, and individual students who approach him. He has succeeded in enabling a "veggie co-op" on campus, where no meat is served.

Recently, a new group of more militant vegan students has founded a "culturally Vegan" magazine, and has made it clear that they want nothing to do with any of the existing structures on campus. Alan has met once with the editor of the magazine and has offered help that has been politely declined. Alan and his supervisor have decided to let the matter rest for the time being.

Toward the end of the semester, Alan was approached by the leadership of the vegetarian student's group and told that "some people" are not happy with the role that Alan is playing on campus. Since the leadership is speaking for others and not for themselves, it is not possible to obtain concrete details on what exactly the issues are, and none of the discontented people are willing to meet with Alan directly to clear the air. Alan was left feeling betrayed by the student leadership for carrying back stories of discontent without any attempt to defend Alan's work and with no way for Alan to clarify or correct the situation. When Alan attempted to speak with the leadership of the magazine, he was informed that they "don't feel comfortable" working with him.

Alan's supervisor continues to be very pleased with his work. The supervisor has been having her own troubles with the founders of the magazine. Alan can count on her support in whatever he decides to do.

Where does Alan go from here? Where do Alan's potential strengths and weaknesses lay in resolving the situation? How can Alan bridge the gap between himself and the dissatisfied students?

Hurt Feelings Lead to Nasty Gossip

A young man from a fundraising organization got upset when the committee rejected a friend he wanted used as a paid speaker for the organization. He made derogatory statements about the organization, and sent nasty letters to supervisors.

How are issues such as these best handled? Who should deal with the young man? What specifically should be said to him? Should anyone speak to the friend? What might be said to him or her, and how (letter, telephone call, in person, etc.)?

Young Staff Member with Elderly Clientele

A young professional who worked with elderly people often ran into conflict due to her age. She tried to create a setting in which she was the professional, staffing a group of volunteers with the goal of meeting their needs. The conflict was that the seniors could not help but see her as another grandchild, and had trouble taking her seriously. Furthermore, they crossed boundaries in terms of wanting her to visit them on weekends and wanting her to advise their real grandchildren on which colleges to go to.

Finally, after a few weeks she managed to change the situation. She started to distribute agendas at meetings and assigned leadership roles to people who agreed to take on positions of authority. Slowly, the seniors began to take her and the group more seriously. The professional also started to lead discussions and programs for the seniors on issues that interested them but in many cases were not familiar to them, so that they looked to her as a teacher, which helped her maintain her professional status.

Do the people involved have respect for each other's time/knowledge/capabilities? How would you have intervened as a staff person?

Role of Staff

A president called the new director of human resources for a large nonprofit agency to lunch to discuss new young leadership. During lunch, the president told the director that staff should have no role other than to implement leadership's wishes, saying, "No agenda should ever originate with the staff."

Do you agree with this statement? As director, how would you respond to the situation at that moment? What would you do to follow up your initial response?

Tools and Exercises

This section includes a number of specific tools related to planning and measuring the effectiveness of meetings, including taking the steps to best plan for meetings, helping members of committees learn and do their jobs, setting expectations for an organization's president and committee chairs, and dealing with various kinds of committee and board members.

The material at the beginning of this section was developed by Mark Salisch, a former professor of social work now working full time as an organizational consultant. That subsection ends with a bibliography related to management meetings.

In that subsection, it is important to note that Salisch does not specifically state the roles that should be performed by board members or staff. Generally, it will be the board president or committee chairperson chairing the meeting, so that when the word "leader" appears, the function would be performed by him or her and not by the staff person. What is implied here is that the staff person would be functioning as a teacher and utilizing this material informally or formally in preparing people to perform well at board or committee meetings.

This section also includes information on leadership. Much of the material on leadership is adapted from material first published in *Building for the Nineties: New Dimensions in Lay-Staff Relations* by Gerald B. Bubis and Jack Dauber (Los Angeles: Hebrew Union College, 1985).

In the research examining professional and lay leaders' attitudes and expectations of one another done by my colleague, Steven Cohen, and me, one of the major findings was the extent to which staff felt volunteers neither possessed the competencies nor applied them in a helpful manner. A remarkably high percentage of volunteer leaders agreed with that assessment.

It remains the challenge for the staff person at the least to informally engage the volunteer leader. Many of the items in this section could be sent by a staff member with a note suggesting the volunteer read it, followed after a respectable time interval with an inquiry as to whether or not the material had been read and whether or not it would be possible to discuss it and its possible use in board and committee training—if only for new members, as a starting place.

It is urgent, in turn, that training for staff takes place at all levels, so that staff members who work with functional boards and committees are knowledgeable about and able to use the material in this section.

This material is based on several premises or assumptions about the relationship between the volunteers and the professional people who make up the team guiding the affairs of a communal agency. *First, both are leaders.* Neither one is always leader and the other the mechanical manager. Neither one is always the "top dog" or "underdog," but each may experience one or the other role during the process of acting out his/her responsibilities. Each must use his or her individual and mutual resources so that the outcome of their work is synergistic, that is, more than either could do alone.

As leaders, both must see the present clearly. Together, they have a better chance of blending their subjective perceptions of an event, process, or structure into a more objective understanding of the realities in which they are engaged. Furthermore, they must impart a sense of continuity, by seeing both the past and future in the present. This sense of continuity needs to be articulated between the partners and communicated to their colleagues.

In this context, the leader is an educator who transforms murky problems into understandable issues, thereby opening the way or ways of involving others in finding acceptable and effective solutions.

The leader is one who is aware of his or her own values, needs, preferences, and prejudices, and is also aware of the same in others.

The leader evokes the best from each person, inviting everyone to be more perfectly the person they are gifted to be. The leader helps others become more freely themselves, and solicits rather than imposes ideas. The leader orchestrates and coordinates the ideas of all and re-orders them into a new plan, workable for all.

The concept that leadership is situational is a contemporary belief derived from research. The concept implies that certain situations call for or create leaders who meet the need of that time and then withdraw. It follows that each of us has the capacity for leadership—the innate talents combined with skill and motivation which move us into the leader role as it meets our needs, the state of the group's development, and the purposes of the organization. Because the task and maintenance needs of a group are at play simultaneously and consistently, it is often necessary for different people to attend to these forces in order to complement each other's efforts toward reaching effective and satisfying outcomes. A lay and professional team must be aware of the interaction between the task and the maintenance needs for themselves as well as for the group with which they are working.

A second premise is that the relationship base between volunteers and professionals is one of mutual learning and education.

Learning from and with each other can meet the growth needs of each, foster open communications, and keep them in tune with each other as well as the changing needs of the agency that they serve. The attitude of mutual education can help soften the expectations, which often derive from notions of "expertise" and "authority." These frequently have negative emotional loadings, which impede and divert appropriate sharing and support. The expectation that we will learn from each other in the accomplishment of mutual goals can make for a useful, wholesome humility and interdependence and create more effective personal and working relationships.

A third premise is that the volunteer and professional relationship is enhanced when experienced as one of mutual support. Such a working relationship would have these characteristics:

1. A sense of reliance on each other to implement agreements that have been reached.

2. Each will back the other as per their agreement. If a change of position is necessary because of unanticipated circumstances, there will be quick and open communication on the matter.

3. Each will grant authority to the other, when needed, in the pursuit of a task.

4. Each has a high degree of self-direction and is bound to the other by mutual beliefs and commitment to the agency and its goals.

5. Each is of help to the other, mainly in the accomplishment of the task, and sometimes on the more personal aspects of the relationship.

6. Knowledge of and respect for each other's similarities and differences.

7. Willingness to express differences and then to work toward resolving them when they relate to the tasks at hand.

8. Understanding that the relationship is a dynamic one, which changes as each grows and as agency requirements change and have their impact. Such changes call for periodic review and stocktaking between the partners.

9. An understanding that the relationship is one of mutual dependence or interdependence.

10. Understanding that all of the above are not ordained or found at the beginning of a relationship, but represent a process of development.

Several inferences or conclusions may be drawn from these premises. The "role" of the volunteer or professional leader is determined as much by the dynamics of the relationship as by the inherent function of either role. For example, the oft-repeated statement that "the board sets policy which the staff implements" is an oversimplification. It ignores the way in which the staff may influence policy or how, frequently, board members implement policies, particularly in such matters as fundraising, nominating procedures, and others. A readiness to define and redefine role and function to meet existential changing situations is particularly important in nonprofit agencies such as community centers, philanthropic organizations, and religious institutions where successful implementation frequently calls for blurring of roles or even their reversal.

This ambiguity calls for skill, especially on the part of the professional, who must take the initiative in modeling open, two-way communications and negotiations. In this instance, negotiation means stating positions and arriving at workable, flexible decisions which help either implementation of a project and/or the procedures for involving others.

Ten Basic Rules for Productive Meetings

1. *Make Sure it is Needed:* Is there a less expensive, more productive alternative to achieve the same purpose? You need to have a clear understanding of what you hope to achieve at the meeting before you decide if a meeting is the best approach. Do not forget that meetings are expensive in that they use people's time and potentially disrupt their schedules.

2. *Schedule with Lead Time:* Few meetings need to be scheduled at the last minute. By giving participants adequate time to study the agenda, prepare for the meeting, and easily work it into their schedules, you will increase their contributions and reduce meeting resistance.

3. *Invite Key Players:* It may seem obvious, but care needs to be taken to include those whose presence is needed in order for the meeting to achieve its objectives. It is all too common for an individual not to be invited who has needed

information or whose support is required. On the other hand, to invite individuals whose input or presence is not required or who cannot help the meeting reach its objectives is also ill advised. A copy of the agenda and the meeting summary is often an excellent substitute for the attendance of some people who need to be informed and aware but need not attend.

4. *Define Desired Outcome(s):* Beyond the general purpose for the meeting, some specific objectives need to be determined in order to give the meeting direction, purpose, and focus. While there are any number of objectives appropriate for a meeting, determining which ones and communicating them to the participants normally increases involvement, commitment, and productivity by giving the meeting a clearer focus.

5. *Plan It:* Use the agenda as a planning tool to set priorities for each item to be discussed. These priorities can be determined by the importance of the item, the complexity of the issue, the available time, or the position (status) of the person proposing the agenda item(s). The agenda should not only indicate items for discussion but specific contributions expected from participants, and should be distributed ahead of the meeting to allow participants to prepare. The agenda is not the only element of the meeting plan. The meeting plan should also outline the various processes by which various agenda items will be dealt with, and indicate whose input and support is needed on a given item.

6. *Provide for Direction and Leadership:* To be productive, a meeting requires that its direction be confirmed before it starts, when it starts, and at appropriate points as it progresses. This approach assures that everyone knows what the meeting is trying to achieve and why he or she has been invited. The discussion needs to be focused on the meeting's objectives at the beginning and kept there by both the convener(s) and the participants.

7. *Encourage Involvement:* The convener often needs to set the tone that encourages involvement, but all participants have a responsibility for this task. Opportunities need to be provided for all participants to contribute and the general discussion (evaluation) of ideas should be positive to encourage participation. People suggesting good ideas should receive immediate public reinforcement. "Off the wall" or unusual ideas should not be treated negatively—they often can become the most valuable input into a meeting.

8. *Provide Follow-up:* A productive meeting will often result in decisions, action plans, and assignments. Some way to reinforce the meeting outputs needs to be developed to assure a common understanding and to make sure that assignments are implemented. One method is to distribute copies of the meeting minutes to participants and other concerned parties. Another means is a follow-up or action timetable indicating agreed upon or anticipated target dates and specific responsibilities.

9. *Start and End on Time:* Avoid the unpardonable sin of starting late or publishing one starting time but actually anticipating starting later. Starting late rewards those who are late and penalizes those who are on time. A meeting that starts late will encourage those on time to be late for the next one. Ending a meeting late can become a problem if it conflicts with other commitments, becomes "too long," or goes beyond the "mental commitment" of the participants. A planned starting and ending time should be included in the agenda. If a meeting reaches closure, it can and should be ended early, but avoid regularly scheduling more time than required because participants will begin assuming an earlier ending time than is scheduled.

10. *Keep it Brief:* Contrary to popular belief, there is not an appropriate or ideal meeting length. The best meeting length depends upon the participants, the meeting objectives, the format, the organization's culture and the meeting setting. If a meeting must be lengthy, then a great deal of attention needs to be paid to timing, structure, and format. The general rule of thumb is that, if feasible, a series of briefer, more narrowly focused meetings are more productive than a long one covering a broad range of topics or requiring a series of complex decisions.

Preparing for a Meeting

1. *Define the Purposes of the Meeting:* A clear notion of what is to be accomplished is the foundation on which everything else rests. Not only should the leader have a good idea of what he or she wants to accomplish, but, equally important, the suggestions of the group members should be solicited. This feedback helps to assure that the meeting will focus on relevant issues. It also promotes anticipation, curiosity, and preparation. If you cannot define a clear purpose, it is often best not to hold the meeting.

2. *Develop an Agenda:* Once considerations are identified, they should be sequenced in a formal agenda so that those topics that are most urgent appear at the beginning of the meeting. This increases the likelihood that the most relevant issues actually will be considered. Clearly separate "for your information" items from items requiring actions. A tentative time allocation is often a useful guide for the participants.

3. *Distribute the Agenda prior to the Meeting:* Keeping the group members informed about the pending meeting increases their sense of responsibility and helps them to be aware of the purposes of the meeting, prepared to attend it, and, one would hope, more enthusiastic about participating. If specific input is expected or responsibility is assigned to individual(s) that should be noted.

Structuring a Meeting

1. *Start on Time:* It is very frustrating for members to have to wait for other members before the meeting can begin. Starting on time, even if only a few people are present, sets a precedent and suggests that members should be more punctual. It also rewards those who arrive on time.

2. *Review the Agenda and Set Priorities:* Initially, agenda items may need to be removed, combined, reordered, or added (as new business at the end of the agenda). This review provides a check on the planning and gives the group members one more opportunity to take responsibility for the meeting.

3. *Stick to the Agenda:* A common problem occurs when the leader allows the members to explore new topics before completing the established agenda. Such a discussion is likely to be unsatisfactory because there has been no opportunity for systematic preparation of information. More important, it is likely that other agenda items will not be explored because discussion of the new topic will take up allotted time. Group members may not like being constrained to agendas, but they are even more dissatisfied when many agenda items remain unexplored. Leaders can minimize this problem by consistently requiring that any topic raised at a meeting be put under "new business" and considered after the listed agenda has been completed (or put on the agenda for the next meeting if no time remains).

4. *Assign Responsibilities and Establish Target Dates for Task Accomplishment:* Decisions that call for tasks to be performed require, either during the meeting or soon thereafter, that members be assigned to carry them out within established time periods. This not only promotes task accomplishment but also provides a clear sign to the group that decisions made at meetings will be pursued. Nothing motivates group members more than seeing that things are done.

5. *Summarize Agreements Reached:* Reviewing the outcomes of a meeting reminds group members about the major decisions that were reached. Assuming that feedback is permitted during the leader's summary, it also enables members to correct any misinterpretations the leader may have made. This activity also provides a sense of completion for the members and increases the potential that members will leave in agreement about what occurred.

6. *Close the Meeting at or before the Agreed-On Time:* Leaders who ask group members to stay for "just a few minutes longer" to complete a "critical" agenda item may be perceived as being insensitive to others. It usually is better to end on time or even a few minutes early. Members will appreciate the leader's concern about their other commitments. If the agenda is organized appropriately, items that are scheduled for the end of the agenda, except in extraordinary circumstances, can be put off until the next meeting. It probably is an indication of insufficient planning if many agenda items are left over on a regular basis.

7. *Keep a Written Record:* Clear, complete, and accurate minutes are important because they provide the group and the leader with the ability to recall decisions that were made, actions that were called for, and responsibilities that were assigned. The minutes remind members to get on with their tasks. Equally important, conflicting interpretations of meeting outcomes can be minimized if complete and accurate minutes are available.

Following Up on a Meeting

1. *Edit and Distribute the Minutes Promptly:* Soon after a meeting, the leader, along with the recorder, should go over the minutes to check them for accuracy, completeness, and clarity. The minutes, once approved by the group at its next meeting, become a definitive record that can help to resolve differing

interpretations and to remind the leader and others of commitments made to pursue certain activities. Therefore, it is a good idea to distribute the minutes to group members while the meeting is still fresh in their memories. The minutes also help to remind group members of the relationship of any given meeting to the purposes of the group or organization.

2. *Encourage the Completion of Tasks:* Nothing promotes belief that meetings are relevant as much as task completion. Leaders should not hesitate to remind members of their commitments and, periodically, to check on the progress being made. It also is good strategy to publicize the progress of work that is being carried out. This gives recognition to those doing the work and encourages them to complete their tasks as expeditiously as possible.

3. *Put Unfinished Business on the Agenda for the Next Meeting:* Each agenda item is of interest to at least one group member or it would not have appeared in the first place. Those who requested discussion of a topic that is not treated at one meeting will watch closely to see whether it appears on the next meeting's agenda. Be sure to include such items on the agenda that is sent to group members for review before the next meeting.

Dealing with Difficult Members

1. *Listen, but Do Not Debate:* Troublesome members cannot simply be turned off or tuned out. Although it is difficult, it is best to work at bringing troublesome members into the mainstream of the discussion. When they feel that their views are respected, such members often begin to accept responsibility for controlling their own behaviors.

2. *Talk Privately with Members Who Continually Exhibit Disruptive Behaviors:* Publicly chastising difficult members can have detrimental effects; they may increase their negative behaviors or withdraw entirely from participation in the group. Public confrontations are best reserved as a last resort. Private conferences in which the leader's concerns are presented and the disruptive members' views are solicited provide confidential opportunities for members as well as leaders to explain their feelings and needs, and promote the potential for agreements to be reached. This strategy preserves the members' sense of dignity, spares the rest of the group from witnessing embarrassing confrontations, and conserves precious meeting time. It is important to remember, during such conferences, that the focus is to be on the members'

disruptive behaviors, not on the members' overall personalities or past histories.

3. *Turn Negative Behaviors into Positive Contributions:* It should not be assumed that all difficult members want to subvert meetings. Some may want to make positive contributions, but have not found the appropriate means to do so. Leaders can help disruptive members to find more productive ways of harnessing their energies to meet the group's needs. For example, leaders can encourage disruptive members to participate in planning sessions, ask for their suggestions during meetings, and give them the responsibility to perform tasks that result from decisions made in the meetings. Although some may not be responsive to such initiatives, many disruptive individuals, when so approached, become active and productive members.

4. *Encourage the Group to Share the Responsibility for Handling Difficult Members:* If the group members share maintenance activities with the leader, it is more likely that negative behaviors will decrease. Group censure puts pressure on disruptive members to modify their behaviors. It is one thing to risk the wrath of the leader and quite another to risk censure by the entire group.

Behind the Scenes in a Meeting

Description of Behavior	Why it Happens	What to Do
Quiet Member	Bored	Gain interest by asking for opinion.
	Indifferent	Question the person next to him or her. Then ask the quiet one to comment on the view expressed.
	Timid	Compliment this person the first time s/he contributes. Be sincere.
	Superior	Indicate respect for the person's experience and then ask for ideas.
Bungler	Can't put good ideas into proper order; needs help in conveying ideas.	Don't call attention to the problem. Say: "Let me see if we're saying the same thing." Then repeat the idea more clearly.
Mule	*Can't or won't* see other perspectives.	Ask other members of the group to comment on the ideas. They will straighten him/her out.
Description of Behavior	*Why it Happens*	*What to Do*
Talker	Highly motivated	Slow this person down with some tough questions.
	Show-off	Say: "That's an interesting point. Now let's see what the rest think of it."
	Well-informed	Draw upon his/her knowledge, but relay to the group.
	Just plain talkative	In general, for all overly talkative folks, let the group take care of them as much as possible.
Ready Answer	Really wants to help but makes it difficult by keeping others from participating.	Cut him/her off tactfully by questioning others. Suggest that "We put others to work." Ask person to summarize; this keeps him/her attentive and capitalizes on his/her enthusiasm.
Conversationalist	Side chatter is often personal, but may relate to topic.	Call by name and ask an easy question. Call by name, restate last opinion expressed and ask his/her opinion of it. Include in the discussion.
Personality Problems	Two or more individuals clash, dividing group into factions & endangering the success of the meeting.	Maximize points of agreement; Minimize disagreements. Draw attention to the objective at hand. Pose a direct question to an uninvolved member on the topic. As a last resort, frankly state that personalities should be left out of the discussion.
Wrong Track	Brings up ideas that are obviously incorrect.	Say: "That's one way of looking at it," and tactfully make any corrections. Say: "I see your point, but can we reconcile that with our current situation?" Handle this tactfully, since you will be contradicting him/her.

Remember, all members of the group will hear how you respond to each individual. And you can encourage or discourage further participation.

Can you (as a committee chairperson, president, or staff person) identify some people like those described above?

Productive/Unproductive Meeting Behaviors

How people behave at a meeting has a definite impact on the meeting. No matter the purpose of the meeting, three elements are involved in every meeting: process (how it is discussed), content (what is discussed), and feelings (reactions to what is discussed). The effective meeting facilitator is aware of those three elements and how individuals' behaviors are either productive or counterproductive to each element.

Process Behaviors

Productive	Counterproductive
Initiating process	Going off topic
Asking for process	Changing the subject
Changing and/or Focusing on process	Assuming everyone understands process
Refocusing on process	Jumping ahead or back
Defining the process	Gate keeping – filtering ideas and roles
Summarizing the process	Circling
Exploring processes	

Content Behaviors

Productive	Counterproductive
Acknowledging input	Making assumptions
Questioning	Stating assumptions as facts
Sharing opinions and points of view	Imbalance of negating or supporting
Initiating	Sarcasm, putdowns, ridicule
Negating	Not being clear
Exploring opinions and points of view	Giving long verbal speeches; interrupting
Supporting	Not participating
Checking that one has understood others	Having side conversations; not acknowledging
Giving information	Blocking – Placing obstacles in the process
Challenging assumptions	
Summarizing	
Clarifying	
Humor Laughing at self Can laugh at something everyone laughs at	

Feelings Behaviors

Productive	Counterproductive
Checking for feelings	Ignoring feelings
Initiating and expressing own feelings	Not checking for feelings Laughing at feelings
Expressing feelings asked for	Dismissing feelings
Refocusing on own and others' feelings	
Exploring feelings	
Acknowledging others' feelings	

Can you think of examples of both productive and counterproductive behaviors for each element that you have either observed or engaged in? Which counterproductive behaviors do you engage in and how can you change your ways?

Three Major Components in a Meeting

Three Key Factors In Meetings	Informational	Advisory	Problem Solving
Purpose – *Why*	To present information	To obtain information & ideas	To develop a solution to a problem
Membership – *Who*	Those who can use information	Those who are qualified to give advice on a problem	Those who have the authority and responsibility to make decisions
Leadership – *How*	The leader communicates information and checks to see how well it is understood	The leader directs the discussion to get the needed information	The leader coordinates the efforts of the group in problem solving

If meetings are only informational, they do the volunteers a disservice. Information can be shared by e-mail, in reports, by fax, or minutes in the mail. A board or committee member has a right to expect to play an advisory and problem-solving function at a meeting. Review recent agendas and/or minutes of meetings you have attended as a member or been the staff person. Was there a mix of the three major components? How can that mix be assured at future meetings? List three things that could be done to assure this in the future. The following pages contain specific helping tools.

Evaluate a Meeting

1. An agenda is prepared prior to the meeting.

2. Meeting participants have an opportunity to contribute to the agenda.

3. Advance notice of meeting time and place is provided to those attending.

4. Meeting facilities are comfortable and adequate for the number of participants.

5. The meeting begins on time.

6. The meeting has a scheduled ending time.

7. The use of time is monitored throughout the meeting.

8. Everyone has an opportunity to present his or her point of view.

9. Participants listen attentively to each other.

10. There are periodic summaries as the meeting progresses.

11. No one tends to dominate the discussion.

12. Everyone has a voice in decisions made at the meeting.

13. The meeting typically ends with a summary of accomplishments.

14. The meeting is periodically evaluated by participants.

15. People can be depended upon to carry out any action agreed to during the meeting.

16. A discussion summary is, or minutes of the meeting are provided to each participant following the meeting.

17. The meeting leader follows up with participants on action agreed to during the meeting.

18. The appropriate and necessary people can be counted on to attend each meeting.

19. The decision process used is appropriate for the size of the group.

20. When used, audiovisual equipment is in good working condition and does not detract from the meeting.

Number of Statements Checked _____ x 6 = Meeting Score

A score of eighty or more indicates you attend a high percentage of quality meetings. A score below sixty suggests work is required to improve the quality of the meetings you attend.

Committee Operations Analysis

A committee system that does not work is worse than no committee system at all. A board makes its committees work just as the board makes itself work—by paying careful attention and doing an annual formal evaluation of committee operation.

Committees should first meet some basic criteria to remain viable. They should be:

- Accountable to the board   • Results-oriented
- Subservient to the board   • Team-oriented

The following short analysis can be applied to most committees and will help you determine how well a committee meets the above criteria:

Yes	No	
		1. The committee has a written job description from the full board.
		2. The committee reports regularly to the full board.
		3. When the committee makes recommendations to the board, a committee member, who serves on the board, is ready with a motion that accepts the committee recommendation.
		4. Each committee meeting is organized around an agenda.
		5. Committee members have a copy of the committee meeting agenda several days prior to the committee meeting.
		6. Actions of this committee could not be accomplished as efficiently by the full board.
		7. The committee is chaired by a member of the board.
		8. The committee chairperson attempts to get all members of the committee involved.
		9. Committee reports are submitted in writing in time to be sent to board members with the board meeting agenda packet.
		10. All board members understand the only power/authority the committee holds is that specifically granted by the full board.
		11. Committee meetings are conducted in the same orderly fashion as board meetings.
		12. The committee meets all deadlines set by the board.
		13. The committee makes great effort to look at all sides of issues it
		14. Committee reports to the board reflect consensus of the committee members and/or present majority and minority reports.
		15. Committee members are chosen for high interest or expertise in this committee's area of responsibility.
		16. The chief administrator, or a staff member delegated by the administrator, staffs the committee. Other staff may serve as voting committee members.
		17. Committee members are appointed by the board president.
		18. The committee chairperson is appointed by the board president. Some organizations, in an attempt to democratize this process, have committees choose their own chairpeople.
		19. Committee members understand that all final decisions rest with the full board.
		20. Committee members are appointed and reappointed every year with attention to maintaining experience as well as bringing in new people.
		21. Committee records are adequate to make committee operations flow smoothly from one year to the next.
		22. The committee functions as a facilitator for the full board, not in place of the full board.
		23. The committee (except the executive committee) recruits and utilizes skills of non-board members.
		24. All members of the committee attend 90% of the committee meetings.

If you checked "No" for any of the above statements, list the actions your board or committee might take to correct the problem so your committee operates effectively.

Meeting Analysis

Participant's Name	Content		Process		Feelings	
	Provide	Build On	Develop	Steer To	Express	Check
1.						
2.						
3.						
4.						
5.						
6.						
7.						
8.						
9.						
10.						

Ask members to go through this exercise and afterward share their private assessments. They can assess each other anonymously by including their own name in the list. Refer to section on *Productive/Unproductive Meeting Behaviors.*

Improving How I Conduct a Meeting

Rate each of the items below in terms of its significance as a concern for **you** when **you** conduct a meeting. Rate 1 = minor to 10 = significant.

What you do When ...

	Minor									Significant
A. Preparing for a Meeting										
1. Define the meeting's purpose	1	2	3	4	5	6	7	8	9	10
2. Develop an agenda	1	2	3	4	5	6	7	8	9	10
3. Distribute agenda before meeting	1	2	3	4	5	6	7	8	9	10
B. Structuring a Meeting										
1. Start on time	1	2	3	4	5	6	7	8	9	10
2. Set priorities	1	2	3	4	5	6	7	8	9	10
3. Stick to the agenda	1	2	3	4	5	6	7	8	9	10
4. Assign responsibilities and dates to complete task	1	2	3	4	5	6	7	8	9	10
5. Summarize agreement	1	2	3	4	5	6	7	8	9	10
6. Close meeting on time	1	2	3	4	5	6	7	8	9	10
7. Provide written record	1	2	3	4	5	6	7	8	9	10
C. Dealing with Difficult Members										
1. Avoid debating them	1	2	3	4	5	6	7	8	9	10
2. Talk with them privately	1	2	3	4	5	6	7	8	9	10
3. Involve them positively	1	2	3	4	5	6	7	8	9	10
4. Involve others in group	1	2	3	4	5	6	7	8	9	10
D. Follow up on Meeting										
1. Distribute minutes promptly	1	2	3	4	5	6	7	8	9	10

| 2. Follow up on uncompleted tasks | 1 | 2 | 3 | 4 | 5 | 6 | 7 | 8 | 9 | 10 |
| 3. Include unfinished items on next agenda | 1 | 2 | 3 | 4 | 5 | 6 | 7 | 8 | 9 | 10 |

Now go back and circle the three concerns to which you give highest ratings, i.e., most significant concerns. These should be your priorities for the next meeting.

Sample Orientation Checklist for New Board Member

Orientation of: _____

(Board Member)

Date Orientation began: _____   Orientation Completed by: _____

(Person and Date)

Describe the Organization to the Board Member: _____

- Who we serve

- What we do

- Other:

Explain and Discuss with Board Member: _____

- Meeting attendance—both full board and committee

- Committee assignment

- Board role and relation to administrator/staff

- Other:

Conduct Tours: _____

- Administrative offices and board room

- Other facilities:

Deliver Important Information to Board Member   _____

- Letter of welcome from the chairperson and administrator

- Mission statement

- Bylaws

- Board policies

- Copies of the minutes of board meetings for the past year
- Annual report and auditor's report for last three years
- Current budget and other financial reports
- Long-range plan
- Goals for the year
- List of all board members including addresses and phone numbers
- List of board officers
- List of committee memberships including committee chairpersons
- Calendar of meetings for the year
- Copies of the organization newsletter for the past year
- Other:

Introduce Board Member To: _____

- Chairperson
- Chairperson of committees to which board member is assigned
- Other board members
- Staff
- Others:

Collect Data: _____

- Address
- Telephone—home and office

- Best time to contact

- Best time for meetings

- Other:

(A board manual can summarize this material but personal orientation is always best.)

An Exercise to Assess Committee Importance and Effectiveness

Consider the stated and unstated functions of many agency committees. To what extent are the functions identified below central or not central to those committees? Code: 1 = very central; 2 = central; 3 = not clear; 4 = not at all central; 5 = not a function at all. Then indicate the extent to which you think these committees have been effective in performing those functions. Code: 1 = very effective; 2 = effective; 3 = neutral; 4 = ineffective; 5 = not at all effective

Functions of Committees	Importance 1 2 3 4 5	Effectiveness 1 2 3 4 5	Comments
Governance (policy making)			
Clearing House (information)			
Education (growth of members)			
Representation (geographic or otherwise)			
Oversight (of staff activities)			
Advice (to staff)			
Task Accomplishment (as assigned around substantive issue)			
Other			
Other			

This scale can be used periodically to revisit what is happening in the agency and committees.

Meeting Management: A Brief List of Readings and Resources

Attard, J. *You Can Organize a Successful Meeting—Large or Small.* Westbury, NY: Caddylak Publishing, 1983.

A brief practical handbook for people who organize meetings including a number of useful forms.

Borman, E. G. *Discussion and Group Methods—Theory and Practice.* New York, NY: Harper & Row, 1969.

A very thorough but somewhat dated analysis.

Cook, C. *76 Ideas for Better Problem Solving and Decision Making.* Old Greenwich, CT: Cook Associates, 1991.

A very helpful and brief pamphlet with lots of specific suggestions on improving meetings, but expensive. Available only from publisher at 203-637-1118, 16 Arcadia Road, Old Greenwich, CT 06870 for $5.00 each.

Daniels, W.R. *Group Power I: A Manager's Guide to Using Task-Force Meetings.* San Diego, CA: University Associates, 1990.
A very useful and easy-to-read guide to meetings of temporary problem-focused groups with an excellent balance between the practical and theoretical.

Daniels, W.R. *Group Power II: A Manager's Guide to Conducting Regular Meetings.* San Diego, CA: University Associates, 1990.
A very useful and easy-to-read guide to committee, board, and department meetings. An excellent balance between the practical and theoretical with numerous useful techniques.

Fox, W.H. *Effective Group Problem Solving.* San Francisco, CA: Jossey-Bass, 1987.
A detailed, current, readable, practical, and scholarly piece of research that provides a detailed analysis of how to improve decision-making in groups.

Goodman, P.S. *Designing Effective Work Groups.* San Francisco, CA: Jossey-Bass, 1986.
Very useful conceptual background reading for understanding the theory behind the design and functioning of those work groups that use meetings to conduct their work.

Harvard Business Review. *What It Takes to be a Leader.* Cambridge, MA: Harvard Business Review, 1981.
Collection of HBR's top articles that provide excellent insight into leadership in the management of organizations. Some are very useful as handouts to selected leaders.

Haynes. H.E. *Effective Meeting Skills.* Los Altos, CA: Crisp Publications, 1988.
Brief, practical, easy-to-use handbook. Tells how, not why. A good publication to provide for chairs.

Meeting Management News. 3M Management Institute, 3M Center, A145-5N-Ol, Austin, TX 78769–2963.
Subscription available on request at no charge. Very valuable, easy to use, readable resource for anybody interested in meeting management. Has a business bias.

Mosvik, R.K. and Nelson, R.B. *We've Got To Start Meeting Like This!* Glenview, IL: Scott, Foresman and Company, 1987.
A very useful, practical, and comprehensive guide for anyone with a serious commitment to improving meetings. Focused on business, but includes universally applicable material.

Rickards, T. *Problem Solving through Creative Analysis.* Epping, Essex, England: Grower Press, 1974.
A comprehensive, serious, in-depth study. Not light reading.

Schindler-Rainman, E. and Lippitt, R. *Taking Your Meetings Out of the Doldrums.* San Diego, CA: University Associates, 1988.
An excellent resource with a great many practical suggestions and tools, but still well-grounded in group theory.

Smith, K.K., and Berg, O.N. *Paradoxes of Group Life.* San Francisco, CA: Jossey-Bass, 1987.
Important, complex, scholarly, current, and very helpful in gaining insight into what really makes groups tick.

3-M Meeting Management Team. *How To Run Better Business Meetings.* New York, NY: McGraw-Hill, 1987.
Clear, practical, easy-to-use, and very helpful, even if it pushes 3M model and products too hard. It tends to focus on business meetings.

Additional Recommended Resources

BoardSource—Formerly the National Center for Nonprofit Boards, this organization serves as a resource center of information to benefit nonprofit Boards. Contact information: BoardSource, 1828 L Street NW Suite 900, Washington DC 20036-5114. 1-800-883-6262. www.boardsource.org

Stanford Social Innovation Review—Stanford Graduate School of Business supports this magazine written for nonprofit and foundation leaders discussing innovative ideas in public and nonprofit management. Contact information: Stanford Social Innovation Review, 518 Memorial Way, Stanford University, Stanford, CA 94305-5016. 1-888-488-6596. www.ssireview.com

Harvard Business Review—Harvard Business School has a large selection of resources for nonprofit organizations including the magazine H*arvard Business Review* and publications from the Harvard Business School Press. Contact information: Harvard Business Review Subscription, Attn: Subscriber Services, P.O. Box 52623, Boulder, CO 80322-2623. 1-800-274-3214. Harvard Business School Publishing, Attn: Customer Service, 60 Harvard Way, Boston, MA 02163. 1-800-988-0886. http://harvardbusinessonline.hbsp.harvard.edu

Leadership in a Nonprofit Organization: Staff and Volunteers

The Traditional Conception of Leadership in Nonprofit Organizations

Some would argue that the principal responsibility for leadership in nonprofit organizations resides with the board. It is the board that must identify the mission of the organization, ensure that effective policies are established, and secure sufficient financial and other resources. From this perspective, the board holds the Chief Executive Officer (CEO) responsible for the exercise of administrative efficiency and the effective delivery of services. The CEO is subordinate to the board in all matters of critical concern to the organization.

Think about the nonprofit organization in which you are involved. Do you agree with this conceptualization? How are the major responsibilities for mission definition, policy determination, resource generation, and administration presently delineated?

An Alternative Model of Leadership in Nonprofit Organizations

This book develops more complex models of leadership of nonprofit organizations than the traditional one. This section emphasizes an active CEO. Leadership is found in the relationship between the CEO and the board. If the leadership of the organization is to be effective, the CEO must assist the board in carrying out its crucial duties and responsibilities. The CEO is held accountable for the success or failure of the organization. The CEO shares with the board in specific ways the formulation of mission, the determination of policy, the generation of resources, and administration of the services and programs of the organization. The CEO does not abrogate the board's responsibilities. Rather, the CEO works to ensure that the board will carry out its responsibility.

Think about the nonprofit organization in which you are CEO, staff, or member of the board. Do you agree with this alternative conceptualization?

Relationship between Lay Board Chair and Chief Executive Officer (CEO)

The first and probably most crucial relationship with which you must be concerned is that between the lay board chair (the title varies from organization, might also be called president) and the CEO. The two of them constitute, in effect, a presidium and a partnership.

I would suggest to you that the shaping of this partnership relationship is more the job of the lay board chair than that of the CEO, because the lay board chair is the only one of the two who has the luxury to make the essential determinations. As the lay board chair is a voluntary position with no salary involved, the CEOs salary is reviewed and recommended (or determined in some places) by committee. The lay board chair has received the recognition of the respect of the organization; the CEO is always subject to "What have you done for us lately?"

Like any partnership that works, however, the essential element is an honest respect on the part of each for the expertise of the other. The CEO is a trained professional, not a hired hand. He has the understanding of process (an occult art which defines the narrow line between the pragmatic planning of controlled response, on the one hand, and devious subterfuge of human propriety, on the other). He has the authority and the ability to assign, handle, and direct staff.

The lay board chair, on the other hand, has the responsibility for the final determinations in ordering the priorities, and has the responsibility for motivating the thousands of individuals in the community whose cooperation and devotion and effort are essential to the success of your overall program.

If the lay board chair is unable or unwilling to be assertive enough to play her proper role, the CEO will be her shield, her crutch, and her mobile teleprompter. But since it is the lay board chair who will receive the credit for accomplishment, it is her own moral integrity which should drive her to hold up her end of the partnership.

Periodic meetings, at least weekly, should take place between the lay board chair and the CEO, and not just as problem-solving sessions. One is aware of what could be; the other is aware of what is. So get together and brainstorm and bounce ideas off each other. These are the navigation sessions for your organization.

The lay board chair does not have the authority to be a martinet; similarly, she does not have the luxury of being a figurehead. The proper relationship is probably best evidenced by the number of times the lay board chair embarks on a course of action where she is really not quite able to figure out if she talked the CEO into it, or he convinced her.

Questionnaire Assessing the Relationship between Chairperson and Staff

This questionnaire could be done individually or as a group activity. If done individually by a lay leader, s/he may wish to ask a staff person to complete the survey to understand the staff perspective. The staff person should read the question as it relates to the individual who asked them to complete the questionnaire (and example is provided in italics in the next paragraph). The two of them should complete the questionnaire individually and then discuss it one question at a time.

To be done as a group activity, this questionnaire should be given to your organization's lay leaders and staff. Individually read through the list and circle the proper letter, as you perceive it. Lay leaders should read the question as written, but staff should read the question as if it is about your lay leaders. *As an example for staff, question #1 would read, "Do your lay leaders understand the purpose, action goals, and objectives of the organization?"* Once everyone has had a chance to complete the questionnaire individually, bring the staff people together in one group and the lay leaders together in another to discuss their individual answers and then create an agreeable group answer. So before the entire group comes together, each group (staff and lay leaders) will have one answer to present to the larger group. Bring the two groups back together in to one large group, and share your group answers with the larger group.

Compare lay leaders' answers and those of the staff's answers, question by question. You may be pleased to find significant congruence—or significant disparity. Whatever you find, the data should be useful in building a strong, trustful relationship.

Y = Yes   N = No   P = Partially   D = Don't Know

	Y	N	P	D
1. Do you understand the purpose, action goals, and objectives of the organization?	Y	N	P	D
2. Are you committed to those purposes, purpose goals, action goals, and objectives?	Y	N	P	D
3. Do you appreciate the operational problems you face?	Y	N	P	D
4. Does your relationship allow sincere, candid interaction?	Y	N	P	D
5. When you are in conference with your organization's staff, do you give the time needed to transact business?	Y	N	P	D
6. Are you willing to listen to staff problems?	Y	N	P	D
7. How knowledgeable are you of the staff and board structure of your organization?	Y	N	P	D
8. Do you encourage your board or committee members to give their best efforts?	Y	N	P	D
9. Do you encourage participation in meetings by board volunteers?	Y	N	P	D
10. Do you encourage participation in meetings by staff?	Y	N	P	D
11. Do you offer new ideas or solutions to problems?	Y	N	P	D
12. Do you assist staff in their own performance improvement?	Y	N	P	D
13. Have you encouraged your board or committee to work as a team?	Y	N	P	D
14. Do you have confidence and trust in your staff?	Y	N	P	D
15. Does the staff have confidence and trust in you?	Y	N	P	D
16. Are you willing to face controversial issues in meetings?	Y	N	P	D
17. Do you allow personal feelings and biases to interfere with the execution of your work and duties?	Y	N	P	D
18. Do you accept responsibility for the performance of your committee or board?	Y	N	P	D
19. Do you take the initiative, keeping the work of the board or committee relevant and on schedule?	Y	N	P	D
20. Do you act as a leader and not as a "Caesar?"	Y	N	P	D
21. Do you delegate tasks to those with the capability of achieving them and assist the inexperienced who accept a tough assignment?	Y	N	P	D
22. Do you rely on a select few for input and decisions?	Y	N	P	D
23. Do staff feel reluctant to use your time?	Y	N	P	D
24. Do your board or committee members fulfill commitments they have made?	Y	N	P	D
25. Are you accessible to staff?	Y	N	P	D

To what extent do you need—?

1. More information on the principles of management of a voluntary organization?

2. More information about how members of your board or committee feel about things?

3. More information about how members of the staff feel about things?

4. A greater ability in handling the work of your board committee in meetings?

5. More insight into how people behave in groups and how to motivate them?

Volunteer/Professional Relations: A Professional's View

This questionnaire is for the professional to use to explore her/his feelings about relationships to the lay leaders s/he works with in the organization.

Roles	Agree	Disagree
My major role is to manage the "process."		
I am more often teacher than enabler.		
Many times I feel like it's a caseworker/client relationship.		
I must master all the facts and be an expert source of information.		
I must never be an advocate of a particular viewpoint. Skill in "facilitation" is crucial to my effectiveness.		
Social Status		
Compared to volunteer leaders I feel "second class."		
I am impressed with the wealth of Board Members and their generous giving. As an employee I feel my status is insecure.		
I make no effort to socialize with Board Members.		
Board Members don't want to socialize with me.		
Norms		
I have a responsibility to help volunteers grow to their full potential.		
I must not let my personal Jewish ideology intrude on my professional role.		
Many volunteers are working out personal problems through their community activity; my role is to work with them on this, to show empathy and understanding.		
Some volunteers bring personal agendas and seek to exploit community activities for business gain or ego needs. This is unacceptable and I must take steps to deal with it.		
Genuine altruism is in very short supply among our volunteers.		
Power and Influence		
I feel powerless most of the time.		
Most volunteers think professionals have the balance of power.		
My strongest source of influence is through my relationships with key leadership.		
Knowledge is power and I must be as knowledgeable as possible.		
Staff derive power from their capacity to influence assignments of status positions to volunteers. My full-time status makes me the ultimate depository of power.		
Responsibility	Agree	Disagree
I am first responsible to my professional supervisor and thereafter to the Board of Directors.		
In the final analysis I am responsible to the community our organization serves.		
My responsibility is to implement Board policy.		
I feel responsible to keep leaders and key givers "happy"; otherwise the community will suffer financial loss and personal disaffection.		

Professional vs. Volunteer Roles: Questions to Stimulate Discussion about Partnership

Who …

1. Determines the agenda for meetings?

2. Prepares the actual agenda for meetings?

3. Puts together the initial list for committee participation selection?

4. Makes follow-up recruitment calls for participation on a committee?

5. Provides the bulk of information and directs the meeting?

6. Provides supportive information and helps troubleshoot during the meeting?

7. Calls the Executive Director of an agency regarding a problem with that agency's budget?

8. Does research on a particular topic which will be discussed at an upcoming meeting?

9. Drafts the cover letter to a committee regarding upcoming meetings and important issues for the committee's consideration?

10. Insures that all contributors are properly thanked?

11. Anticipates problems and tries to come up with creative solutions to problems before they actually arise?

12. Does research to determine several potential speakers for an event?

13. Prepares the first draft of department or program budgets?

14. Explains the budget to the committee?

15. Speaks to the board regarding the budget and the committee's recommendations?

16. Keeps records of all interactions and correspondence for the committee?

17. First scrutinizes agency budgets that come to Federation or Fund for review?

18. Is responsible for knowing and informing committees about policy issues that may affect their decision-making?

19. Generates new ideas for committee consideration and voices them during committee brainstorming sessions?

20. Is responsible to correct a volunteer leader when they have made a mistake in relaying information to their committee? Under what circumstances?

Additionally …

21. Under what circumstances should a professional take over a meeting from a volunteer leader?

22. Do professionals have a vote on agency or Federation committees and boards?

23. Under what circumstances would a Federation/agency professional "cc" an agency President on a letter to an agency Executive Director?

24. To whom does the Federation/agency Executive Director report?

25. Does the Federation/agency Executive Director or the Federation/agency board have final say over the budget?

26. Does the Federation/agency Executive Director or the Federation/agency board have final say over individual salaries within the approved budget?

27. Who hires Federation/agency staff, the Federation/agency Executive Director, or volunteer leaders?

28. Can Federation/agency professionals serve on other beneficiary agency boards?

29. Who is more important to the functioning and success of the Federation/agency, professionals or volunteer leaders? Why?

Professional vs. Volunteer Roles: Checklist of Duties

This exercise can be used by an individual, shared with volunteers or staff, or used in a volunteer or staff training session. As with all the materials in this section, discussion with participants is essential in order to ascertain degrees of consensus or difference on who is expected to perform the various roles and functions to assure effective and efficient delivery of services. Listed below are various functions, which are ascribed primarily to either the lay board chair (or volunteer leaders) or CEO (or staff). For each function, select who handles it in your organization or who you believe should handle the function.

Staff	Volunteer	
		1. Appoints members of the community to committees and Boards
		2. Keeps and organizes service related data for backup to decision making
		3. Sets policy for the agency
		4. Makes determination to phase out a particular service
		5. Determines when staff takes a vacation
		6. Accounts for expenditure of funds
		7. Determines when expenses get charged
		8. Sets agenda for Board meeting
		9. Hires staff who work with the executive
		10. Calls members of committee and Board to determine attendance
		11. Prepares backup material on issues for Board deliberation
		12. Decides to close agency due to inclement weather
		13. Solicits prospective donor's annual gift.
		14. Makes budget presentation to United Way
		15. "Chairs" meetings of Board and committees
		16. Makes final policy decisions
		17. Responsible for agency's day-by-day management
		18. Responsible for spreading good word of the agency throughout the community
		19. Represents the organization at meetings throughout the community
		20. Alerts Board as to potential crisis in area of function
		21. Deals with angry donors around role of Federation
		22. Accountable for Federation operating budget
		23. Develops leadership programs in order to build leadership base
		24. Handles emergency allocations
		25. Insures that all points of view are adequately aired at appropriate time
		26. Determines which meetings and/or conferences staff should attend
		27. Creates goals and objectives for Federation activities
		28. Defines and clarifies issues that need policy clarification
		29. Helps to select resources as a backup to process
		30. Has the legal responsibility for nonprofit corporation
		31. Implements policy of Board

Questions for Organization's Volunteer and Professional Leadership on Relevant Organizational Issues

Regarding the Mission of the Organization

How do you respond to the following questions?

1. What is the role of the board in determining the purpose of the organization and its role in the community? What is the role of the CEO in this regard? Do the CEO and board agree about the present statement of mission?

2. About what matters relating to the mission should the CEO advise the board?

3. What is the role of the board in cultivating opportunities and maintaining relationships with external funders, corporate donors, and important government entities that may affect the mission of the organization? What is the role of the CEO in this regard?

4. What responsibilities does the CEO have in probing the environment of the organization for opportunities to advance the organization's interests? What is the role of the board?

5. Are the board and CEO clear with each other about who is responsible for the boundary-spanning activities of the organization?

6. In what ways do the responsibilities of the CEO intersect with those of the board in maintaining and enhancing the network of stakeholders for the organization?

Regarding the Role of the Board Volunteer

How do you respond to the following questions?

1. Differentiate between those roles that are advising, operational (performing), policy-making, and supervising.

2. How do board members lend sanction to the organization?

3. Which roles can the board member perform on his or her own and which require board or committee approval?

4. Which roles can be designated primarily for the input, output, or through-put processes or systems?

5. What responsibilities do board members have to each other?

6. What criteria should be used to create a balance in the board which would cover all the roles?

7. What satisfactions should volunteers gain from their service on a board?

Regarding the Policies and the Generation of Resources for the Organization

How do you respond to the following questions?

1. Who should determine the allocation of resources to programs? What are the responsibilities of the board? What are those of the CEO?

2. Who should determine the plan for resource distribution and decide about the elimination or creation of new programs and services?

3. What responsibilities have the board for determining where resources are to be found? What is the responsibility of the CEO?

4. Who determines fundraising and marketing strategies?

Regarding the Administration & Management of the Organization

How do you respond to the following questions?

1. What administrative functions should be performed by the board?

2. Over what programs, materials, and human resources should the board preside or have oversight? Which should they review? How often should the reviews occur? In what form?

3. What administrative changes should the board instigate, and under what circumstances?

4. What critical information must the CEO provide the board, in what format, and how often?

5. Whom should the board hire and fire?

Management System

LEVEL OF INFLUENCE	PROFESSIONAL STAFF
BOARD	

1.	2.	3.	4.	5.	6.	7.
Mission	Goals and Objectives	Strategies and Planning	Resource Development and Allocation	Operational Programs	Administration — Fiscal and Personnel	Day-to-Day Management

Place the number of each function at the position that indicates your assessment of who is primarily performing these functions. The diagonal line suggests "conventional wisdom." Would you agree?

Concepts of Leadership

Objectives: 1. To present a systematic way of looking at the phenomena of leadership.
2. To give an understanding of the functional approach to leadership and its meaning in a variety of settings.

Content: Both laymen and scientists hold different views about leadership. In considering the various approaches which have been made to understanding leadership, the following conceptual model might be useful.

Continuum of Leader Behavior

Leader-centered _____ Group-centered

USE OF AUTHORITY BY LEADER	
	AREA OF FREEDOM OF THE GROUP

Leadership is not a single form of behavior. The leader chooses among a range of behaviors, depending on the situation, the nature of the group and/or his own competencies, etc.

Discussion of Styles of Leadership

Trait Approach

Hundreds of studies have been done comparing the physical, intellectual, or personality traits of leaders and followers. For example, leaders tend to be bigger and brighter, better adjusted, and have more accurate social perceptions than followers (but not so much as to be unacceptable to the group).

On the whole, trait approach has been disappointing. Only five percent of the traits identified in over one hundred studies appeared in four or more of those studies. This trait approach has led to selection procedures based upon paper and pencil test and/or performance test.

Situational Approach

This could best be described as an insight rather than an approach to understanding leadership. It is based upon the hypothesis that behavior of leaders in one setting may be different from those in another. Those which are needed vary from one situation to another. This is recognized by the Air Force which allows "mutinies" to occur in emergency situations, involving the lives of survivors following a crash. That is, although the pilot is in command of the flight, during a crash and struggle for survival in enemy territory, the group may select a different commanding officer whose leadership skills better meet the situation. Although there has been little research on this, these situational factors do suggest the need for flexibility in the principles of selection, training, and sensitivity of leaders.

There are a good many variables that enter into producing leaders. There are, however, two types of forces which influence how a leader arrives at a leadership position. One of these types includes personal drives and hungers—it is motivational. Probably vitality to survive the pressures brought to bear on people in leadership positions is important also. Then there are external forces that present men and women with the opportunity to be leaders. Sometimes, in other words, people are motivated by personal drives to become leaders; other times they find themselves in leadership positions as the result of external forces, and they may or may not be aware of the forces influencing them. Usually both factors are at work. There are both motivational and social forces which tend to produce leaders.

Styles of Leadership

The three styles of leadership are: autocratic, democratic, and laissez faire leadership. These are complex terms which refer variously to leadership style or group climate. In attempting to find adequate definitions for these terms, one might try to place them on a scale representing amount of freedom. When one suggests "freedom" as a continuum along which these terms might be ranged, the autocratic leaders should be placed low on the scale and the other two higher (see *Continuum of Leader Behavior* diagram). However, there is considerable disagreement as to whether democratic or laissez faire permitted more freedom, and among those who placed laissez faire leadership higher there was disagreement as to where along the continuum democracy belonged. Freedom, then, seems to be inadequate as a criterion for defining these terms.

A second possible criterion for defining these terms is efficiency. This, too, seems inadequate. Laissez-faire leadership should be placed low on such a scale and the other two higher. We would not agree on the relative positions of autocracy and democracy.

There is a third way of defining leadership: in terms of the *location* of the decision-making function. In this case, we can all agree that the decision-making function resided in the *leader* in the autocratic group, in the *individual* in the laissez-faire group, and in the *group* in the democratic group.

All possible leadership styles can be defined by placing them at some point along the connecting lines. When forces move a group away from any one of these, two directions are possible. For example, a group moving away from laissez faire may move toward autocracy or democracy.

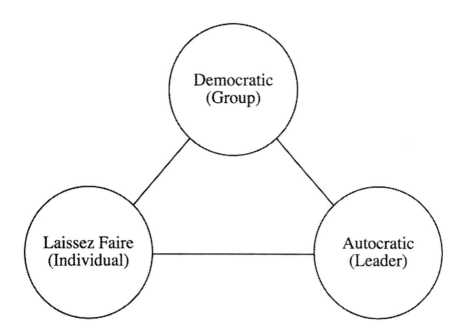

Major Experiments

Three major studies have been made of leadership style and climate. The first two were done in 1938 and 1940 at Iowa, the third in 1942 at Stanford. All were done with clubs of youths with adult leaders. The two general purposes of the clubs were achievement and recreation. The boys were engaged in activities such as building furniture, making papier maché masks, etc. The same club had all types of leaders, and the same leader used at least two of the styles mentioned previously, after extensive training. The results showed six kinds of differences:

1. Democratic leadership resulted in a more satisfying, efficient leadership than did laissez faire.

2. A democratic social climate can also be efficient.

3. An autocratic style creates hostility and aggressiveness among its members.

4. Discontentment, which does not appear on the surface, occurred in some of the autocratic groups. Four of the six autocratic groups showed no overt discontent, but:

5. There was more dependency and less individuality in the autocratic than in the democratic group.

6. There was more orientation to the needs of the group and more acceptance of each other in the democratic groups.

Functional Leadership

This concept of leadership seeks to discover what actions are required by groups under various conditions, if they are to achieve their objectives, and how different members take part in these actions. Leadership is viewed as the performance of those acts which are required by the group. The group-functions approach to leadership takes into account the other approaches discussed. Groups differ from one another in a variety of ways. Actions vary from one group to another. The nature of leadership traits or acts will accordingly vary from group to group. Situational aspects will determine what functions are needed and who will do them: i.e., the nature of group goals, structure of group, attitudes of members, and similar situational factors.

Many classifications of leadership functions in the group have been proposed. Cattell offers: "Anyone who modifies the properties of the group." Administrators refer to planning, decision-making, coordination, etc. Basically, there appear to be two main classifications of leadership functions in groups:

1. Achievement of the group goals.

2. Maintenance or strengthening of the group itself.

In this respect, it is important to note that any specific behavior may be helpful for both or favor one at the expense of the other: i.e., a group may be so intent upon maintaining good relations that it avoids friction at all costs, thereby retarding its problem-solving process. On the other hand, a wise solution may solve a problem and also help the solidarity of the group.

The distribution of leadership functions in a group occurs in several ways. Usually in a well-organized group, certain functions are assigned to certain members, or granted to them. Distribution may be centralized or spread among many members. There has been little research on the consequences of restricting or spreading distribution of leadership. In studies and experiments, those who distributed functions got "better" results: i.e., productivity, morale, etc.

There are many factors that determine the distribution of leadership functions. Leadership is:

1. Provided by members to meet a need of the group. This is a group maintenance function, which is, in effect, shared leadership.

2. Granted to persons who held central positions in the communications system.

3. Granted to persons of high power or prestige by those of lower status.

4. Granted to persons of greater visibility. Members who talk a lot are chosen for leadership positions, a decision which the group sometimes regrets.

5. Assumed by those who are "hungry for power."

6. Assumed by conscientious members. An experiment by Pepitone illustrated when members who are told that their tasks are important to the group performed with a higher quality than those told that their task were not important to the group.

7. Granted to persons seen by the group as able to meet their needs.

In summary, problems of leadership cannot be separated from problems of group functioning. If we are to understand leadership we must understand groups. In training effective members, we are doing the best training for effective leadership, since a leader can be no more effective than his group members.

Communal Leadership: Reaction Sheet

	Strongly Agree	Agree	Disagree	Strongly Disagree
Leadership in the contemporary organization must be exercised by a relatively small elite.				
Leaders should subordinate their own visions and values to those of the institution they serve.				
Volunteer communal leaders must be prepared to serve as role models for other communal members.				
Volunteer leaders should be willing to defer to their professional expertise in decision-making.				
Nonprofit organizations need a representative leadership to speak for it authoritatively on important issues.				
The nonprofit organization really belongs to the non-professionals.				
A good knowledge of organizational history and traditions should be a requisite for serving as a volunteer leader today.				
The most important attribute of a volunteer communal leader today is the ability to get along with others.				
In communal organizations today, volunteer leaders should make decisions and professionals should carry them out.				
Leadership by consensus is the only way organizations can operate today.				
Volunteer organizations are really run by the professional staff.				
Large contributors play a disproportionate role in communal decision-making.				
Voluntary organizations are as "democratic" as they can be.				
Organizational professional staff should take a stronger leadership role in decision-making.				

Continuing Professional Education Management II, August, 1985.

On Being a Group Leader—I

As you read this material, you will have several opportunities to learn about how to be a group leader. Try to use this material and practice, practice, practice.

There are some simple rules to follow that will help you be more skillful in getting others to talk and maintaining control of a conversation. By using these as a group leader, any group you work with will get more out of the projects you handle.

1. *Ask "open-ended questions."* These are questions that cannot be answered by yes or no. "What are your thoughts about this?" or "How do you feel about that?" are examples of open-ended questions.

2. *Wait for a response.* Do not feel you have to fill the silences. If you wait, the participants will take the initiative.

3. *Get everyone to participate.* Do not let one person monopolize the entire discussion. Get everyone to join in by directing questions to the ones holding back.

4. *Keep control.* Hold to the subject. Do not let the conversation stray to unrelated subjects. Do not get "hung up" on a small point for a long time.

5. *Give recognition.* If you are impressed with a remark or an insight offered by another, say so. Avoid "putting down" another because that person's opinion is different from yours. Do not criticize or make fun of another. This tends to inhibit response.

6. *Keep yourself out of it as much as possible.* Do not dominate the conversation. Let everyone express themselves.

7. *Find key points and summarize.* Your report should be no longer than one minute. Be selective about the items in your group's discussion and report their conclusions.

8. *Remember that a good listener listens for the ideas first and details second.* Being the group leader will give you opportunities to practice listening with understanding and discernment. Extract the real meaning from the discussions. Check your perceptions with the group by summarizing a point and asking if

it is an accurate reflection of what was said. This helps to arrive at a consensus. Practicing listening should be your first priority.

On Being a Group Leader—II

An introductory presentation by the leader might include materials with an emphasis on the concepts of facilitating, indirect leadership, the situational aspects of leadership and the need to be flexible and adaptive.

Following the introduction, distribute copies of the page "On Being a Group Leader" (previous page). First, ask the group to discuss the handout as general guidelines, and then ask how they might use them to prepare a chairperson to conduct a meeting of a committee. Questions suggested for discussion are:

1. Which rules would be most important for the chairperson?

2. How might the staff member be of help during the course of the meeting?

3. Should the chairperson call on the staff member during the meeting? For what purpose?

4. Should the staff member intervene without being called on by the chair? Under what circumstances?

5. Are there differences in the way these rules would apply—at committee meetings? Board meetings? Staff meetings? Social groups (clubs)? Highly task-oriented groups?

Leadership Effectiveness Grid

Place a dot or an "X" under the number that you feel most accurately describes your level of effectiveness in each factor, 1 being the lowest rating and 100 the highest.

Leadership Factors	1	10	20	30	40	50	60	70	80	90	100
Developing trust											
Listening to problems											
Patience											
Giving praise when deserved											
Being consistent											
Establishing job descriptions											
Setting a good example											
Positive expectations											
Adaptability											
Being supportive											
Understanding others											
Making decisions											
Being open to others' opinions											
Positive attitudes											
Showing appreciation											
Handling stress calmly											
Delegating responsibility											
Giving constructive correction											
Managing conflicts											
Dependability											

Start at the top and connect the dots (or "X's") down the page to form a line. That which is to the left of this line is your degree of success in each of the factors. That which is to the right of this line is your potential.

1. What is your general opinion of your leadership effectiveness from the grid? What do you feel are your strong areas in leadership? Which are the areas that have the most potential?

2. Which of the above factors are *most* important in being an effective leader? In what kinds of work environments might some of these factors be more important than in others?

3. How do you visualize a strong leader? How could you develop those characteristics? What steps could you take to move your grid from the left over to the right?

Styles of Leadership

Warren Schmidt and Robert Tannenbaum of UCLA developed the diagram below. It is a continuum which portrays the range of choices and responses which both leader and group member have available to them in the group experience. Each of us develops a pattern of behaviors, which we will use most often and which could be our normative style. However, there are situations to which we respond differently either as leader or follower. An awareness of our normative style and how we adapt to changing conditions and people is important to our knowledge of ourselves and to group process.

Place an "x" on the diagonal line at the point that you consider to be the style that you generally use when in a leadership capacity. Think of an incident when you have or tend to behave differently and place an "o" on the diagonal line at a point that describes your response to that situation.

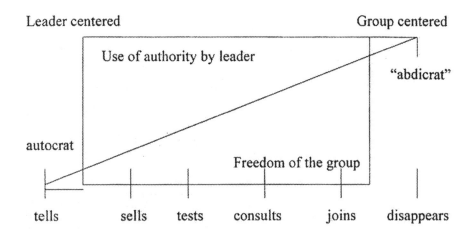

Make some notes about the following:

    A. What factors have shaped or influenced my normative style?

    B. What forces cause me to use a different approach?

Leadership Questionnaire

Name _____   Group _____

Directions: The following items describe aspects of leadership behavior. Respond to each item according to the way you would most likely act if you were the leader of a work group. Circle whether you would most likely behave in the described way: always (A), frequently (F), occasionally (O), seldom (S), or never (N).

A	F	O	S	N	
A	F	O	S	N	1. I would most likely act as the spokesman of the group.
A	F	O	S	N	2. I would encourage overtime work.
A	F	O	S	N	3. I would allow members complete freedom in their work.
A	F	O	S	N	4. I would encourage the use of uniform procedures.
A	F	O	S	N	5. I would permit the members to use their own judgment in solving problems.
A	F	O	S	N	6. I would stress being ahead of competing groups.
A	F	O	S	N	7. I would speak as a representative of the group.
A	F	O	S	N	8. I would needle members for greater effort.
A	F	O	S	N	9. I would try out my ideas in the group.
A	F	O	S	N	10. I would let the members do their work the way they think best.
A	F	O	S	N	11. I would be working hard for a promotion.
A	F	O	S	N	12. I would tolerate postponement and uncertainty.
A	F	O	S	N	13. I would speak for the group if there were visitors present.
A	F	O	S	N	14. I would keep the work moving at a rapid pace.
A	F	O	S	N	15. I would turn the members loose on a job and let them go to it.
A	F	O	S	N	16. I would settle conflicts when they occur in the group.
A	F	O	S	N	17. I would get swamped by details.
A	F	O	S	N	18. I would represent the group at outside meetings.
A	F	O	S	N	19. I would be reluctant to allow the members any freedom of action.
A	F	O	S	N	20. I would decide what should be done and how it should be done.
A	F	O	S	N	21. I would push for increased production.
A	F	O	S	N	22. I would let some members have authority, which I could keep.
A	F	O	S	N	23. Things would usually turn out as I had predicted.
A	F	O	S	N	24. I would allow the group a high degree of initiative.
A	F	O	S	N	25. I would assign group members to particular tasks.
A	F	O	S	N	26. I would be willing to make changes.
A	F	O	S	N	27. I would ask the members to work harder.
A	F	O	S	N	28. I would trust the group members to exercise good judgment.
A	F	O	S	N	29. I would schedule the work to be done.
A	F	O	S	N	30. I would refuse to explain my actions.
A	F	O	S	N	31. I would persuade others that my ideas are to their advantage.
A	F	O	S	N	32. I would permit the group to set its own pace.
A	F	O	S	N	33. I would urge the group to beat its previous record.
A	F	O	S	N	34. I would act without consulting the group.
A	F	O	S	N	35. I would ask that group members follow standard rules and regulations.

Reproduced from J. William Pfeiffer and John E. Jones, eds., *A Handbook of Structured Experiences for Human Relations Training*, vol. 1 (rev.).

Leadership-Style Profile Sheet

Name _____ Group _____

Directions: To determine your style of leadership, mark your score
                   on the *concern for task dimension* (T) on the left-hand
                   arrow below. Next, move to the right-hand arrow and
                   mark your score on the *concern for people* dimension
                   (P). Draw a straight line that intersects the P and T
                   scores. The point at which that line crosses the *shared
                   leadership* arrow indicates your score on that dimension.

**Shared Leadership Results from
Balancing Concern for Task and Concern for People**

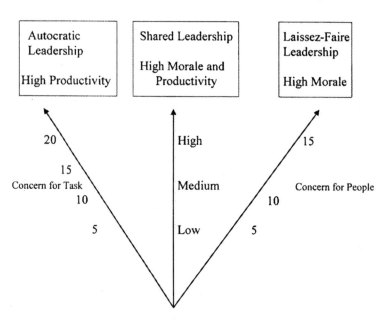

Reproduced from J. William Pfeiffer and John E. Jones, eds., *A Handbook of
Structured Experiences for Human Relations Training,* vol. 1 (rev.). La Jolla,
CA: University Associates, 1974.

Leaders and Followers

The "Leaders and Followers" exercise is intended:

1. To identify ambivalences about being a leader and/or follower.

2. To introduce a view of changing attitudes toward authority.

3. To become aware of attitudes toward volunteer and professional leaders.

Discussion with the participants will be directed toward and connected to the opinions and attitudes which may have been expressed with respect to both the staff and volunteer leadership roles and responsibilities. Potential ambivalences need to be explained as they may be expressed about staff leadership responsibility, or concerns about use of authority by worker or volunteer.

Questions about how one should lead or follow have been matters of concern throughout history, and are particularly important in these days, when attitudes toward authority and leaders have changed toward less trust and confidence. Ambivalent attitudes are pervasive about leadership in all arenas of organization work—in business, industry, government, and the nonprofit sector. Understanding these attitudes and learning how to work effectively in this atmosphere is a challenging condition.

The paired statements below have been selected from biblical sources because they bear on the matter of leadership and following styles, responsibilities, and attitudes.

Each participant should check the statement with which s/he most agrees. After the individual choices have been made, the group should discuss the pairs of statements with these questions as guidelines:

1. What is your interpretation of the statements?

2. What is your preference for one or another of the statements? Is either close to your personal style at some time?

3. Which statement seems more applicable to the exercise of leadership or follower-ship in your class, group, work, or supervisory setting? Does it help or hinder the work to be done and the relationships between people?

Leaders and Followers Questionnaire

After reading each paired statement, check the statement with which you most agree.

A   1. In the place where there is a leader, do not seek to become a leader.

2. In the place where there is no leader, strive to become a leader.

B   1. Like generation, like leader.

2. What can the great ones do if their generation is evil?

C   1. "Be rather a tail to a lion than the head of a fox."

2. "Be rather a head to a fox than a tail to a lion."

D   1. When the shepherd is enraged at the flock, he blinds the eyes of the lead sheep.

2. When the shepherd blunders along his way, his flock blunders after him.

E   1. Be exceedingly lowly of spirit since the hope of man is but the worm.

2. Condemn no man and consider nothing impossible, for there is no man who does not have a future and there is nothing that does not have its hour.

Tzimtzum: Group Processes and Leadership

The *Tzimtzum* theory is a theory of leadership derived from Jewish sources in order to show how the alternation of assertion and "letting go" applies in the organizational setting. Brief versions of the Luria theory and its contemporary relevance as seen by Eugene Borowitz and Jack Dauber are presented, followed by some review and discussions of the theories. Three experiential activities follow which are designed to involve people you work with in identifying the three phases through the use of texts, personal experiences, and organizational perceptions. Instructions and questions for discussion are included in each project. Issues for consideration will be:

1. Similarities and differences between the democratic, authoritative, and laissez faire leadership styles and phases in *Tzimtzum*.

2. Comparison of the value systems in *Tzimtzum*, the three leadership styles, and those that the participants hold.

3. How the situational concept of leadership fits with the others.

4. How the flow of a board's work fits *Tzimtzum* phases.

5. Personal styles and resources which may be used most effectively in the various phases of the organization's work.

6. The concerns and the effects of "letting go and letting others in," i.e., control, assisting, abdicating, transmitting, being remembered, freeing, and being freed.

Our constant experience is that we have not been consulted, or have not been listened to, or have not really had a voice in matters which deeply affect our lives. In short, we exist in the continuing consciousness of being the object of someone else's power rather than being a person in our own right, though we are involved with people of greater status than ours.

We seek a leadership construed not primarily in terms of the accomplishment of plans but equally in terms of its humanizing effect on the people being led. Our ethics demand a leader who uses power to enable people to be persons while they work together. Such a leader, as against the stereotype of the cruel general or ruthless executive, is not essentially goal-oriented but recognizes that people are always as important, if not more important, than the current undertaking.

The Lurianic model of leadership has, as its first step, contraction. The leader withholds presence and power so that the followers may have some place in which to be.

Leadership in the Lurianic style is particularly difficult because it requires a continuing alternation of the application of our power. Now we hold back; now we act. To do either in the right way is difficult enough. To develop a sense when to stop one and do the other and then reverse that in due turn, is to involve one in endless inner conflict.

Those who lead by *tzimtzum* must quickly reconcile themselves to the fact that leaving room for others to act is likely to mean their own purposes will be accomplished only in blemished form.

Lurianic leadership depends not only on an exquisite sense of inter-personal rhythm but a capacity to forgive and go on working with those whose need for independence is a major cause of the frustration of our plans. The strength to persist in so frustrating a role can come from recognizing that the leader's *tzimtzum* and the resulting *shevirah* ("shattering") are the occasion for the followers' work to *tikkun,* restoration and completion. The group's objectives may not have been accomplished now but the leader may be confident that the effort will go on.

Tzimtzum: A Group Dynamic Model

Jack Dauber

In 1974, Eugene Borowitz proposed some ideas about leadership which grew out of Isaac Luria's theory of creation. The article stimulated experimentation with applications of the theory to group dynamics, staff training, leadership development, and organization work. Major concentration of effort was in the Confluent Education Teacher Training Program at Hebrew Union College in Los Angeles. Practical applications of the Luria model led to theory building on the phases of growth which groups experience as they move toward the accomplishment of their respective tasks. Here we will describe the current status of this group development theory.

The reference in Borowitz's article is to a theory of creation propounded by the great mystic, Rabbi Isaac Luria (1534-1572). His theory is a radical explanation of the theological dilemma regarding the understanding of the nature of God and of the biblical statements about the Creation. Simply put, "If God is everywhere, how can there be any place outside him to create in?" We believe that creation takes place outside of ourselves—an external extension of our being. The quandary, therefore, was to explain where creation could take place if God filled all space.

A second aspect of the dilemma "in its ontological form is … if God is a fundamental, fully realized (perfect and infinite), how can there be a secondary being, that is, a being only partly realized (imperfect and finite). Or, if God is all-in-all, how can the partial or the transitory, which must depend upon him for their being, ever come to exist?"

The presence of good and evil in the world is a third dilemma. How could the ultimate "Goodness" suffer evil to co-exist in the world which He created?

Luria's response is to suggest that Creation must begin with an act of contraction or concentration within Himself or *tzimtzum*. "God must, so to speak, make Himself less than He is so that other things can come into being." Thus, the first step in the creative process becomes an internal one, rather than an extension as was previously noted.

Tzimtzum is followed by the **Shevirah** phase, which is one of "shattering" or catastrophe. God cannot withdraw completely and leaves a residue of Himself in the void. A beam of energy grows from the contraction of the infinite light which stimulates the creative process. Luria's analogy is that the "vessels," which are in the void, are inadequate to cope with the "beam" and are broken and sundered.

The "Divine" sparks remain among the "husks" and "shards," thereby providing the stimulus for the next step in creation which is *Tikkun*.

Tikkun means "restoration, the reintegration of the organic wholeness of creation." Out of chaos comes mending, healing, re-creation and creation of the "new."

Some interesting implications flow from Luria's theory:

- Man is co-creator with God.

- There is an inevitable coursing of the creative process—an act of withdrawal causes a period of chaos which precedes creation.

- God provides energy and a trace of himself which influences man in the work of creation.

- God is prepared to accept lesser accomplishment from man than the ideal or "perfect."

- Out of the "bad" in events can come good.

When these concepts are transposed into human terms, i.e., what they mean when applied to the exercise of leadership, to group process, and to training programs in organizations, there are compelling teachings and values.

1. Leaders must allow space in which their associates may establish their own solutions and directions.

2. What happens to people is as important, if not more important, than the task at hand or the "product."

3. Leaders provide a resource, "trace," or contribution which the followers (co-creators) will blend into their works as they carry on with the organization's functions. They never fully leave.

4. What the followers accomplish in terms of the end products will most likely be different from the visions and goals of the leader.

5. The phases of creation—*Tzimtzum, Shevirah* and *Tikkun*, are as inevitable in the development of the organization as they are in the mystical theory.

6. Therefore, the leadership "style" which is called for, is like an alternating current of contraction and assertiveness which reconnects the leader with his people.

7. The "Great Man" or "Born Leader" concepts of leadership are not supported by this theory. Rather, God is the "Great Delegator" or co-creator, which is more closely related to the concept of "Situational Leadership." That is to say, certain situations call for or create leaders who meet the need of that time and then withdraw. Also, it is rare that a leader can meet both the "task" and "maintenance" needs of a group or organization simultaneously and consistently, and, therefore, must find others to complement his efforts.

My first association when I read the Borowitz article was with my experience in a group some years before. The leader, or trainer, as I learned to understand the title later, opened the first session by saying, in effect, "we all know what we're here for so why don't we begin." Following that, he waited silently without giving any further direction.

The people in the group, confronted with a leader who was not performing in the stereotyped notion which all of us had, that is, that the leader should give direction and guide us through the program which had been planned for us, were thrown into a state of confusion. During that period of chaos, each of us responded in a different way. Some withdrew into silence with the facilitator. Others expressed anger and hostility which was directed either at the leader or displaced on to others in the group. Others asked leading questions in order to get some of our colleagues to begin the discussions. Several competed for the leadership of the group. It is interesting to note that sensitivity training literature describes this "opening" as the necessary first step toward enabling the participants in the group to create a new community which will represent their own beliefs, attitudes, and aspirations.

Other examples on both personal and organization levels which may serve to illustrate the phases in the Luria theory are:

1. Parents easing their control in order to help the child to grow.

2. The struggles and ambivalences between parent and teenager, as they try to work out the emergence of the adult from the child.

3. The ambiguities and confusions which occur when a new administration takes over the reins of governance, be it the state, an agency, synagogue or committee.

4. The strategy developed by revolutionary movements in which they first develop an "infrastructure" of both ideas and people, then create a revolution in order to depose the rulers, which causes chaos and which they hope leaves them free to move into positions of power in order to recreate the society according to the image which they hold.

5. The process of divorce, i.e., effecting the separation and then building new lives for individuals and families.

6. The process of delegation in which a supervisor asks a subordinate to assume certain responsibilities or to develop some new approaches to accomplishing certain tasks.

7. The process of delegation in which the board develops a "charge" to a committee to accomplish a certain agreed upon project.

8. The struggle of the teacher, who is expert in a particular field of knowledge, is severe as he restrains himself in order to encourage students to find their own way into the teacher's ideas and knowledge.

In order to apply this theory to the training of educators, to leadership development programs, and to classroom teaching, the first challenge was to find an appropriate adaptation of the "God" concept in the attempt to make a group dynamic theory. Since God came before the creation of the world, He represents the "past." From this came the notion of "antecedents," that is, the past history, beliefs, attitudes, etc., of individuals, groups, and organizations. No group or organization is ever completely "new." The participants and/or organizers bring with them their own life experience, aspirations, and ways of doing which need to be blended in some operational form so that a functional entity will result.

(Drawn from Eugene B. Borowitz, *Tzimtzum: A Mystic Model for Contemporary Leadership*.)

Exercise One: Delegating

If you are using this with a group, read aloud:

The first phase of the Luria theory of creation is *Tzimtzum*, in which God "concentrated" or withdrew in order to make creation possible. God made space for other things to come into being, so that humans could engage in the creative process. Here we will begin to translate the Luria theory into human and organization terms. The question for us, which flows from the theory, is how to determine ways in which we may behave in order to "let others in." That is to say, how might we "contract" or withdraw so that other leaders may find space for themselves in helping to make the organization progress cooperatively.

Listed below are some ways of withdrawing from group situations. Check those with which you are familiar—those which you have seen in others or those which you may practice yourself. There are probably other behaviors which you have experienced.

Feeling sick
Delegating
Taking time off
Withholding attention
Walking away from the situation
Being silent
Stay on the job, but don't perform required tasks
Ask questions
Be negative
Other
Select two or three of the behaviors and describe the effects on:
Yourself
Others
Which methods are effective, under what circumstances? Think of ways to use this material as a volunteer or staff person.

Changing the Organization

This material is intended for any staff or volunteer who will be training others. If you are a facilitator, this can be used if you are working with a group. Divide it into teams of four to six participants, each with a group leader, and read the following paragraph, asking the group leaders to proceed according to the instructions.

In Exodus 18:13-27, Jethro advises his son-in-law Moses, that he will "surely wear away" if he continues to be the sole judge for the people of Israel, that he should teach them the statutes and laws; that he should provide "able men, men of truth to be rulers of thousands, rulers of hundreds, rulers of fifties and rulers of tens." They should judge the people in "small" matters. Great matters should be brought to Moses. Moses harkened to his father-in-law and did all that Jethro had said.

1. Is this situation on example of the *Tzimtzum*, *Shevirah*, or *Tikkun* phase?

2. Is this a change in Moses' style of leadership? From what to what? What would you imagine the effects of the change to be on Moses? On the Israelites?

3. What actions or processes would have to precede the selection of judges?

4. What would you imagine the effects of the withdrawal of Moses from his accustomed role of the sole judge to be on him? On the people?

◆   ◆   ◆

1. Write a two-paragraph memorandum from Moses to the "rulers of thousands" in which he outlines their responsibilities.

2. Write an advertisement for judges to be announced at public assemblies of the people.

3. Write a job description for a "judge of tens."

4. Write a publicity release to the people of Israel advising them of this new system and why it is being put into practice.

Tzimtzum—Withdrawing

This exercise is meant for group participation. A trained volunteer or staff can lead this as is the case with the bulk of the exercises in this section of the book. The more emphasis is given to prepare volunteers for these roles, the more intense the commitment to agency is likely to result.

Self-Assessment Questionnaire

The Luria theory suggests that a period of confusion follows the "withdrawal" of the leader and that this is a natural succession which makes it possible for the creation to take place. If this is true, then there must be skills, knowledge, experience, and will. These represent strengths and resources which may be the seeds for creation and consensus in the *Tikkun* phase. In our experience in organizational work we may be familiar with the "chaos" of the *Shevirah* phase, but not aware of the potentials in those situations—that point to solutions which can be creative, satisfying, and productive for those who are involved.

1. Choose an event or situation you have observed in an organization which you feel represents a time of confusion, chaos or ambiguity (*Shevirah*).

2. Describe it in a few sentences.

3. Do you recall a feeling you had as you perceived or experienced this event? What was the feeling?

4. Was there a lesser or different feeling as well? What was it?

5. Was there a leading character? How did you experience that person's actions and/or demeanor? Were there feelings of resentment or application?

6. Can you associate a sound, a rhythm, or a color with this event?

7. How did you perceive others to respond in this situation? Was there support for a leader? Was there competition for leadership? Did group members withdraw? How?

8. As you reflect on this situation now, were there strengths or resources which were called on or emerged which helped move things to a resolution?

9. Were there resources which were present but untapped or not offered?

10. If you could rewrite the "scenario" for this event, would you repeat it as it happened? Would you have people do things differently either as leaders or followers?

Decision-Making and Conflict-Management

Objectives:

1. Study concepts of decision-making and conflict management.

2. Learn to apply the concepts to ease material and real experiences.

3. Understand the professional role in managing conflict.

4. Understand decision-making appropriate to various levels in the organization.In his book, *Management—Tasks, Responsibilities, Practices*, Peter Drucker (1993)[1] has a chapter on "The Effective Decision," which is the basis of this section. He describes the Japanese system as follows:

What are the essentials of the Japanese method of decision-making? First the focus is on deciding what the decision is all about. The Japanese do not focus on giving an answer until there is consensus, (and) a wide variety of opinions and approaches is being explored. The focus is on alternatives rather than the "right solution." The process further brings out at what level and by whom a certain decision should be made, and finally, it eliminates selling a decision. It builds effective execution into the decision-making process (p. 470).

The process, which Drucker recommends for management in this country, is summarized as follows:

1. *Gather opinions* with the goal of stimulating the expression of many divergent ideas. Involve people at all levels of the organization who will ultimately have anything to do with the decision or its implementation, encouraging all of them to have a voice. Drucker's goal here is to stimulate clash and conflict to promote the emergence of a variety of alternative opinions.

---

1. New York: Harper Business Publisher.

2. *Select or make hypotheses* about the nature of the problem that is being addressed, creating a preliminary formulation of the problem.

3. *Collect data* relevant to step two.

4. *Define alternative solutions* to the problems that have been raised.

5. *Create dissent about the alternative solutions* among the participants. "[T]he executive who wants to make the right decision forces himself to see opposition as *his* means to think through the alternatives (p. 474)."

6. *Consider whether or not to make a decision.* Drucker's guidelines are, "act if, on balance, the benefits greatly outweigh cost and risk: and act or don't act, but do not hedge or compromise."

7. *Who does the work?*—"The first rule is to make sure that everyone who will have to do something to make the decision effective—or who could sabotage it—has been forced to participate responsibly in the discussion…. In fact, no decision has been made unless carrying it out in specific steps has become someone's work assignment and responsibility (p. 477)."

8. *A decision is now ready to be made.* It requires courage as well as judgment—most effective decisions are distasteful to someone. The best decision is only an approximation and a risk. Don't start with: "What is acceptable?"

9. *Plan for feedback.* Few decisions work out as intended, therefore, expectations need to be spelled out clearly, in writing, in advance, and an organized effort for follow-up designed as part of the decision-making package.

Trust-Building Concepts

This material is intended for group leadership training and should begin with presentation and discussion on trust-building using concepts in the bibliography or examples from the participants' experience which support or differ from the presented concepts. Examples should not be limited to readings on the volunteer-professional relationship, but should include references to friendships, family, work, and school. A leader may have to use his or her own personal experiences in order to set a tone for discussion and sharing.

Values Which Affect Trust Levels

The list of statements which follow are taken from biblical sources and represent values which guide most of us. Some are ideal goals and others are more specific. Some set forth values and concepts that are in conflict with others on the list. The task is to identify those values which influence trust for a group in a general way, those which are more specific to the volunteer/professional relationship, and those which people hold as individuals and which guide their behavior.

After the leader's introduction there could be individual review and analysis of the value statements below and discussion of them by pairs of group members. Then the group as a whole should select those values which they feel have the greatest impact on the volunteer/professional trust level.

Values and Trust Questionnaire

Below are statements from biblical sources that reflect beliefs and attitudes influencing trust levels between individuals. Select five that you feel could contribute to the building of a high level of trust between the volunteer and the professional.

1. "None may want superiority over his fellow man."

2. "Nobody is more alone than a man in pain."

3. "Keep thy tongue from evil and thy lips from guile."

4. "Do not bear false witness against thy neighbor."

5. "Give thy neighbor the benefit of the doubt as long as there is no incontrovertible evidence to show that he has acted or spoken wrongly."

6. "Any statement which, if it's spread, may cause to one's fellow man physical damage, financial loss, grief or fear is gossip."

7. "He that blesses his friends in a loud voice in the morning, it should be counted as a curse to him."

8. "Spare a fellow embarrassment. Treat his imperfections with grace."

9. "Put not your trust in princes."

10. "Trust not in yourself till the day of your death."

11. "Excessive confidence throws men off their guard, whereas fear teaches precaution."

12. "Love work; hate lordship; and seek no intimacy with the ruling power."

13. "Be ye guarded in your relations with the ruling power; for they who exercise it draw no man near to them except for their own interests; appearing as friends when it is to their own advantage, they stand not by a man in the hour of his need."

14. "Be submissive to a superior, affable to a suppliant, and receive all men with cheerfulness."

Value Systems

The values choices in the questionnaire included here provide an opportunity for them to:

1. Project themselves into the values, which they perceive volunteer leaders and staff to have.

2. Compare their values as staff with those of volunteers, and vice versa.

3. See if the value systems are compatible with the agency's goals and supportive of them.

4. Identify value conflicts between volunteers and professional workers and determine which need to be resolved and how this should be done.

5. Relate value choices to change taking place in the larger community.

Not all the value choices need to be used. A questionnaire with a shorter selection can be made, but should include at least one of each of the following:

1. Personal/family

2. Leadership attitudes

3. Board functions

4. Expectations of staff

The leader should divide the group in half and ask one half to rank the statements as though they were volunteer leaders. It might be helpful to have them think of a person whom they know and do the rankings as though they were that person.

The other half of the group should make the rankings as though they were staff.

The rankings should be done individually and without discussion. When each has completed the task, each group should tabulate the individuals' rankings to see if their priority choices are similar. Each group, working separately, should identify a "values profile," i.e., those values which are essential for them as volunteer leaders or staff.

The "profiles" of the two groups should then be compared for similarities and differences.

Another "mind set" from which the rankings could be made would be to ask that participants to use an agency as their frame of reference in filling out the questionnaire. This might make differences sharper between the staff in the different agencies and create the opportunity for seeing if any of the staff are closer in their value systems to the volunteer leadership.

Values Clarification

Rank each set of statements in accordance with your sense of their importance to you. Use the number one for the most important. Be spontaneous and don't think too much about the value choices. Thinking about "why" you choose a particular value may make you select a "should" rather than the one that is really your value.

1. I am an/a:

- American

- Good Person

- Human being

- Man/Woman

2. Things that make my house a home are:

- Personal belongings

- Celebrating holidays together

- Peace in the family
- Presence of children, parents, and grandparents

3. Which is the most important quality for a communal leader?

- Practicing what one preaches
- Financial generosity
- Being articulate and persuasive
- Possess a philosophy shared by the organization s/he serves

4. The most critical issue facing volunteer leadership today is:

- Apathy or indifference within the community
- Raising adequate funds to serve local and overseas financial needs
- Leadership development
- Preserving culture and tradition

5. The most important function of a board member is to:

- Determine policies
- Take responsibility for chairing a committee
- Make financial contributions
- Help shape the organization's vision and mission
- Interpret the work of the agency to friends and community.
- Recruit new board members
- Participate actively in agency programs
- Represent the agency to the community
- Work in the fundraising campaign

6. All people should:

- Be responsible for one another
- Be united in fellowship
- Not be separate from the community

- Perform acts of loving-kindness

7. The most important function of a staff member to me, as a board member, is to:

- Share his or her professional expertise with me
- Be fiscally responsible
- Prepare me thoroughly for meetings in which I have a leadership role
- Coordinate my activities with those of other board members
- Help in shaping the organization's vision and mission
- Treat my views and actions with respect
- Help me be successful in the projects and responsibilities which I undertake
- Be candid about individual and organizational relationships
- Respect my time requirements

8. As a board member, I expect a staff member to:

- Give precedence to his or her professional responsibility over his or her personal interest
- Be responsible for the quality and extent of the services he or she performs
- Work toward the creation and maintenance of conditions which strengthen the community
- Give equal treatment to men and women of all beliefs, ages, and social status

Selecting a Board for a Nonprofit Organization or Institution

Objectives:

1. Determine the make-up of a board which will meet the organization/institution's needs for the tasks which are current and which lie ahead.

2. Determine the balance of human resources which should be included on the board.

3. Have the participants struggle with the need to develop a viable working entity out of the diversity of backgrounds.

Group Exercise for Board Composition

The task to which the groups should address themselves is to assume that they are in a new community, perhaps a suburban area of a large metropolitan city, where they feel a new community planning organization should be created.(This is adapted from *Reform is a Verb, Part II* a report made to the Union for Reform Judaism)

The current Board of Director consists of:

1. Divorced parent (woman) with one child who had been an involved member in the community.

2. Former president of large agency in town.

3. Parent, about thirty-five years old, with two children, interested in day school.

4. President of the local Women's Organization (in her fifties).

5. Wealthy real estate developer in the area.

6. Woman, MBA, early thirties, single, youth activities and camping background.

7. Active civil rights leader.

Each of the members will have met others in the neighborhood whom they consider to be possible additions to the board of directors. None of the people on the list, which follows, have been approached as yet, since it had been decided that a careful selection would have to be made in order to develop a small but effective board. The board has agreed to expand their number to a total of fifteen individuals. Here is the list of potential board members:

1. A wealthy, elderly man who is inactive in the community.

2. A young married man of about thirty-two with two children. He has been a religious school teacher.

3. A socially prominent woman in the community.

4. A seventy year old man who is very knowledgeable about his culture and religion.

5. A writer who has not been affiliated with the community.

6. A young dynamic lawyer in a large firm.

7. A nonprofit organization executive.

8. A community center worker.

9. A manager of a large business.

10. A famous local artist.

11. A construction man

12. A professor of philosophy.

13. A woman who is accustomed to attending religious services regularly.

The participants should work on this project in groups of four to six. Each should be asked to select the preferred eight candidates, ranking them in order of preference. These selections should be made without discussion. When the individual choices have been made, the facilitator should present the objectives for the project. The task for each group is to:

1. Select a slate of candidates.

2. Write the criteria upon which they made their determination.

3. Write the objectives which they think the temple has at the time.

Discussion after the groups have completed their tasks, should center on:

A. The objectives for the lesson.

B. The participants' own values as they influenced the selections.

C. Differences and similarities in group slates, criteria, and objectives.

About the Authors

Gerald Bubis is the Founding Director of the School of Jewish Communal Service and Alfred Gottschalk Professor Emeritus of Jewish Communal Studies at Hebrew Union College-Jewish Institute of Religion in Los Angeles, where he served from 1968 to 1989. He has been a Fellow at the Jerusalem Center for Public Affairs since 1977 and a Vice-president of the Center and later its Steering Committee since 1984. He has written, edited and/or co-authored 13 books and monographs and published nearly 100 articles. He continues as a trainer, lecturer and consultant. Over the years he functioned in one of those capacities in over 100 communities throughout the world. He served as a faculty member in the Council of Jewish Federations' (now UJC) Continuing Education Program and in the Wexner Program for graduate training. He has been honored by a dozen organizations locally, nationally and internationally. He has served on many local, national and international boards of directors, a number of which have elected him to the presidency.

Rev. Lee Barker is the President and a Professor of Ministry at Meadville Lombard Theological Seminary. A lifelong Unitarian Universalist, he has served as a congregational pastor in Pennsylvania, New Jersey, and, most recently, in Pasadena, CA. His life's work has been to work through the UU community to better the world, both through social justice and through far-ranging religious and spiritual vision.

Richard Chait and **Barbara Taylor** are both involved in issues of governance in the nonprofit sector. Chait served as executive director of the National Center for Post-secondary Governance and Finance and as professor higher education and management at the University of Maryland. Taylor served as director of programs and research at the Association of Governing Boards of Universities and Colleges, have co-authored many books and articles and served as consultants to the boards of many nonprofit organizations.

Peter Drucker is Professor at the Drucker School of Management at Claremont College, Claremont, California. He has published innumerable books and articles on organizational behavior in the profit and nonprofit sectors. He is one of the foremost organizational theoreticians in the world.

Rabbi Arthur Gross-Schaefer is both a rabbi and a lawyer. He is a Professor of business law and ethics at Loyola Marymount University in Los Angeles, and rabbi of the Ojai Jewish Community. He has written extensively on rabbinic, legal and business ethics.

Rev. Stefan M. Jonasson has been the Coordinator of Services for Large Congregations with the Unitarian Universalist Association (UUA) since 1999. Over the years he has also served as the UUA's District Executive for Western Canada, minister of churches in Arborg and Gimli, Manitoba, and a personnel manager for the T. Eaton Company. He holds a Bachelor of Arts degree (Religious Studies) from the University of Winnipeg and a Master of Divinity degree from the same institution, for which he was awarded the Governor-General of Canada's Gold Medal for the highest standing in a graduate degree.

Ralph Kramer is professor emeritus at the School of Social Welfare, University of California Berkeley. He was a communal executive in both Jewish and Non-Jewish settings. He has written extensively, conducted extensive research, and served as a consultant in the U.S. and abroad.

Jean Quam, Ph.D. is a Professor and the Director of the University of Minnesota, School of Social Work. The author or co-author of numerous articles and books, she is a noted leader in social work education in America.

David Teutsch is a rabbi and holds a Ph.D. in organizational behavior. He was president of the Reconstructionist College and has written very extensively in addition to editing a new Reconstructionist prayer book. He teaches and consults throughout North America.

Rabbi Eric Weiss is presently the Director of the Bay Area Jewish Healing Center in San Francisco. He has lectured and written on many different subjects.

Miriam Wood is on the faculty of the Institute for Social and Policy Studies at Yale University in the Program on Nonprofit Organization. She has conducted extensive research and written extensively on the subject of nonprofit governance.

978-0-595-41878-
0-595-41878-3

Printed in the United States
125996LV00003B/14/A

9 780595 418787